Scottish Orientalism and the Bengal Renaissance

The Continuum of Ideas

Rabindranath Tagore

Scottish Orientalism and the Bengal Renaissance

The Continuum of Ideas

Edited by
BASHABI FRASER, TAPATI MUKHERJEE
and
AMRIT SEN

Special Advisor
NEIL FRASER

Luath Press Limited
EDINBURGH
www.luath.co.uk

First published in India 2017 by The Director, Granthan Vibhaga, Visva-Bharati

Revised edition first published in the UK 2018 by Luath Press

ISBN: 978-1-912147-11-3

The paper used in this book is recyclable. It is made from low chlorine pulps produced in a low energy, low emission manner from renewable forests.

Printed and bound by Bell & Bain Ltd, Glasgow

Typeset in 11 point Sabon by Lapiz

Photographs (except where indicated) courtesy of the Rabindra-Bhavana Archives

Contents

The Poet and the East-West Encounter

Scientific Innovation in India

Acknowledgements

THIS BOOK IS THE outcome of a collaborative project between the Scottish Centre of Tagore Studies (ScoTs) at Edinburgh Napier University and Rabindra Bhavana at Visva-Bharati in the UK and India respectively, co-funded by the British Council and the University Grants Commission (UGC) of India as a UK India Educational Research Initiatives (UKIERI) project. We are grateful to the UKIERI for their generous research grant and support.

As a Knowledge Exchange programme, this project was an interchange of ideas and personnel with staff and research students travelling from the UK to India and vice versa to engage in intensive research in diverse areas of the research topic and participate in an intellectual interchange with colleagues and students of the partner institution. Without their participation and contribution, the research could not have been conducted, completed and brought together in this book. We are thus grateful to our research students, Kathryn Simpson and Thomas Crosby for travelling from Edinburgh Napier University to Visva-Bharati and consulting the Rabindra-Bhavana archives and library, investigating various materials in different Indian archives and libraries and consulting leading intellectuals for their respective chapters. We have benefitted from the work of our Indian research students, Biswanath Banerjee and Saptarshi Mallick, who have made research trips to the UK to do dedicated research in UK libraries and archives for writing their contributory chapters for this book.

At seminars held as part of this UKIERI project at Visva-Bharati and Edinburgh, several scholars have interacted with the researchers on the research theme and contributed to the scholarly debate that has informed this book. We are thus thankful to Rosinka Chaudhuri (Institute of Social Science, Kolkata), Mary Ellis Gibson and Nigel Leask (Glasgow University), Roger Jeffery, Crispin Bates (University of Edinburgh), Friederike Voigt (National Museum of Scotland), Aya Ikegami (the Open University) and Murdo Macdonald (Dundee University) for their incisive comments and reflections which have enriched the project. We value the contribution of Dikshit Sinha (Sriniketan, Visva-Bharati) in a significant chapter to this volume.

Tom Kane (Edinburgh Napier University) was involved in advancing the research at the Rabindra Bhavana archives and at institutions in and around Santiniketan and in Kolkata to assess the educational links between Scotland and India, which have enriched this research project. Christine Kupfer (Edinburgh Napier University), conducted workshops in Scotland to assess the current relevance and efficacy of Rabindranath Tagore's ideas on education in school classrooms in Scotland, which have proved useful for researchers contributing to this book. We value the work of Kaberi Chatterjee who has travelled to Scotland to follow the trail of Alexander Duff and pour over relevant records in libraries and archives in the UK for her specific subject.

The Special Advisor for this book is Neil Fraser (University of Edinburgh) whose dedicated research in both countries and intellectual advice have proved invaluable for this book. He too, like Dikshit Sinha, has brought his social scientist's evaluation of Rabindranath's pragmatic projects in a chapter for the book.

This book would not have been possible without the generous help and co-operation of the staff at the Nehru Museum Library and Archives (Delhi) , the Sahitya Akademi Library (Delhi), the National Library of India (Kolkata), the Victoria Memorial Library and Archives (Kolkata), Goethal's Library and Archives (Kolkata), Asiatic Society Library and Archives (Kolkata), Bishop's College Library and Archives (Kolkata) and Scottish Church College Library and Archives (Kolkata) in India. In the UK, our project members are deeply grateful to the knowledge, advice and support of staff members of the National Library of Scotland, University of Edinburgh Library, Stathclyde University Archives, Dundee University Archives, St Andrews University Library and Archives, the Devon Record Office (for Elmhirst's papers from the Dartington Trust) and the India Office Library at the British Library.

This project has benefitted from the rich collections at the Rabindra Bhavana Library and Archives at Visva-Bharati and the Tagore Collection at the Scottish Centre of Tagore Studies at Edinburgh Napier University. We owe the Tagore Collection largely to the generous donation of William Radice and Indra Nath Choudhuri.

We would like to express our deep gratitude to Utpal Mitra who made many of the resources at the Rabindra Bhavana Archives available to us, to Madhumita Roy for her dedication and help with formatting the chapters and to Priyabrata Roy for his technological help in expertly typesetting the manuscript. He has done a brilliant job. A special thanks to Saptarshi Mallick who has not only been an excellent researcher, but has always been there to assist the team members in multiple ways, including locating relevant documents and providing expert technical help. He has been our invaluable trouble-shooter.

Since this was a Knowledge Exchange project, it involved the travel and stay of researchers from one country to the other. As such, it required meticulous planning and administrative support to ensure accommodation, subsistence overseas and internal travel arrangements for which we are sincerely grateful to the staff of Ratan Kuthi and Purba Palli Guest House at Santiniketan and Debjani and Kamal Sharma in Kolkata for making our research members welcome and comfortable in their guest flat. We would like to specially thank Marguerite Le Riche, the Administrator of our Research Centre, the Scottish Centre for Tagore Studies (SCOTS, under CLAW) for her continuous help with making travel and accommodation arrangements for our research partners in the UK and the smooth administration of the entire UKIERI project. Our research work in Delhi was made possible by Indra Nath and Usha Chaudhuri, who not only provided warm hospitality in their home, but made all the arrangements to facilitate our library work and meetings with key intellectuals who could advise on our project. It is not possible to name all those who have helped us directly and indirectly during the research period. This book would not have seen completion without the co-operation and support of our colleagues at Edinburgh Napier University and at Visva-Bharati who let us have the space and time to devote to the research for this book. Thanks also to our friends in Visva-Bharati who have gone out of their way to help all the researchers on this project.

We would like to thank Prof Swapan Kumar Datta, Vice Chancellor, Visva-Bharati and the Registrar, Prof Amit Hazra and the Director of the School of Arts and Creative Industries, Edinburgh Napier University, Pauline Miller Judd for their administrative support for the project and the book.

We appreciate the British Council's permission to use a part of our funding towards publication costs of this book.

We are grateful to Gavin MacDougall, the Director of Luath Press (Edinburgh) and to Visva-Bharati Press for agreeing to publish *Scottish Orientalism and the Bengal Renaissance: the Continuum of Ideas* in the UK and India, respectively, bringing the ideas, thought and work of two great men on education and the environment to a global audience.

Tapati Mukherjee
Bashabi Fraser
Amrit Sen

Santiniketan

From the West to the East

Raja Rammohan Roy

Scottish Orientalists and the Bengal Renaissance:
An Introduction

Bashabi Fraser

THIS BOOK CONSIDERS the work of Scottish Orientalists who are significant in Indian history, having contributed to India's socio-cultural developments. The intention is to understand their special significance within the context of British Orientalism. This study is not about the emergence and history of the Bengal Renaissance per se, but about the impetus prominent Scottish Orientalists lent to the tide that changed Bengal/India and propelled her on this unstoppable crest into the modern era. The Indo-Scottish interface generated a continuum of ideas as evident in the work of Bengal Renaissance figures who worked closely with Scottish Orientalists, effecting the transformation of the socio-cultural fabric of Bengal through the implementation of their epoch changing ideas in a period of creative transition.

In order to gauge the special approach of Scottish Orientalists in and to India, it is necessary to go back to the significance of the ideas generated during the Scottish Enlightenment in the 18th century which were reinterpreted and reshaped by Scottish Orientalists, the legatees of the Scottish Enlightenment, who contributed to the socio-cultural, religious and literary debates that affected the social reality and ideology of the times in Scotland and India from around the mid-19th century to the 1930s. Jane Rendall has said 'the extent to which the Scottish Enlightenment offered a conceptual framework for the understanding of complex and alien Asian societies has been underestimated' (Rendall 'Scottish Orientalism from Robertson' 69). This introductory chapter thus addresses and assesses this hitherto largely unexplored field and considers the socio-historic significance of the debates that were generated in the discourse that inspired and informed the Bengal/Indian Renaissance Movement. The prevailing debates emanating from Scottish Orientalists in India will be considered, inasmuch as they affected and informed the wave of change influenced by certain Scots whose interventions affected religious thinking, education and Bengali society, which would affect India as the nationalist consciousness gained momentum.

For the purposes of this study, we will first look at the major ideas that were established during the period of the Scottish Enlightenment on which later modernity is based (*The Scottish Enlightenment: The Scots' Invention of the Modern World*). The Act of Union in 1707 gave Scotland the opportunity to work within, and benefit from, the British colonial enterprise. They did pay higher taxes but gained from a better governance. The Scottish Reformation (1638) introduced an egalitarian democratic spirit to Scottish culture with the setting up of Scottish Presbyterianism, followed at the end of that century by instituting schools in every parish. The Scottish idea of history then became important as it was fundamentally based on the idea of progress.

The Scottish Enlightenment presented man as the product of history and a creature of his environment. It shared with the broad spirit of the European Enlightenment the thirst for knowledge and the willingness to challenge dogmas. Scottish Universities, at this time, played a key role in framing and generating transformative ideas. Scots invented the social sciences and the establishment of different branches of learning into disciplines; Edinburgh and Glasgow were the vanguard of bringing new disciplines into universities.

Moving away from the Hobbesian moral law and view of life being 'nasty, brutish and short' for the majority (and that power corrupts and absolute power corrupts absolutely), Scottish intellectuals were influenced by the Scottish philosopher, Francis Hutcheson (1694-1746). Hutcheson believed that people are born with an innate moral sense of what is right and wrong, that man is not inherently selfish and his search for personal and public happiness is justified from this sense of moral judgement (Herman 73). Hutcheson was the first to teach in English rather than Latin at Glasgow University. As a moral philosopher, he has had a lasting impact on Scottish thinking as he advocated the universal right of freedom, attacking all slavery and was Europe's first liberal thinker. An example of this liberal thinking is evident in India many years later in the formation and thinking of the Indian National Congress. Two Scots, Allan Octavian Hume (1829–1912) and Sir William Wedderburn (1838–1918) were founders of the Indian National Congress as a body that pressed for greater Indian representation and a stronger voice in India's governance. Wedderburn and another Scot, the wealthy businessman, George Yule (1829–1892), were Presidents of the Indian National Congress.

Lord Kaimes (Harry Home), the Patron of David Hume and William Robertson, used a four stage analysis of human society and its progression: 1. Hunting, 2. Pastoral, 3. Agricultural, 4. Commerce/Industry. He proposed that changes in the means of production bring in historical change, so, for example, institutions like law have to alter as society alters. All of this led several leading Scotsmen to refrain from racial interpretations of history (not accepting slavery in Scotland).

David Hume, arguing against Hutcheson, radically said that reason is, and ought to be, the slave of the passions. The most basic human passion was self-gratification. Society's problem was to channel passions in a constructive direction, meaning that liberty had to be counterbalanced by authority. In answer to Hume, Adam Smith referred to the inborn moral sense of human beings, speaking of a 'fellow feeling' which enabled one to place oneself in another's position. In *The Wealth of Nations* (1776) Smith explored the nature of human progress, the notion of specialization and division of labour, whose importance grows with each stage in society. He also applied this notion to intellectual labour. However, he was critical of the British government's defence of producers and pointed out the costs of capitalism. The sociologist, Adam Ferguson, recognized the danger of subservience to profit, while Smith believed that the benefits of capitalism were worth the price.

The polymath, Dugald Stewart, who replaced Adam Ferguson in the Chair of Moral Philosophy at Edinburgh University in 1785, was the intellectual bridge between the Scottish Enlightenment and the Victorian era as he 'put the disparate works of the Scottish school together as a system, a system of classical liberalism' (Powell 9). He promulgated a liberal optimism, and was the teacher of Lord Minto, 'providing the 'conceptual tools they could use as a framework for their analysis of Asian cultures', creating some 'distinctive Scottish paradigms of empire' (Ibid.). In conclusion, the great insight of the Scottish Enlightenment was to insist that human beings need to free themselves from myths and see the world as it truly is.

Encyclopaedia Britannica, which was first published in Edinburgh from 1768 to 1771 in three volumes, was a product of the Scottish Enlightenment, the age of 'new ideas' (Powell 8) – as a compendium of knowledge which remains highly regarded, even today.

The Scottish Orientalist project, if one may call it so, goes back to a seminal Orientalist figure in the historian William Robertson (1721–1793), Principal of the University of Edinburgh, who wrote of a sophisticated civilization in India while resident in the Scottish metropole in Edinburgh. His 1791 volume, *An Historical Disquisition Concerning the Knowledge which the Ancients had of India,* traces the commercial links that facilitated a cultural exchange between the West and India. In this West meets East study, Orientalists who were writing in India like Quintin Craufurd (1743–1819) and his *Sketches Chiefly Relating to the History, Religion, Learning and Manners, of the Hindoos* (1792), become significant, who endorse a similar perspective, very much in the spirit of the scholar-administrators like Sir Thomas Munro (1761–1827), Sir John Malcolm (1769–1833) and Hon Mountstuart Elphinstone (1779–1859) and the Muir brothers of Kilmarnock, John Muir (1810–1882) and Sir William Muir (1819–1905). The Muir brothers' study of the original sources of Vedic and Arabic civilizations (Powell 10), are seminal works of Scottish Orientalists.

However, one notes a narrative shift in the change in perception of India in Western discourse, effected by another Scot, James Mill (1773–1836), through his significant six volume text, *The History of British India* (1817). Mill was deeply influenced by Dugald Stewart (1753–1828) who was his teacher at the University of Edinburgh. This *History* became a source of 'knowledge' for British personnel who came out to serve and rule India, as it was their recommended text. Mill's *History* told them of the inherent 'evil' and 'corrupt' nature of the Hindu and his 'depravity', fuelled by his superstition and 'primitive' religion. The initial use of 'Hindu' in British discourse was a synonym for everything 'Indian', which, only in later times, was used for the religious majority of the sub-continent. The misreading of Indian civilization by Mill justified the sense of the colonisers' 'superiority', which led to a disinterest amongst East India Company servants, and later employees, of the Raj in Indian culture, literature and the historical continuity of an old civilization that had been validated by earlier 'Orientalists' like Robertson. This project will study how the reading of history and interpretations of culture and literature have been instrumental in forming the minds of generations responsible for governing India, establishing business houses, managing plantations and trade in Indian produce in a global market.

Mill had never set foot in India and had no linguistic acquaintance with Indian languages, claiming his 'expertise' in India's history from the distance of the metropole, in an act that marginalises India's history through a written discourse based on second-hand knowledge, which takes on the aura of 'authenticity' associated with the written word. Mill's treatise was further consolidated by another Scot, Thomas Babington Macaulay (1800–1859, who lived in India between 1834 and 1838) whose 'Minute on Indian Education' of 1835, passed the judgement that 'a single shelf of a good European library was worth the whole native literature of India and Arabia' (Sharp 109); sweeping statement made by a Member of the Governor-General's Council, who, like Mill, did not possess any first-hand knowledge of Indian Languages or of Arabic. These texts were instrumental in constructing perceived notions as 'facts' about India, and the reality on the ground became secondary in an assessment of far-flung colonies, which could thus be written about, assessed and branded as 'inferior' without association with the people or the land that was being described–negating the human association so necessary for a fuller understanding of the people and their context. By these means, another 'myth' was constructed, the myth of Indian barbarism and decadence against Western rationality and superiority, negating and dismantling the view that was prevalent and practised during the Scottish Enlightenment. As Subrata Dasgupta has said, 'the Scottish Enlightenment embodied not only rationalism but also a solid dose of Scottish practicality' (*Dasgupta, Awakening* 146), which would be exemplified by the work on the ground carried out in the educational sphere by significant Scottish thinkers and pragmatists as will be discussed below.

Robertson did not visit India, but he preceded the Victorian, evangelist views, when there was still a certain respect for the wonder that was India and the sophistication of her civilization.

And as we have seen, Mill wrote about Indian history and made sweeping, definitive statements about India and Indians (and of Indian art, which will be discussed below) without ever visiting India. Macaulay dismissed all Arabic and Sanskrit literature without having any knowledge of any of the Indian languages and its continuous literary history that was over 3,000 years old. Later, Ruskin's dismissal of the beauty, meaning and deep philosophy of Indian art and architecture would be based on secondary sources and information without any direct contact with examples of Indian art or debates with Indian art critiques (Mitter 244).

However, Mill's representation of India continued to be challenged in subsequent publications, (e.g., in thoughtful analyses by John Crawfurd (1783–1868) in his *History of the Indian Archipelago* (1820) and, in *A View of the Present State and Future Prospects of the Free Trade and Colonisation of India* (1828).) There was also the French account by Anquetil-Duperron (1731–1805) who came to India in 1754, and whose work was rediscovered by Raymond Schwab in 1950. His *La Renaissance Orientale* was later translated into English in 1984 by Patterson-Black and Reinking entitled, *The Oriental Renaissance: Europe's Rediscovery of India and the East 1680–1880* (1984). This Orientalist perspective of India is considered a seminal text by Edward Said in his *Orientalism* (1978).

What we are looking at here, however, is pre-Saidian Orientalism (with a capital O) as opposed to Saidian/post-Saidian orientalism (with a lower case), in relation to India where Scots played a pivotal role in the civil, military, maritime and medical services at the beginning of the 19th century, in private businesses, in partnerships in agency houses in the Presidencies, particularly in Calcutta (Powell 6). The Saidian thesis that all orientalist endeavours were for the advancement and empowerment of the colonial state, as discussed by Michael Dodson in his *Orientalism, Empire, and National Culture: India 1770–1880* (2007) establishing a discourse which was aimed at representing, speaking for, dominating and ruling the Orient, is not pertinent to this particular study. The pre-Saidian Orientalism was, in many cases, a self-fulfilling scholarly venture to gather knowledge and indulge in a cultural exchange with native scholars, which Bayly called 'constructive orientalism' in his *Empire and Information: Intelligence Gathering and Social Communication in India 1780–1870* (1996), a term Dodson also uses with reference to the educational scene. This form of Orientalism has been called 'neo-orientalism'.

The idea of a 'Scottish School' of Indian governance has been mooted by Martha McLaren in her *British India and British Scotland, 1780–1830: Career Building, Empire Building and a Scottish School of Thought on Indian Governance* (2001) and Michael Fry in his *The Scottish Empire* (2001). There is a general consensus about a Scottish 'distinctiveness' 'in such spheres as governance, militarism and trade' (Powell, 7) as has been noted by Philip Constable in 'Scottish Missionaries' (Constable 278-313). Michael Fry also speaks of a 'discrete Scottish attitude to empire linked in general to the intellectual climate' practised by Governor-Generals like Munro, Malcolm and Elphinstone (Powell 7). However, the idea of tracing a distinctive Scottish School or paradigm has been challenged by scholars like Jane Rendall in her article 'Scottish Orientalism from Robertson to James Mill', where she speaks of the intellectual influences of Scots in 'a second "generation" of philologists and historians, who worked in the spirit of Robertson's liberal humanism rather than under James Mill's racist construct of India and her people (Rendall). The Muir brothers' (Ibid.) generation of Scots did have some links with Rendall's scholars like: Alexander Hamilton (1762–1864), James Mackintosh (1765–1832), John Crawfurd (1783–1868) and Mountstuart Elphinstone (all Haileybury pupils through their contacts in India). However, as Powell points out, a putative 'third generation' of Scottish scholar-administrators in the Muir brothers can be identified 'at a considerable chronological remove from the original idea' (Powell 9).

Warren Hastings (1732–1818), who came to Bengal in 1772 as Governor, was appointed Bengal's first Governor-General from 1774 until 1785. Hastings was a key figure of this constructive orientalist group who believed that the British official serving in India should 'think and act like an Asian', having a good knowledge of the country's literature, culture, its laws and history (Kopf 18). The Orientalists familiarized themselves with various facets of the Indian knowledge domain. Calcutta, as the capital of the Bengal Presidency, became a beehive of scholarly activity under Hasting's Governorship. These Indophiles included the Sanskritists William Jones (1746–1794, founder of the Asiatic Society in 1784), Henry Colebrook (1765–1836 who wrote Sanskrit Grammar and translated Indian law texts), Nathaniel Halhed (1751–1830) who wrote the first Bengali grammar), Charles Wilkins (1749–1836 who translated the *Bhagvat Gita* into English), James Princep (1799–1840 who deciphered the Bramhi script of ancient India) and Robert Chambers (1737–1803, third President of the Asiatic Society, who was interested in law and literature) (Dasgupta, *The Bengal Renaissance* 24, 31).

These eighteenth century men actually preached and practised such a professional cosmopolitanism, a scholarly ideal perhaps best exemplified by the Asiatic Society (Curley 370).

According to David Kopf, these scholar administrators were 'classicists', cosmopolitan and rationalists rather than 'progressives', nationalist and romantics; they were very much products of the European Enlightenment (*British Orientalism* 22).

They were all Englishmen, apart from Sir William Jones, who was Welsh. Their Scottish counterparts, who were legatees of the Scottish Enlightenment and are identified by many scholars as Scottish Orientalists, may be described in Kopf's terms as progressives, nationalist and romantics. They fell into a different category of men who would influence the 'Awakening' of the Bengali mind (Ibid. 19; Dasgupta, *Awakening* 2) in no uncertain terms as they moved away from a focus on classical Sanskrit scholarship to vernacular Bengali and to education in English. It is in the area of educational and cultural reform and in their association with Indian reformers, that Scottish Orientalists influenced and facilitated the Bengal Renaissance, which would later affect all of India. Though they did not study William Robertson's history of India at University, his book was available and read and his views on India were well known: 'to him (Robertson), the cave temple–one of the earliest forms of architecture–indicated a developed state of society, as equally the sculptures in them reflected considerable achievement for the period (Mitter 177).

These Scottish Orientalists were not influenced by James Mill's *The History of India*. According to Mill, India's crudeness and barbarism could be detected in her art. In his estimation, not only was Indian art 'primitive, unattractive, rude in taste and genius', but 'unnatural, offensive and not infrequently disgusting… The Hindus copy with great exactness, even from nature. By consequence they draw portraits, both of individuals and groups, with a minute likeness; but peculiarly devoid of grace and expression…They are entirely without a knowledge of perspective, and by consequence of all those finer and nobler parts of the art of painting, which have perspective for their requisite basis' (Ibid. 176, 177). This strong indictment of Indian artistic expression, the culmination of her civilization according to Mill, is not evident in the consciousness of Scottish Orientalists.

George Davie in his work, *The Democratic Intellect: Scotland and Her Universities in the Nineteenth Century* (1961), speaks of the generalist education in secondary schools in Scotland, which offered a Universalist body of knowledge–very school worth mentioning at this higher education today. The Scottish secondary schooling system had philosophy at its core, rather than the classics, which, Davie notes, marked the English system. In Scotland, a general education that covered poetry, philosophy, science and mathematics, did not see these subjects as competitors, but together they accounted for an intellect that was philosophical, scientific and humanist, hence 'democratic'. Murdo Macdonald in his 'Introduction' to the 2013 edition of Davie's book, links the intellectual traditions of the Scottish Enlightenment to those of today. Patrick

Geddes (1854–1932), a generalist who will be discussed later, welcomed this scientific approach to teaching, affirming that any aspect of knowledge, culture or society benefits from illumination of all other aspects, (Macdonald 77). Davie's idea of the Democratic Intellect has been challenged as too simplistic by some scholars, while hailed and accepted by others like Macdonald and the Indian historian, Barun Dey.

We have already discussed one Scot who was responsible for the introduction of English education and Western science first in Bengal, which soon spread across India, namely Thomas Babington Macaulay. This clever but audacious proposal to create a band of brown sahibs (there is no mention of brown memsahibs here) in India, 'Indian in blood and colour, but English in taste, in opinions, in morals, and in intellect' (Sharp 116) so that the British could create a brand of loyalists amongst the natives and continue to rule by proxy, reaped tremendous benefits for British rule for over a century. However, this step also generated ideas of modernity, of democracy – humanist ideas emanating from the British and Scottish Enlightenment, ideas of freedom, the dignity of man and the right to question and challenge as thinking, debating individuals and societies – questioning and answering the British in their own words, in a language they understood, English.

This brings us to the discussion of two Scots, David Hare and Alexander Duff, who were central figures in Calcutta, influential in the education sector and who contributed to the developments that would become the cornerstone of higher education in modern India. We have the story from Peary Chand Mitra (1814–1883) that on one occasion when Raja Rammohan Roy (founder of the Bramha Samaj in 1828 and the leading spirit of the Bengal Renaissance) was with his friends in his Calcutta home, he mooted the idea of forming an 'Atmiya Sabha' to discuss and address the 'moral condition' in Hindu society.

One person who was present at this gathering was David Hare (1814–1883), a Scottish watchmaker and philosopher from Edinburgh. Hare was an atheist, outside the Presbyterian/Anglican fold of missionary activity in India. It was Hare who came up with the proposal of educating 'native' youths in Western/English literature and science to enlighten them effectively and free their minds of 'pernicious cants' (Mitra, XII). Dasgupta calls the Scottish Orientalists 'tinkers as well as thinkers' (*Awakening* 146). Thus Hindu College, the forerunner of Presidency College (now Presidency University), was conceived by David Hare and supported warmly by Raja Rammohan Roy. It was established on 20 January 1817 and it celebrated 200 years of its anniversary in January 2017. Its fundamental objective was 'the tuition of the sons of respectable Hindoos in the English and Indian language (sic) and in the literature and science of Europe and Asia' (Ibid. 147). However, the religio-caste-class imperative meant that Raja Rammohan Roy, who was shunned by a section of prominent Orthodox Hindus as a Bramho, had to distance himself from the actual foundation of the

College. David Hare's proposal of educating 'native' youths in Western/English literature and science was practised at Hindu College, which in 1828 had 400 students receiving English education. By 1835 there were 24 schools offering English education. Hare School remains a testimony to his role in Education (Ibid. 150). He was also the founder of the School Book Society and an initial force behind the idea of promoting the education of women in Bengal.

Of Raja Rammohan Roy, one can say that he did not just belong to a great epoch of change that would help India to become a modern nation, but was the creator of an epoch, responsible for its epochal revolution through his untiring advocacy for religious, social and educational reforms. He was the initiator of the Bengal/Indian Renaissance and we owe the study of English, of education in English in India to Raja Rammohan Roy's initiative. He has been considered 'The Father of Modern India' (Bruce Carlisle Robertson, 1999). The Director of the East India Company had set aside one lakh rupees for education, which the Orientalists wanted for Maulvis, Pundits, Sanskrit and Arabic scholars to use. It was Rammohan Roy who changed the course of our socio-cultural history with his famous letter to Lord Amherst, dated 11 December 1823, in which he wrote:

> We now find that the government is establishing a Sanskrit school under Hindu *pundits* to impart knowledge as is already current in India. This seminary can only be expected to load the minds of the physical distinctions of little or no practical use to the society... The Sanskrit system of education would be best calculated to keep this country in darkness... But as the improvement of the British native population is the object of the government it will consequently promote a more liberal and enlightened system of instruction, embracing mathematics, natural philosophy, chemistry and anatomy with other useful sciences which may be accomplished with the sum proposed by employing a few gentlemen of talent and learning educated in Europe, and providing a college furnished with the necessary books, instruments and other apparatus (Sharp 99, 100, 101).

Rammohan Roy did not receive an answer to his letter. Sanskrit College, which was established in 1823, remains an institution which is a great part of India's heritage and is of contemporary relevance. However, the ripples Rammohan Roy caused had phenomenal effects. Twelve years later, on 7 March 1835, Lord William Bentinck passed a Resolution on Education which was based on Macaulay's 'Minute' written earlier on 2 February 1835. Rammohan Roy's letter was part of what was called the 'Anglicist-Orientalist controversy' where 'Orientalist' refers to the proponents of Sanskritist classical learning and education in India.

Raja Rammohan Roy's close associate and friend was Prince Dwarakanath Tagore (1794–1846, Rabindranath Tagore's grandfather), the appellation of Prince signifying his philanthropy and generosity. Dwarakanath studied at Sherbourne's School in Calcutta. In fact, he was so grateful to Sherbourne, that he gave them a life stipend after his teacher retired. Dwarakanath was, also, taught by several Scottish teachers – William Adams, J.G. Gordon, James Calder–and later on, he gained proficiency in law under the guidance of the Scottish Barrister, Robert Culler Fergusson. Dwarakanath financed several educational institutions in his lifetime. While Raja Rammohan Roy is known as the Father of the modern Indian nation, one can say that he and Dwarakanath, who spearheaded the Bengal Renaissance, were architects of modern India with the impetus they lent to religious, social and educational reform and in Dwarakanath's case, to economic entrepreneurship.

One school worth mentioning at this juncture was the Dhurromtollah Academy run by David Drummond (1785–1843) – a Scot and a theological dissenter. He objected strongly to Phrenology and his students imbibed his way of freethinking and analysis. Both Hare and Drummond carried the legacy of the Scottish Enlightenment in their sceptical rationalist approach (Drummond was the author of *Objections to Phrenology*, 1829), which is evident in their work in education in India. Henry Derozio, the brilliant firebrand poet and Indian nationalist who taught at Hindu College between 1828 and 1831 (dismissed in 1831) had studied at Drummond's school. The band of Derozio's followers at Hindu College, called 'Young Bengal', vociferously dismissed traditional Hindu ways and Bengali culture and literature as they espoused western ways. What is significant for us today is the Academic Association which was set up by the Derozians for their discussions and debates, mainly on poetry and philosophy, all of which were conducted in English. Derozio signified the spirit of a new age in his brief academic life and career; where the freedom of thought and expression, the nationalist spirit of India and the gateway to the West and the world, through the medium of English, steered a section of society in Calcutta on a tide that would spread and embrace the whole country.

The role that education played in the evolution of modern India was further exemplified in an estimation of the contribution the first Scottish Free Church Mission missionary, Rev Alexander Duff (1806–1878). Duff spent three periods in India: 1830–1834, 1840–1851 and 1855–1863. He was a friend and associate of Raja Rammohan Roy's before the latter sailed for England. Rammohan Roy was a close associate of both David Hare and Alexander Duff. At the General Assembly institution (later Scottish Church College), where Duff was superintendent, science and English were taught with a view to introducing a progressive value system to Indian students, very much in the same vein as Hare had suggested. In spite of Duff's missionary zeal and proselytizing mission, he engaged the students in secular debates at Hindu College where he taught, encouraging freedom of thought and expression. Duff worked with William Carey at the Serampore Press and published books on Bengali Grammar and the Bible in Bengali. We see a marked shift in Duff from the earlier school of British Orientalists, as Duff valued vernacular language and education alongside English education, while the classicists of Hasting's time went back to what they considered the classical 'golden age of India' exemplified in its Sanskrit literature. The Scottish intervention in modern education in India helped to shape much of the intellectual horizon of the Bengal Renaissance.

The West had travelled to India, and a reverse track was in turn initiated during the early years of the Bengal Renaissance by Raja Rammohan Roy and Dwarakanath Tagore who both travelled to England where they died and were cremated. At the heart of a Bengal Renaissance reform movement for social and educational reform, stands the Tagore family, emanating from Prince Dwarakanath Tagore, continuing in his son, Maharshi Debendranath Tagore (1817–1905), who was the leader of the Bramho Samaj, a monotheistic movement, which gave fresh impetus (1842–43 onwards) to validating the Upanishadic tenets of Hindu philosophy and had a deep interest in Unitarianism. The dissenting voices reflected amongst Bramho activists, and the role of the Tattwabodhini Sabha and the journal, the *Tattwabodhini Patrika,* embody the centrality of ideas in a society that was confronting the challenges of transformation on the socio-religious front. One can say that Debendranath's son, the Nobel Laureate, Rabindranath Tagore (1861–1941), is the grand figure who, with his grandfather, Dwarakanath, bookended the Bengal Renaissance. Rabindranath was a pivotal figure who contributed substantially to bringing India to its modern status, willing to see the modern validation of ancient and medieval Indian thought, while welcoming the meeting of minds from the West and East in a mutually beneficial syncreticism.

As has been said before, this study is not about the Bengal Renaissance, but about the impact of Scottish Orientalists on this transitional epoch. We have highlighted the influential role some Scots have played in English education in India. We will end with a reference to the opinions of some Scottish critics on Indian art and architecture, which are suggestive of an appreciation of an Indian heritage and its aesthetic expression, which is very different from the Western 'standard' of what is beautiful, moral and acceptable as postulated by John Ruskin. Ruskin wrote in the league of scholars who took their cue from James Mill's *History of India*. While Ruskin's dismissal of the beauty, meaning and deep philosophy of Indian art and architecture was based on secondary sources and information without any direct contact with examples of Indian art or debates with Indian art critiques, some significant Scottish Orientalists' descriptions and critiques of Indian art and edifices were written on first-hand experience. Thus, Alexander Cunningham (1814–1893) says of the Khajuraho temple, 'the general effect of this great luxury of embellishment is extremely pleasing although the eye is often distracted by the multiplicity of detail' (Keay 128). James Fergusson (1808–1886, son of an Ayrshire doctor), was 'the historian of India's architecture' (Ibid. 118) and author of *History of Indian and Eastern Architecture* (1876); he gathered photographs of 3000 Indian buildings, praising them 'for an exuberance of fancy, a lavishness of labour and an elaboration of detail' (Ibid. 147). He notes 'the glory of Hindu architecture' (Ibid. 156) in Bhubaneswar temples and speaks of the temple at Halebid as 'a masterpiece of design in its class'. He comments that 'the artistic combination of horizontal with vertical lines, and the play of outline and of light and shade, far surpass anything in Gothic art' (Ibid.). He goes on to say, 'all that is wild in human faith and warm in human feeling is found portrayed on these walls' (Ibid.). However, there is an echo of Ruskin when he concludes that 'but of pure intellect there is little' (Ibid.). However, he is appreciative of the Qutab Minar (Ibid. 160) and of the Taj Mahal; he says, 'what made the Taj unique was its sculptural quality' (Ibid. 165). These art historians go back to medieval India in their appreciation of her aesthetic splendour and achievements. What is significant here is that they were writing and commenting on India's 'human faith' and 'warm human feeling' during the period of the Bengal/Indian Renaissance, affecting public opinion on India in the West.

Scotland remained a destination for many Indian scientists, engineers and teachers. Scottish researchers, like Sir Ronald Ross (1857–1932) who was born in India and won the Nobel Prize in 1902, and the botanist, William Roxburgh (1751–1815), the first Superintendent of the Botanical Gardens in Calcutta (1793–1813), who conducted their research in India, made significant contributions to the Indian scientific field. The philanthropist, Sir Daniel Hamilton from Arran, settled in India and was involved in establishing cooperatives, introducing microcredit and working for the rural regeneration of communities in the Sundarbans.

The East-West dialogue that was generated as a result of this encounter in India, would be continued by several Renaissance figures who travelled from India to the West in the earlier 20th century, like Acharya Prafulla Chandra Ray who studied at Edinburgh and Sir Jagadish Chandra Bose and Rabindranath Tagore were friends and close associates of the Scottish polymath, Sir Patrick Geddes. To Geddes, we owe the preservation and conservation plans of around 50 towns and cities in India, markedly Varanasi. In India, the clock that had been deftly wound and set ticking by Scottish Orientalists like David Hare, would continue to witness fresh developments and the expansion of education in India that is in tune with global trends today.

The subsequent chapters in this book have been arranged into four sections. The first section covers the period before, and leading up to, the Bengal Renaissance. The second section concentrates on stalwarts who contributed to education during the early and middle period of the Bengal Renaissance. The third, looks at the later period in which Rabindranath Tagore is the interweaving thread who binds some leading minds together in a narrative of creative experiment and development. The final section of the book also has the figure of Rabindranath at its core, as his advocacy for science in Indian education as a nation building imperative made him the friend of two leading scientists whose inventions and discoveries were significant for India and the rest of the world.

This book exemplifies certain positive results of the Indo-Scottish encounter in a discussion of the continuum of ideas evident in the work of key figures who dominated this period of transition to the modern era in India.

However, this period of intellectual and pragmatic interchange was preceded by travelling Scots, whose interest in the bustling port city of Calcutta, its architecture and its people in the early part of the 19th century is exemplified in Fraser's text, 'A Sojourner's Calcutta: through the colonial lens', which looks at the travel journals of the observers and recorders, Maria Graham, Walter Hamilton and LT RG (Robert Grenville) Wallace in this book. Their work on their Calcutta experience frame the later wave of Scots in the colonial/imperial capital, accounting for a narrative shift that is inevitable between itinerants/transients who are passing through and others who come with the intention of becoming part of a socio-cultural fabric, between ones who hold themselves apart from the 'native' population and those who immerse themselves in the projects for socio-cultural transformation(s).

What is significant about these travel narratives is their continuum with perceived ideas of Calcutta that is commensurate with other British narratives, which are marked by their Saidian Orientalist perspective of a 'black' town as separate from the European quarters. The latter, in turn, are segmented into groups which cascade from the superior ones who hold themselves apart from the 'natives' to those who live in close proximity with the indigenous population in a critically perceived association, thus perpetuating a hierarchical reading of the traits of diverse groups in this cosmopolitan city. The nature and influence of post-Saidian Orientalism, evident in the work and ideas of Scottish Orientalists, can be seen as a counter-narrative to this estimation of Calcutta through a colonial lens, which can be seen as different from the association that developed during the time of the Bengal Renaissance.

The gap that exists in any sustained analysis of this 'Scottish interaction' in India is addressed by Tapati Mukherjee in 'East Meets West: A Vibrant Encounter Between Indian Orthodoxy and Scottish Enlightenment', who notes the significant number of Scots who were at the helm of affairs in colonial India. The role of Scottish Viceroys, like Mountstuart Elphinstone, Lord Minto and Lord Dalhousie, in the transformation of Bengali society through governance; the work of educationists, like David Hare and Revd Alexander Duff (who were both friends of Raja Rammohan Roy), and path-breaking studies by experts in medicine, like Sir James Renald Martin, Sir Joseph Fayer and James Macnab

Cunningham, are considered in this overview of a transformatory period. Mukherjee traces the impact of Scottish Orientalists to the ideas they inherited from the Scottish Enlightenment. This chapter reiterates the historical overview provided in the Introduction and in its particular studies of the contribution of Scots to India; it reaffirms the positive side of the colonial encounter. Mukherjee goes back to the path being laid for this interchange by Rabindranath Tagore's grandfather, Prince Dwarakanath Tagore, an enterprising business entrepreneur and visionary, philanthropist and modernist, who travelled to Western metropolises – London, Paris and Edinburgh – and was honoured in the Scottish capital by being made a Freeman of the city.

This chapter also explores inter-continental friendships and association in several Scottish and Indian Renaissance figures, who are discussed at length in subsequent sections of this book. Thus Sir Patrick Geddes' contribution to the conservation work of towns and cities in India and to the planning of Rabindranath Tagore's International University, Visva-Bharati at Santiniketan, the work of Arthur Geddes at Rabindranath's rural institution at Sriniketan, the impact of Sir Daniel Hamilton's cooperative movement at Rabindranath's institution, establish the fruits borne of the dialogue between friends from the East and the West.

In 'The Scotland-India Interaction: Scottish Impact on a so-called native stalwart in India–Dwarakanath Tagore', Mukherjee expands on the subject of addressing and challenging Hindu orthodoxy in a study of the life and contribution of Dwarakanath Tagore, as she takes into account his humanism and liberalism in his attempts to break Hindu barriers of ostracism. Mukherjee shows how Dwarakanath's education and training under Scottish Orientalists widened his world view. Dwarakanath's diversification into different avenues of trade and business with the British make him the leading entrepreneurial Indian figure in his time. His friendship with India's modern architect, Raja Rammohan Roy, accounts for the impetus he gave to the monotheistic religious movement led by the Bramho Samaj. Mukherjee speaks of Dwarakanath's munificence as he promoted education amongst Indians through his contribution to educational institutions and student scholarships, his multifarious charitable activities, his dedication to consolidating landowners rights in colonial India, need to be revisited and remembered in any account of this period in Indian colonial history. Dwarakanath's association with Scots like David Hare, the educationist and Mr Holecroft, the proprietor of the *Calcutta Journal,* highlight the filtering of ideas from the Scottish Enlightenment which subsequently affected the thought and work of Scottish Orientalists. Dwarakanath's journeys to England and Scotland follows a reverse track from the colonial Scottish travellers. However, what signifies his visit in 1842 is the honour with which he was received by Queen Victoria and by the City of Edinburgh (made a Freeman in the latter) in spite of being from a subject nation. As Mukherjee affirms, Dwarakanath remains 'an icon of the Scotland-India encounter and intercourse'.

In all of these essays, the towering figure of Raja Rammohan Roy looms large on the Bengal horizon as he interacts with key Scottish personages during the Bengal Renaissance, like David Hare and Revd Alexander Duff, a trio who form the subject of essays which focus on their role in education in dedicated studies by Kathryn Simpson, Kaberi Chatterjee and Saptarshi Mallick.

David Hare, Roy's friend and collaborator on the implementation of English education in India, is the central persona in Saptarshi Mallick's discussion of the Serampore Missionaries, entitled 'Serampore Missionaries and David Hare: On the Penury of Education in Nineteenth-Century Bengal'. In his study, Mallick gives a brief overview of the Bengal Renaissance to place the two educationists in their context. This is followed by a detailed account of the contribution of the 'Serampore Trio', William Carey, Joshua Marshman and William Ward to vernacular and English education. The trio established schools for girls as well as boys, structured and expanded on the curriculum and published texts books to facilitate learning amongst the indigenous population. Mallick evidences his findings with references to various reports and shows how the 'Trio' compromised on imparting a Christian education by incorporating ethics as the fourth 'r' to reading, writing and arithmetic, moving away from their proselytizing mission. David Hare's contribution to education and the establishment of schools, his role in the Hindu College and the Medical College, were facilitated by Carey's work, as the latter was a precursor in the field of education for Indian children and youths, laying the path ready for Hare's subsequent endeavours. Mallick speaks about the role of the School Society and the School Book Society in the educational sphere. The difference between Carey's Christian faith and Hare's atheism is noted, but as Mallick points out, this does not deter the two from maintaining a close association in their educational and philanthropic projects. Hare, like Carey, spent his working life in India, never returning to his homeland. They remain an indelible part of Indian socio-cultural history inasmuch as they contributed to the nation-building process through their modernizing methods.

In 'Understanding the Renaissance in Nineteenth Century Bengal', Kathryn Simpson uses Clifford Geertz idea of 'Thick Description' and Max Weber's 'Webs of Significance' to analyse how a new historiography is formed in an estimation of an encounter in a peripheral community, which, on the one hand, is ascribed by and on the other resists the 'imperial'/colonial metropole. Simpson attempts to understand the macro-narrative through micro-narratives in a study of a 'Scottish Bengali comradeship' as a counterpoint to the overarching theme of 'English subjugation'. While key figures like Dwarakanath are focused on by Mukherjee as ones who promoted '"Man" and his welfare', Simpson shows – after Sudhir Chandra (1998) – how the

Renaissance deals with 'aspects of man-in-society' during a time of change/flux. At these transformational times, Duff's own dual language background (Gaelic and English), equipped him with the understanding of the Bengali-English dualism in Bengal, where he advocated education in English with Roy. His ideas were in tune with other Bengal Renaissance figures like Dwarakanath Tagore, Ram Komul Sen and Raja Radhakanta Deb. With Roy, Duff advocated and worked to effect a holistic educational environment in an atmosphere of debate and interchange between teacher and student through a new pedagogy. Both Roy and Duff promulgated English education and the sciences as they mapped what Simpson calls an 'Indian literary historiography'.

Alexander Duff's role in deciding on the pedagogic methodology in India is studied at length by Kaberi Chatterjee in 'The Caledonian Legacy: Of the Scottish Church College in Kolkata' who shows that missionary activity continued but did not impinge upon or impede Duff's pursuit of a 'quality' education in the English language. The debate between the vernacularists and the advocates of English was (and remains) ongoing. What marks Duff is his holistic approach to education is that he not only includes literature, history and philosophy, but also natural history, mathematics and the sciences in his curriculum, thus fulfilling the requisites of the Committee of Edinburgh for the first Scottish missionary's work in India. Duff's close association with Raja Rammohan Roy, his view of India as a 'fellow subject' of Britain in line with the Hebridian and Irish Catholic community, imbue his work in Calcutta with a sense of social inclusion that is directed at Indian youths in his institution(s). The Scottish-Indian encounter is enumerated in the outcome of the meetings between Rev Hastie and Swami Vivekanada, and between Netaji Subhas Chandra Bose and WS Urquhart at Duff's institution, by Chatterjee. This essay places Duff in the historical account of the changes in the nomenclature which signified the journey made by Duff's institution from the General Assembly Institution to Scottish Church College, by which name it is still known today.

After the two sections on Scottish Orientalists and Raja Rammohan Roy and his associates, we have essays on Rabindranath Tagore and his encounter and interaction with some leading Scottish minds. Burns' influence on Rabindranath and the latter's evolving estimation of and response to Scotland's national bard, are probingly dissected by Amrit Sen in 'A Complex Interface: Rabindranath and Burns'. Sen shows how the knowledge of Burns was brought to India in the wake of a sizeable Scottish presence in colonial times. Other links with Burns, both material and familial, are traced in this study of an inter-continental imperial project. Derozio's indebtedness to Burns in his nationalistic poetry found a continuum later in Rabindranath's bardic nationalism. Burns' songs, his collection of folk tunes in a nationalistic mission, are echoed in Rabindranath's work, especially in his appreciation of Burns' work, and the inspiration he drew from the medieval tradition of Vaishnava poetry and the Bauls (wandering minstrels) of Bengal. This analysis takes into account the biographical details in both poets' lives as it looks chronologically at Rabindranath's translations of Scottish and Irish melodies, weighing their significance against Rabindranath's poetic oeuvre, tracing his development from a Romantic lyrical poet's response to a poet confident in wielding his imaginative craft as he voiced a nation's soul and desire for freedom in the spirit of Burns' world view.

In Thomas Crosby's 'An Assessment of Sir Daniel Hamilton's Political Philosophy: The Panacea of Scottish Capitalism and Utilitarianism' there is no mention of Rabindranath; however, Hamilton visited Santiniketan on Rabindranath's invitation and, if one goes to Hamilton's bungalow today, there is a photograph of the wooden bungalow that Hamilton built for Rabindranath's visit, which has been washed away in this tide country. The two Rural Reconstructionists, Hamilton and Rabindranath, shared an interest in and fostered the cooperative movement. In Crosby's essay, he shows how microcredit through the introduction of paper currency in one rupee notes, follows the Scottish banking model which Hamilton implements in his Gosaba project in the Sundarbans. Hamilton's utopian project of an agricultural society where caste, class and religious differences were put aside, and self-reliance and interdependence were practised, was a socialist endeavour. Hamilton's Christian beliefs made him a strong opponent of communist ideology. Crosby notes ambivalences in Hamilton as he encouraged self-dependence and an internal, participatory resolution of disputes, while he remained opposed to Indian independence, as he believed that India had not resolved her own differences and was thus not ready for self-rule. Crosby traces a Scottish brand of Reconstructionist implementation in Hamilton's project. What was desirable were 'men of conscience', with an inherent reliability, both of which Hamilton possessed, making him the benefactor that he was, on whom his people relied and whom they trusted. What Hamilton set out to establish, and succeeded in, was implementing 'his "Scottish" brand of compassionate co-operative capitalism' within the prevalent English paradigm.

This vision of a rural Bengal with self-reliant communities was a vision shared by Hamilton and Rabindranath. It was at his rural reconstruction centre at Sriniketan (Birbhum district) that Rabindranath, with the help of the agriculturalist, Leonard K Elmhirst (an Englishman) and the Scottish geographer, Arthur Geddes (Patrick Geddes' son), implemented his regeneration scheme. There are two essays on the work of Arthur Geddes in this volume, by Neil Fraser and Dixit Sinha. In 'A Scotsman at Sriniketan', Neil Fraser shows how Arthur Geddes and Elmhirst shared Rabindranath's philosophy that people had to work in close bond with nature, replenishing, not robbing, the soil which nurtures us, and that there needs to be full collaboration between 'the scholars, the poets, the musicians, the artists as well as the scientists'. Fraser also notes that Rabindranath's modernity made him welcome Patrick Geddes's scientific approach to 'village reconstruction and land regeneration'. In his analysis, Fraser takes Elmhirst's list of principles as the cornerstone to the success of the Sriniketan experiment, winning the trust of villagers through settling feuds and problem solving, providing training to farmers and craftsmen, working with boy scouts (*bratidal*) and implementing profitable farming. Both Hamilton in Gosaba, and Arthur Geddes and Elmhirst in Birbhum, encountered the prevalence of preventable diseases, especially malaria, which was a killer and a serious deterrent to regeneration plans.

Fraser notes four major areas in which Arthur contributed to Rabindranath's institution: through his rural reconstruction work; his village surveys which informed his doctoral thesis, *Au Pays de Tagore* (*In the Land of Tagore*); acting as a conduit for his father's plans for Rabindranath's university on the ground; and his translation (with notations) of Rabindranath's songs. Here we find the fruits of a friendship between the older Renaissance man, Rabindranath, and a young visionary Scot, which engendered a multifaceted project that contributed to India's aspirations as a modern nation.

The polymath in Arthur Geddes is reaffirmed by Dikshit Sinha in his essay, 'Arthur Geddes and Sriniketan: Explaining Underdevelopment' as he 'effortlessly' straddled geography, sociology, folklore, and town planning, music and literature. Sinha is conscious of the fact that Arthur Geddes's reputation as the translator of some of Rabindranath's songs, and the prominence of Elmhirst have overshadowed the truth about Arthur Geddes' effective work in rural regeneration. Sinha points out that both Arthur Geddes and Elmhirst believed in 'sovereignty and freedom of reason' for all people and all civilizations as evident in their efforts to encourage self-help, self-reflexivity and self-governance in the village community for a sustainable future. Theirs was a holistic approach to education, as they not only built the infrastructure of Sriniketan, but facilitated an environment of knowledge-sharing between the institution and the surrounding villages. In Arthur Geddes one finds an exemplary example of one who was able to build bridges between western culture and the eastern reality as he addressed the local issues with his geographical and sociological expertise, involving students and using creative methods in his teaching at Santiniketan and Sriniketan, which was in tune with Rabindranath's educational project. On Rabindranath's advice, Arthur Geddes taught his students Patrick Geddes' 'graphic method', a diagrammatic sociological interpretation of history and culture. Both Arthur Geddes and Elmhirst carried out intensive research to understand the people, life and nature of the hinterland of the university and implement their ideas through empathetic methods, addressing issues like poverty, poor nutrition and ill health in collaborative, collective projects. Dixit provides a detailed analysis of the focus and significance of Arthur Geddes's PhD thesis. Amidst all the work carried out by the geographer, the 'personality of the poet' was a pervading influence in this space where the local and global, the regional and international met and where Rabindranath's philosophy of *samagrata* (ecological bonding of man with the environment) was implemented by his collaborator Arthur Geddes who, like Elmhirst, maintained a friendship he valued with Rabindranath, who he addressed as 'Gurudev', even after he had left Santiniketan/Sriniketan, through correspondence.

The final section of this book has two essays which dwell on the life and work of two leading scientists, both Renaissance men who were men of science. Acharya Prafulla Chandra Ray was a chemist, who was known to Rabindranath and Sir Jagadish Chandra Bose, a biologist who was a close friend of Rabindranath's. Both were educated in Britain: Ray at the University of Edinburgh (where he obtained a BSc and a DPhil in Chemistry) and Bose at Cambridge. Both scientists were engaged in original scientific research in Calcutta, the seat of the Bengal Renaissance. In 'The East's Writing Back to the West: Acharya Prafulla Chandra Ray and Postcoloniality', Biswanath Banerjee offers a postcolonial analysis of the ambivalence in Ray to Western attitudes, where Ray was critical of and rejected the West's sense of superiority and its dismissal of the tradition of Indian sciences as emanating from an irrational mind, while he remained respectful of the enquiring mind and investigative scientific research carried out at Western institutions. Ray's syncretic approach as he willingly imbibed good Western practices and recognized the value of indigenous scientific knowledge, in addition to his postcolonial vision of contributing to development and industry in India through his training and research work in chemistry, made him a nationalist who was international in outlook. He was deeply critical of Indian superstitious beliefs, the degree-seeking Indian and the divisive caste system. Ray's critique of British stringent economic and political policies in India find voice in an essay he wrote for a competition at Edinburgh with the intention of raising awareness amongst the British in Britain of what was happening in India, an opinion he would hold throughout his life while he continued to have a deep respect for leading Western scientists in his field, seeking their association and collaboration. Ray went on to found the first chemical industry of India. For Ray, empirical science was the tool for dismantling Western hegemony: the key to India's prosperous future, the path to her economic recovery, her liberation and modernization.

The final chapter in this book considers Patrick Geddes' biography of the pioneering biologist in JC Bose, where Bose's professional ideals and standards, his intellectual integrity, his struggle against colonial obstacles to recognition, where the scientist as hero is discussed by Patrick Geddes, who believed that India would progress through 'impassioned inquiry and research' as embodied by Bose's life and work. The colonial encounter comes full circle in Geddes's friendships with Rabindranath and JC Bose in India, nurtured through mutual respect and understanding, facilitating the continuum of ideas in a meeting of minds, between the East and the West. Geddes and Bose had met in Paris through Margaret Noble, the Irish spiritual thinker and social worker, who is more popularly known as Sister Nivedita, the disciple of Swami Vivekananda, mentioned in Kaberi Chatterjee's chapter on 'The Caledonian Legacy'. We find a new respect and hope for India in Geddes' perceptive estimation of and advocacy for one of India's greatest minds in Sir JC Bose. This advocacy is analysed by Amrit Sen in his chapter on 'The Scientist as Hero: The Fashioning of the Self in Patrick Geddes's *The Life and Work of Sir Jagadish. C. Bose* (1920)', and where Sen probingly asks why Geddes was drawn to Bose. He finds the answers in Bose's intrepid personality, his creative thinking and inventions, his multidisciplinarity and his complete indifference to patenting his findings and seeking personal materialistic gains. In this chapter, Sen establishes how science would have benefitted if the West had heeded and recognized Bose's discoveries as the valid work of a brilliant and reliable pioneer in the East and if Bose himself had resorted to patenting his discoveries, which were epoch changing. Ray's Bengal Chemical and Pharmaceutical Works and the Bose Institute for scientific research were their respective contributions to India as Renaissance men. They were both products of a positive synthesis of the West and the East, participants in a dialogue that began during the Scottish Enlightenment and continued in Renaissance Bengal which saw the transformation of India as a modern nation, moving towards self-realisation and expression, given impetus by the spirit of Scottish Orientalist thought.

Works Cited:

Bayly, Christopher A. Empire and Information: *Intelligence Gathering and Social Communication in India 1780–1870.* Cambridge: Cambridge University Press, 1996. Print.

—. "Orientalists, informants and critics in Benares, 1790–1860." *Perspectives of Mutual Encounters in South Asian History 1760–1860.* Ed. Jamal Malik. Leiden: Koninklijke Brill NV, 2000. 97-127. Print.

Bruce. Carlisle Robertson. *Raja Rammohan Roy: The Father of Modern India.* New Delhi: Oxford University Press, 1999. Print.

Bureau of Education, (ed. H. Sharp) *Selections from Educational records, Part 1* (1781–1839) (Calcutta: Superintendent, Government Printing, 1920; reprinted National Archives of India, 1965).

Constable, Philip. "Scottish Missionaries, 'Protestant Hinduism' and the Scottish sense of empire in nineteenth and early twentieth century India." *Scottish Historical Review* 86. 2 (October 2007): 278-313. Print.

Crauford, Quintin. *Sketches Chiefly relating to the History, Religion, Learning, and Manners, of the Hindoos.* 2 vols. London, T. Cadell, 1792. Print.

Crawfurd, James. *History of the Indian Archipelago.* Edinburgh: Constable, 1820. Print.

Crawfurd, James. *A View of the Present State and Future Prospects of the Free Trade and Colonisation of India.* London: J. Ridgeway, 1828. Print.

Curley, Thomas M. *Sir Robert Chambers: Law, Literature and Empire in the Age of Johnson.* Wisconsin: University of Wisconsin Press, 1998. Print.

Dasgupta, Subrata. *The Bengal Renaissance: Identity and Creativity from Rammohun Roy to Rabindranath Tagore.* Ranikhet: Permanent Black, 2007. Print.

—. *Awakening: The Story of the Bengal Renaissance.* Noida: Random House, 2011. Print.

Davie, George. *The Democratic Intellect: Scotland and her Universities in the Nineteenth Century.* 2nd rev. ed. Edinburgh: Edinburgh University Press, 2013. Print.

Defries, Amelia. *The Interpreter: Geddes: The Man and his Gospel.* New York: Boni & Liveright, 1928. Print.

Devine, Tom M. *Scotland's Empire 1600–1815.* London: Penguin. 2004. Print.

Dodson, Michael. *Orientalism, Empire, and National Culture: India 1770–1880.* Basingstoke: Palgrave-Macmillan, 2007. Print.

Fry, Michael. *The Scottish Empire.* Edinburgh: Tuckwell/Berlinn, 2001. Print.

Herman, Arthur. *The Scottish Enlightenment: The Scots' Invention of the Modern World.* London: Harper Collins, 2001. Print.

Keay, John. *India Discovered.* Glasgow: Collins, 1988. Print.

Kopf, David. *British Orientalism and the Bengal Renaissance: The Dynamics of Indian Modernization, 1773–1835.* Berkeley: University of California Press, 1969. Print.

MacKenzie, John. "Essay and Reflection on Scotland and the Empire." *International History Review* 15: 4 (1993): 714-739. Print.

—. *Orientalism: History, theory and the arts.* Manchester: Manchester University Press, 1995. Print.

Macdonald, Murdo. 'Patrick Geddes and the Tradition of Scottish Generalism', *Journal of Scottish Thought,* 2012, Vol 5: Special issue on Patrick Geddes. Aberdeen: Aberdeen University Press; 73-87. ISSN 1755 9928.

McLaren, Martha *British India and British Scotland, 1780–1830 : Career Building, Empire Building and a Scottish School of Thought on Indian Governance.* Akron: University of Akron, 2001. Print.

Mill, James. *The History of British India.* London: Baldwin, Cradock and Joy, 1817. Print.

Mitter, Partha. *Much Maligned Monsters: History of European Reactions to Indian Art.* Oxford: Clarendon Press, 1977. Print.

Mitra, Peary Chand. *A Biographical Sketch of David Hare.* Calcutta: W. Newman and Co. 1877. Print.

Powell, Averil A. *Scottish Orientalists and India: The Muir Brothers, Religion, Education and Empire.* Woodbridge, Suffolk UK: Boydell Press, 2010. Print.

Rendall, Jane. "Scottish Orientalism from Robertson to James Mill." *Historical Journal* 25. 1 (March 1982): 43-69. Print.

Robertson, William. *An Historical Disquisition Concerning The Knowledge which the Ancients had of India; And the Progress of Trade with that Country prior to the Discovery of the Passage to it by the Cape of Good Hope.* London: Cadell and Davies, 1791. Print.

Said, Edward W. *Orientalism.* London: Routledge and Kegan-Paul, 1978. Print.

Schwab, Raymond. *The Oriental Renaissance: Europe's Rediscovery of India and the East 1680–1880.* Trans. G. Patterson-Black and V. Reinking. New York: Columbia University Press, 1984. Print.

Sharp, H., comp. and ed. *Selections From Educational Records Part I 1781–1839.* Calcutta: Superintendent Government Printing, 1920. Print.

Young, Richard Fox. *Resistant Hinduism: Sanskrit Sources on Anti-Christian Apologetics in Early Nineteenth-Century India.*

A Sojourner's Calcutta: Through the Colonial Lens

Bashabi Fraser

'THE EAST', as is noted in *Tancred* by Disraeli, 'is a career' (II: XIV) and India signified this place for adventure, trade and professional advancement. Once the three villages of Gobindapur, Sutanuti and Kalikuta were occupied and united under the umbrella term, Kalikata, by Job Charnock in the last decade of the 17th century, the nucleus of a port township emerged on a crucial trade route through what became, in British descriptions, the city of Calcutta. Marked differences emerge in colonial discourse in perspectives of Calcutta, the cradle of British governance in India, as it was first settled, then transformed into a bustling global trading *bandar*/port, the East India Company's powerhouse, and then as it effortlessly donned the mantle of the imperial capital of the British Raj after the Indian Revolt in 1857–58. This study will consider some travel journals written in the earlier part of the 19th century by Scots travelling to Calcutta; observing, describing and assessing the city, its architecture, its people, and its multiculturalism. The Scot in India was part of the colonial presence, the hegemonic dominant group considered as belonging to the privileged British group, which was numerically a very small group amongst a heavily populated majority of 'natives'. The Scots, in the same vein as their British compatriots, held themselves apart in a stratum above the other European presences in Calcutta, as the journals reviewed in this paper will illustrate.

The three journals that are considered for the purposes of this study are by Maria Graham, 'Calcutta in 1810', Walter Hamilton, 'Calcutta in 1821' and Lieut RG (Robert Grenville) Wallace, 'Calcutta in 1823'. All these journals on Calcutta are dedicated pages from longer works. Graham's descriptions are from *Journal of a Residence in India*. As the title indicates, she was a resident in India, but the entries confirm she always had the vision of returning 'home' to 'England'. Graham's journal does not claim a view beyond the personal response to the places she visits, the society and customs she encounters. Hamilton's Calcutta pages are part of *A Geographical, Statistical and Historical Description of Hindostan and The Adjacent Countries* (London, 1820), Vols 1 & 2, Vol, 1, pp. 48-61. [220-244] and his description is acknowledged in the *East India Company Gazeteer*. The third journal by

Lieut RG Wallace, entitled 'Fifteen Years in India: Or Sketches of a Soldier's Life, Being and attempt to describe Persons and Things in various parts of Hindotsan', appears in the *Journal of an Officer in His Majesty's Service*. The three journal entries on Calcutta are included in P. Thankappan's Nair's anthology of travel writing.[1] As they span the earlier part of the 19th century, they offer an Orientalist view of Calcutta in the William Jonesian sense, that will be revised and altered in the second half of the 19th century as a result of the exigencies of colonial policy subsequent to the Indian Revolt in 1857–58.

The post-Indian Revolt view of Calcutta is very different from the reference to its enchanting prospect, magnificence and luxuriance which we encounter in the early 19th century travel journals. The imperial construct of an unsavoury Calcutta has persisted in many British perspectives, and can be seen as late as the mid-1980s in an Introduction by MM Kaye to an edition of Eliza Fay's travel journal, edited by EM Forster. Kaye is at a loss to understand why Fay would even want to travel to Calcutta and cannot fathom her 'obsession' with the city to which she returned more than once. Of Calcutta he says:

> It can never have been a salubrious city, and although its imposing public buildings and the Georgian mansions of the merchant princes of the East India Company built for themselves on the banks of the Hoogli at Garden Reach may have looked impressive enough in the latter half of the eighteenth century, when they were spanking new, the climate must have been just as bad then as it is now. While the smell was probably worse – if that is possible.[2]

The dismissal of the trade capital of the East India Company is complete in Kaye's estimation. Graham, Wallace and Hamilton would probably have understood Fay's fascination for the city of Calcutta.

Wallace's work, like Graham's, has an official documentation agenda, while Hamilton's work retains the personal response in its life writing avocation 'Journal', and the informal nature of his account is suggested by its claim to being 'Sketches'. While Graham and Hamilton appear to have the freedom of a personal documentation, Wallace's 'Description' has a more official intention as indicated by the title. Like Graham, Hamilton had been a resident in India, while Wallace's document does not affirm this.

This study will consider the significance of some key descriptions in view of Scottish travellers in Calcutta in the 19th century. In this context, it is pertinent to consider a term that has been used for another group of travellers (or migrants?) to another continent, in this case, the Chinese in the USA. Paul Siu has used the term 'sojourner' for the Chinese immigrant to America who 'clings to the culture of his own group' and who 'is unwilling to organize himself as a permanent resident in the country of his sojourn' (sojourner). Like the marginal man, the sojourner is also a deviant; but, unlike the marginal man, the sojourner does not 'seek status in the society of the dominant group' (Siu, Chinese Laundryman 294). He 'spends many years of his lifetime in a foreign country without being assimilated by it' (Ibid.) In the case of the Scot in India, the Scot was part of the imperial presence, the hegemonic dominant group considered as part of the privileged British group, which was numerically a very small group amongst a heavily populated majority of 'natives'. The British, as the journals reviewed in this paper illustrate, held themselves apart in a stratum above the other European presences in Calcutta.

In her consideration of diaspora, sojourn and migration, Deboarah L. Madsen quotes Wang Gungwu's keynote address at the fifth international conference of the International Society for the Study of Chinese Overseas held on 11 May 2004. She highlights the difference of the two terms, 'sojourning' and 'migration' in the view of their return to the country of origin stating:

> ...the key difference [between migration and sojourning] lies in that sojourning always implied the readiness to return to China. Migranthood makes no such commitment. It is both flexible and unpredictable where notions of home and nationality are concerned ('Diaspora, Sojourn, Migration' 43).

The word 'sojourner' evokes the figure of the traveller, the one who is forever passing through and remains an observer but never a real participant.

This brings us to another term, this time used by Michael Fry of Scots in India.[3] He calls him the transient, one who has the sense of being a temporary resident in a country not his own, marked by the inevitability of imminent change. The last word I would like to consider is the itinerant, the travelling, peripatetic, wandering migrant, who is assailed by wanderlust. All these terms – sojourner, transient, itinerant – lay emphasis on the concept of 'scattering,' which is inherent in the original Greek term, diaspora (diaspeirein 'disperse', from dia 'across' + speirein 'scatter', rather than the meaning pertinent to settler colonies in to 'sow'). It therefore highlights, in these particular instances, the unstable nature of colonial journeys, which nevertheless, have helped to construct a discourse emerging from the colonial gaze as it charts and describes Calcutta.

There is nothing to demarcate these travel journals as distinctively Scottish apart from the names of the authors, as they write in a genre that was shared by British travellers from the 17th century and which continued through the 19th century as the collected journals in the three volumes complied by Nair show.

All three journals are part of a prevalent colonial discourse and, to adopt Homi K. Bhabha's position, they are 'crucial to a range of differences and discriminations that inform the discursive and political practices of racial and cultural hierarchisation', which is an 'exercise of colonial power through discourse, demand[ing] an articulation of forms of difference – (both) racial and sexual' (Bhabha 37). This review of the three selected journals will explore how the racial and cultural hierarchisation and difference become evident through the colonial lens as Calcutta and its location, space and society are described by the travel writers.

In *Orientalism*, Said notes how the near East became known to the West, through charting the trade routes/travels and accounts of Marco Polo, Lodovico di Varthema and Pietro della Valle and through fabulists like Mandeville. He says:

> Altogether an internally structured archive is built up from the literature that belongs to these experiences. Out of this comes a restricted number of typical encapsulations: the journey, the history, the fable, the stereotype, the polemical confrontation. These are the lenses through which the Orient is experienced, and they shape the language perception, and form of the encounter between the East and West. What gives these immense encounters some unity, however, is the vacillation...Something patently foreign and distant acquires, for one reason or another, a status more rather than less familiar (Said, *Orientalism* 58).

The unity that emerges in this literature as a result of this encounter with the Orient and the resultant account, as it makes the distant more familiar, will be considered in a critical scrutiny of Graham, Wallace and Hamilton's journals.

The ground for these journals had been laid by Alexander Dow's translation of Firishta's *History of Hindostan* in 1768 and *The History, Religion, Learning and Manners of the Hindus* by Quintin Craufurd in 1790 which were generated by a focus of Scottish Orientalist interest in India or 'Hindostan'. William Robertson's respectful estimation and India and her civilisation in *An Historical Disquisition Concerning the Knowledge which the Ancients had of India*, 1791 was a key text that had shaped the British/ Scottish imagination for travellers/adventurers/traders coming to India in the late 18th and early 19th centuries. The art historian, Partha Mitter has noted that William Robertson,

> ...while discussing the progress of arts and sciences, [William Robertson] had regarded India as one of their earliest homes. To him the cave temple, one of the earliest forms of architecture, indicated a developed state of society as equally the sculptures in them reflected considerable achievement for the period (Mitter, *Much Maligned Monsters* 177).

These travel accounts chart a city as the flaneur/flaneuse would in London or Paris[4] in Modernist texts almost a century later with an objectivity that embodies the metropolitan consciousness of a cosmopolitan observer, in this case, an itinerant, a sojourner, a transient.

A poem in Wallace's account conveys the impact Calcutta has on itinerants/sojourners/transients:

> **View from Champaul Ghaut** (Chandpal Ghat)
> […]We stand at Champaul Ghaut's refreshing green,
> And contemplate the grandeur of the scene.
> Aurora's hand had spread the genial feast,
> Of golden morning o'er the silver east;
> While crowds of Hindoos, at the dawn of day,
> With Gunga's tears to lave their sins away,
> Plunge in the Hoogly's deep majestic flow,
> Whose curling waves move past sublimely slow.
> A wood of lofty masts, Britannia's pride,
> From ships well moor'd along Calcutta's side,
> Extends to where Fort William's flag unfurl'd,
> Proclaims our glory to the eastern world.
> Far spreading thence the city's rich display,
> O'er which appears the splendid car of day,
> Of lofty structures, pleased we to behold,
> Like orient pearls that glow in burnished gold.

The reference to the Calcutta edifices as 'orient pearls' is interesting, the echoes of Shakespearean descriptions of eastern beauty and opulence in 'burnished gold'(in this case, of Cleopatra's resplendence) as recalled in the section two ie 'A Game of Chess' in T Eliot's in *The Waste Land* (1922), reflecting a long established and familiar discourse on India.

However, there is a sharp contrast in the depiction of native life at the beginning of Wallace's poem which is repeated right through the texts in all the journals:

> Here Gunga's banks terrific scenes display,
> Idolatry stalks forth in open day (Wallace 301).

The dichotomised description continues, 'The luxuriance of nature and the grandeur of the scene pleases his eye, while the customs and manners of men make his heart bleed' (Ibid.).

The approach to Calcutta, however, is perilous with the 'murky' Hoogly, 'whose water looked like thick mud' (Nair 86), infested with crocodiles and sharks. The proximity of Saugor Island in the west – 'a nest of serpents and a den of tigers' – is where superstitious devotees of Kali perform their unmentionable acts of violence. Saugor now has British troops to prevent the natives from resorting to their 'horrific practices' (Ibid. 86-87). Saugor is mentioned by Wallace in 1823 as a 'poor place [...]' adjacent to Kedgeree and Diamond Harbour (Ibid. 309), without the details we encounter in Graham's 1810 account.

But as one nears Calcutta, the 'scene becomes enchanting, all cultivated, all busy', and Graham feels 'we were approaching a great capital' (Ibid. 87). 'On landing' she is 'struck with the general appearance of grandeur in all buildings' (Ibid.). Buildings with 'columns, porticos, domes and fine gateways, interspersed with trees, and the Broad river crowded with shipping, made the whole picture magnificent' (Ibid.). Wallace echoes Graham's description when as records, 'nothing can[...] be imagined finer than the approach to Calcutta.' These houses which 'rise upon the sight, like so many scenes of enchantment, one after the other' (Ibid. 307) have 'large and airy rooms' and one cannot 'conceive the magnificence and extent of these dwelling' (Ibid.). He comments on 'palaces on the Chowringhee side of the Esplanade', and comments on the skyline of 'monuments, mosques, pagodas and churches of the city (which) have a beautiful effect' (Ibid. 303). The buildings in the second city of Empire, the metropolis of Calcutta, are European, while the majority of native dwellings occur at the margins/the periphery, emphasising the racial difference that Bhabha speaks of, as engendered by colonial discourse. Hamilton, too , uses the term 'magnificent' for the panorama that embraces the Hoogly in 'magnificent structures of the Government House, Town-Hall, Supreme Court, Fort William, Kidderpore School, Theatre, and the fine range of palaces along the Chouringhee side of the esplanade' (Ibid.). Hamilton comments on the architecture along the Chowringhee being Grecian (Ibid. 222).

In Graham's account, we hear of her visit to a native palace, the Maharaja Rajkissen Bahadur's residence (Sova Bazar Rajbati) to attend the cultural evening during Durga Puja, where she is struck by the artistic splendour of the residence and the gracious hospitality of her host, and especially struck by his warm welcome to all his guests as he paid the same attention to all his guests, 'whether Hindoos, Christians, or Mussalmans' (Ibid. 90).

The city is the intellectual and cultural hub where 'English' society offers 'greater variety of character and greater portion of intellectual refinement than... other presidencies' (Graham 87). Hamilton documents the intellectual accreditation through the establishment of The Asiatic Society founded by Sir William Jones on 15 Jan 1815:

Its principal object is to concentrate in one focus the valuable knowledge that may be occasionally attained of Asia, or at least to preserve many little tracts and essays, the writers of which might think them of sufficient importance for separate publication. From this period may be dated the commencement of all accurate information regarding India in general, and Hindustan in particular, which even at the present day is but very imperfectly known (Hamilton 232).

This embodies, as Said posits, the culmination of earlier scholarship and the commencement of an internally structured archive which provides the lenses through which the Orient is experienced as the distant is brought near and the exotic is made familiar.

The social life of European society is, as Graham notes in the cold season, full of 'gaieties' with 'public and private balls and masquerades, besides dinners and innumerable parties' (98). However, as the halls are not big enough for the Christmas parties and dances, Calcutta's lively western world assembles in Barrackpore. Hamilton too records the social life of Europeans who are 'numerous, gay, and convivial' (230) with the Governor-General's fetes and principal government officers giving dinners for 30-40 people where the claret and Madeira flow freely (231) and excellent 'viands' are served 'in great profusion' (230). What is striking is the declaration that the 'waste (is) tremendous' which is commensurate with the picture of decadence that is associated with the east (231) in this journal.

The Black Town, however, as Hamilton says, offers 'a remarkable contrast' (224) to this grandeur and opulence. Its 'streets are narrow, dirty, and unpaved; the houses of two stories are of brick, with flat terraced roofs; but the majority are mud cottages, covered with small tiles, with side walls of mats, bamboos, and other combustible materials... swarming with population' (Ibid.). The frequent fires decimate life and property in the native quarters as both Hamilton and Wallace note. The security of European lives living in incombustible dwellings against the precarious existence of natives is captured in these observations. Wallace records the effect of these destructive fires on combustible habitations, 'After these fires, the melancholy spectacle... is (so) frequently seen... that the eye becomes familiarised by habit, and feels a shock every time of less painful disgust'(320). What shocks the itinerant even more is the seeming callous attitude of the native citizens to those affected and made destitute by these fires which do not affect the non-combustible houses of the European city.

In fact, this sense of apathy and indifference is noted by Wallace amongst the native bathers in the Hoogly and in their attitude to floating corpses. Graham refers to 'the passive submission, the apathy, and the degrading superstition of the Hindoos, the more active fanaticism of the Mussalmans, the avarice, the prodigality, the ignorance, and the vulgarity of most the white people, seem to place them all on a level, infinitely below that of the least refined nations of Europe' (88). Further down, she notes the plight of the lower caste Hindus, who 'seem resigned to all that I call evils of life. Yet I feel degraded, when, seeing them half-clothed, half-fed, covered with loathsome disease'; their response being that this is the custom, and they never venture to 'overstep the boundaries that confine them' (96). The hierarchisation and difference are at different levels in this teeming city, not just between the Europeans and natives and but also within Indian society, demarcated by religion and caste.

The cosmopolitan hub of Calcutta is witnessed by the writers. Graham speaks of 'inhabitants from every country in the world. Chinese and Frenchmen, Persians and Germans, Arabs and Spaniards, Americans and Portuguese, Jews and Dutchmen, are seen mixing with the Hindoos and English, the original inhabitants and the actual possessors of the country' (92). The qualifier – 'actual' – is telling as this is the time of the Company Raj. Graham is surprised that this colonial encounter and association, which should have lessened prejudices has instead created a sense of outrageous pride in the British resident: 'every Briton appears to pride himself on being a John Bull' (92). Hamilton corroborates the reality of the world meeting in Calcutta. He refers to Sir Henry Russel, Chief Justice's estimate of the population of Calcutta as being 1 million and he goes on to quote General Kyd's estimation of the town population as 4-500,000 with houses occupied by the British (4300), Armenian (640), Portuguese and other Christians (2650), Hindoos (56,460), Mohammedan (17,700) and Chinese (10) (310).

The contrast and variety, the racial difference and hierarchy in the imperial city are comically caught by Wallace:

Many a young Bondstreet dandy struts with inconceivable self-satisfaction; and youthful British, Portuguese, and French half-cast, with tawny face, and neck stiffened almost to suffocation, jumps from the sublime to the ridiculous in attempts at imitation. A stranger's eye would next, perhaps, rest upon a Capuchin friar, with a beard and costume of the 14th century; and soon remove to a British missionary, who, in deepest black and countenance of longest sorrow, musing on the state of man, marches against a grave Turk, who jostles a Persian, who discomposes a Seik (sic), who insults an Arabian, who electrifies a Chinese, who contaminates a Hindoo, who upsets a dancing-master, and terrifies an Armenian' (Wallace, 'Fifteen Years in India' 310).

The world meets in the second city of colonial heyday, yet nations remain demarcated by notions of superiority/inferiority in this metropolis. The Portuguese form the lowest section amongst the Europeans, more so because of their free association and mingling with the local inhabitants. They are slotted with the amorphous 'other Christians' as they 'have approximated very closely to the natives in appearance and manners' (233). Through close interaction with the natives 'they have learned all the mean arts of chicanery, imposture, and litigiousness, to which they are by nature sufficiently prone; without acquiring a particle of plain dealing, firmness independence of spirit or useful knowledge.' They have imbibed 'natives' insolence, ill nature, coarseness brutality or drunkenness, qualities hostile to their national character... traced to intercourse with low Europeans' (Hamilton 235).

The greatest contempt is reserved for the Hindu *sirkar/banyans* who replaces the Jew in Calcutta, a city, which, as Hamilton and Wallace claim, has no Jews, the 'only opulent town (which is) free of them' We are told that 'their practices and occupations are engrossed by the native *sirkars, banyans*, and writers; most of whom are quite a match for any Jew' (233). Wallace's poem captures the reviled image:

The Sircar

Behold the Sircar sly, inured to guile,
Mark the persuasive cringe and ready smile;
The blackest vice is easy to the knave;
Bribe him, he sits as silent as the grave:
Lure him with gold, he swears that black is white,
A plunge in the Gunga sets his conscience right (315-16).

The shops of these petty traffickers although better than their houses, 'are mean and disagreeable'. The contrast with European shops is sharp, as the latter 'are singularly splendid' (Hamilton 234). The felicity of the Hindoo/the Oriental at duplicity and lying, is corroborated by Wallace, as the '*shroff* or *sircar* would out-Isaac Isaac... truth is not in them; and they are so addicted to gratuitous falsehood' that one is cautioned when an inferior says 'Such bola' (315). His progeny inherits his deviousness as 'crannies' (a misappropriation of the Bengali word, *kerani*, meaning a clerk) who helps every European to keep his accounts. The 'crannies' in their uneducated positions, nevertheless, picked up their master's language with alacrity, which found expression in letters which have become stereotypical of a certain brand of 'Indian English' as in the following example of a missive sent by a 'cranny' to his employer:

Honourable Sir,
    Yesterday vesper arrive great hurricane, valve of little aperture not fasten; first make great trepidation and palpitation, then precipitate into precinct. God grant master more long life and more great post.

I remain, honourable Sir,
In all token of respect,
Master's writer,
Bissonaut Maitre
P.S. no tranquillity in house since valve adjourn; I sent for carpenter to
make re-unite (317).

Wallace has a postscript to this, acknowledging another group of *sircars*
who 'make a considerable advance towards an accurate knowledge of the
grammatical construction of English' (Ibid.).

The young new arrival from Europe often falls prey to such men,
especially to their dewans, as the former strives to maintain the status
of the senior civil servants who has around 200 servants each, while a
magistrate in Britain would have ten. His juniors, in trying to emulate
their superior's standard (civil servants haven a 'princely allowance', see
Hamilton 232), 'involve themselves in embarrassment' (Hamilton 232)
borrowing from their dewans to maintain horses, carriages, servants and
their 'imprudence' then takes years to clear. It is the nature of the Oriental
to ensnare the hapless young European in his pernicious net. In this city,
'the morals of the native inhabitants are worse in Calcutta, than in the
provincial districts. Natives have 'a skill in the arts of collusion, intrigue,
subordination, and perjury, which enables them to perplex and baffle the
magistrate with infinite facility' (Hamilton 236). The natives' 'wages are
low, for living costs them little', an assumption that is made and confirmed
in colonial discourse' (Wallace 325).

The Hindu, is, by nature, disparagingly 'timid', but the trading
opportunities have allowed him to engage in speculation, lending money for
'distant voyages... to remote parts of the world' (Hamilton 228). Interestingly,
it is again this 'extreme timidity' (Hamilton 236) which prevents the 30-40
servants sleeping within the grounds of a European employer in passages and
verandas to refrain from theft and burglary in spite of the temptations open
to them from valuable items being left in unlocked rooms. True to their petty
nature, they are only given to 'small pilfering and cheating', confirming their
'racial traits of faithlessness' (Ibid.).

One does detect a sense of regret on Graham's account as she feels she
misses out on any real contact with Indians in Calcutta:

I grieve that the distance kept up between the Europeans and the
natives, both here and at Madras, is such that I have not been able
to get acquainted with any native families as I did in Bombay. There
seems to be little difference in their manner of living. Their houses
appear to be more commodious at Calcutta that at either of the
other presidencies (Graham 90).

On witnessing bathers in the Hoogly, the women are singled out for praise by Wallace. The sari is described as a garment which 'flows in graceful folds down to the ankle… the other end is drawn tastefully round their breasts, so as to cover their back also, and serve as a veil, flowing over their black hair' (Wallace 304). Their 'jewellery and hairstyle are closely observed through the appreciative male gaze. Do they signify the object of dangerous desire that Bhabha writes about? Their silence and passivity are telling as they stand still when strangers pass. They are like Flaubert's Kuchuk Hanem, "They have bright dark eyes, the glance of which they strive to increase, by painting their eyelashes jet black" (Ibid.) However, there is an admiration and respect in the detection 'of (their) commanding deportment, from the erect and majestic step common among the females of Hindostan' (Ibid.) – a sweeping statement.

European women, however, are singled out for Wallace's ironic jabs, as they reflect the social stratification and exclusion practised in the provincial capital: 'In Calcutta, a civilian's lady considers herself a superior being to the wife of a military officer; the latter looks down with contempt on the partner of a country captain, who, in her turn, despises the shopkeeper, and frets if neglected by the merchant's wife' (Wallace 334).

In relation to Bengali men, Wallace has categorised them as resembling those of other flat and marshy countries. They 'are of portly stature, and have those large joints, prominent bones, swelling muscles, and round elastic integuments, which have been called property of a soldier' (Wallace 304). Of the Bengal sepoys, he says, they 'are the finest looking in the Company's services, nearly all grenadiers, and individually very brave (though not as hardy as natives of Madras and Bombay)' (305). This estimation would change in post-1857-8 India when Bengali men would be constructed as belonging to the non-martial races to effectively carry out the divide and rule policy of abstaining to recruit local men into the army in the Provinces, Bengalis in Bengal, Marattas in Bombay and Madrasis in Madras.

The description of Bengal's inhabitants by Wallace as having 'a countenance, (which) with the exception of colour, is the same as our own' (Wallace 304) would be echoed in Macaulay's *Minute on Education* in 1835, when he proposed that English education would produce people who would be 'Indian in blood and colour, but English in tastes', the brown sahib, who would carry on the task of assisting the administration of India. Indians are recorded by Hamilton as being in 'inferior situations of clerks, overseers… necessarily occupied by the natives… With English education they would refrain from writing like the uneducated 'crannies', replacing earlier epistles with more grammatical compositions' (Hamilton 234).

In this city whose very skyline reflects its diversity, with its 'monuments, mosques, pagodas, and churches' (Wallace 303), the colonial space of multiple encounters has created a society which is defined by racial difference and hierarchy. 'Claret and champagne circulate, and song and good humour prevail' (Wallace 313). However, this is a society where class and race create marked social divisions. 'There are numberless exclusions from society in Bengal; and, perhaps, rank, precedence, and etiquette are not so much attended to at Carlton Palace as in the Chowringhee' (Wallace 313). The marginalised are not just the Indians. The Anglo-Indians are described as half-castes. Girls born of mixed parentage are the *chee chee* (fie fie) girls; they and the descendants of the Portuguese and other Christians, are the marginal (wo)men, who are the racial other in this stratified society of jostling humanity. However, here the European transients and sojourners – the clergymen, merchants, medical professionals, shopkeepers, schoolmasters, tradesmen and speculators 'who come out under the free mariner's indentures' (Wallace 309). And, as Wallace reports, they are not granted leave to remain and must move back to their country by government decree. Law enforcement is harsh: 'The government shows a decided dislike to colonisation; and the permission to remain, in all cases, is refused to adventurers, without authority from the Court of Directors, some of who resisted an order to depart, have been forced on board a ship by the bayonets of a military escort' (Wallace 309). The itinerant/wanderer in Hamilton, who is not a resident, the transient or sojourner in Graham and Wallace who are residents, all return to Britain. But the 'Old Indian' in each of them retains a nostalgia for the life in India: 'The ease and splendour in which Europeans live in India attach many of them to the country; and for a long time after an old Indian returns home, he secretly sighs on remembering the past' in this second city of empire (Wallace 324).

The first phase of Orientalist views framed by Firishtha/Alexander Dow and the Quintin Craufurd's journals and William Robertson's history would be overturned by James Mill's *History of India* and Thomas Babington Macaulay's *The Minute on Education*. It is true that Robertson never visited India, but his idea of India was framed/formed by an existent regard for India's heritage and culture. Mill made sweeping, definitive statements about India and Indians and Indian art without setting foot in India, at a point in time when it was necessary to justify Britain's economic hold over India and her population. Macaulay had dismissed all Arabic and Sanskrit literature[5] without having any knowledge of any of the Indian languages and its 3,000-5,000-year continuous literary tradition. In the sphere of aesthetics, John Ruskin's dismissal of the beauty, meaning and deep philosophy of Indian art and architecture was based on secondary sources and information without any direct contact with examples of Indian art or debates with Indian art critiques. But the Scottish travellers writing before Mill's History subverted and distorted Robertson's estimation of India, present a pre-imperial perspective of the colonial capital of Calcutta. These writers are writing for an audience in Britain, for possible recruits to India. The question is, are these travel journals written to vouch for the good life of Europeans in India, with the assurance that they had no danger of being challenged by the 'timid' Hindu or the 'fanatic' Mussalman or the apathetic lower castes? Together they contribute to a colonial discourse that observed and assessed India and, in this case, Calcutta, through the lens of a dominant nation whose capital flowed from India. I would like to end with a proposition – that these travel accounts chart a city as the flaneur/flaneuse would in London or Paris in Modernist texts almost a century later with an objectivity that embodies the metropolitan consciousness of a cosmopolitan observer.

End Notes:

1. All the page numbers of these travel accounts refer to P. Thankappan Nair's *Calcutta in the 19th Century (Company's Days)*.

2. See 'Introduction' by MM Kaye to Eliza Fay, *Original Letters from India (1779–1815)*, ed. EM Forster (1925, London: The Hogarth Press, 1986), p. 1.

3. Michael Fry, *The Scottish Empire*. Edinburgh: Birlinn Ltd, 2002. Print.

4. For a discussion of the flaneur in a modern urbanscape, see Martina Lauster, 'Walter Benjamin's Myth of the "Flâneur"' in the Volume 102, No. 1 of *The Modern Language Review*.

5. The passage in question reads,

> I am quite ready to take the Oriental learning at the valuation of the Orientalists themselves. I have never found one among them who could deny that a single shelf of a good European library was worth the whole native literature of India and Arabia. The intrinsic superiority of the Western literature, is indeed, fully admitted by those members of the committee who support the Oriental plan of education (Lees 91).

Works Cited:

Bhabha, Homi K. "The Other Question." *Contemporary Postcolonial Theory: A Reader*. Ed. Padmini Mongia. New Delhi: OUP, 2000. 37-54. Print.

Craufurd. Quintin. *The History, Religion, Learning and Manners of the Hindus*, 1790.

Disraeli, Benjamin. *Tancred: The New Crusade*. 3 vols. Leipzig: Bernard Tauchnitz, 1847. Print.

Alexander Dow, trans from the Persian. *History of Hindostan* by Muhammad Qâsim Hindû Shâh Astarâbâdî Firishtah, 1768; 1803–1812, Vols I-III.

Eliot, T. S. *The Waste Land and Other Poems*. London: Faber & Faber, 2002. Print.

Fay, Eliza. *Original Letters from India (1779–1815)*. Ed. E. M. Forster. London: The Hogarth Press, 1925. Print.

Fry, Michael. *The Scottish Empire*. Edinburgh: Birlinn Ltd, 2002. Print.

Graham, Maria. *Journal of a Residence in India*. Edinburgh: Archibald Constable & Co, 1812. 1-211. Print.

Hamilton, Walter. *A Geographical, Statistical and Historical Description of Hindostan, and The Adjacent Countries*. 2 vols. London: John Murray, 1820. Print.

Journal of an Officer in His Majesty's Service. 2nd ed. London: Longman, Hurst, Rees, Orme and Brown, 1823. Print.

Kaye, M. M. Introduction. *Original Letters from India (1779–1815)*. By Eliza May. London: The Hogarth Press, 1986. N. Print.

Lauster, Martina. "Walter Benjamin's Myth of the "Flâneur"." *The Modern Language Review* 102. 1 (January 2007): 139-156. Print.

Lees, Nassau W. *Indian Mussalmans: Being Three Letters Reprinted From The "Times." With An Article on the late Prince Consort, And Four Articles on Education, Reprinted from the "Calcutta Englishman." With an Appendix containing Lord Macaulay's Minute.* London: Williams and Norgate, 1871. Print.

Madsen, Deborah L. "Diaspora, Sojourn, Migration: The Transnational Dynamics of "Chineseness"." *Diasporic Histories: Cultural Archives of Chinese Transnationalism*, Ed. Deborah L. Madsen and Andrea Riemenschnitter. Hong Kong: Hong Kong University Press, 2009. 43-54. Print.

Mill. James. *The History of British India*. London: Baldwin, Craddock and Joy, 1817, 1820, 1826. Print.

Mitter, Partha. *Much Maligned Monsters: History of European Reactions in Indian Art.* Oxford: Clarendon Press, 1977. Print.

Nair, P. Thankappan. *Calcutta in the 19th Century (Company's Days)*. Calcutta: Firma KLM Private Limited, 1989. Print.

Said, Edward. *Orientalism*. 1978. Harmondsworth: Penguin, 2001. Print.

Shakespeare, William. *The Arden Shakespeare: Antony and Cleopatra*. Ed. John Wilders. London: Routledge, 1995. Print.

Siu, Paul C. P. "The Sojourner." *American Journal of Sociology* 58 (July 1952): 34-36. Print.

—. *The Chinese Laundryman: A Study of Social Isolation*. Ed. John Kuo Wei Tchen. New York: New York University Press, 1987. Print.

Walter Hamilton, *East India Company Gazeteer*, Vols I-II, 28 London 18.

Wallace, Lieut RG "Fifteen Years in India: Or Sketches of a Soldier's Life, Being and attempt to describe Persons and Things in various parts of Hindotsan." *Journal of an Officer in His Majesty's Service*. 2nd ed. London: Longman, Hurst, Rees, Orme, and Brown, 1823. Print.

William Robertson. *An Historical Disquisition Concerning the Knowledge which the Ancients had of India; and the Progress of Trade with that Country prior to the Discovery of the Passage to it by the Cape of Good Hope.* London: A. Strahan and T. Cadell, 1791. Print.

Hamilton, Walter. *A Geographical, Statistical and Historical Description of Hindostan and The Adjacent Countries* (London, 1820), Vols 1 & 2, Vol, 1, pp. 48-61. [220-244]

East Meets West:
A Vibrant Encounter between Indian Orthodoxy
and the Scottish Enlightenment

Tapati Mukherjee

IT IS RATHER QUEER and, to this day, still unexplained that the Scottish interaction with India throughout the centuries has hardly been recognized as an issue of academic and pratical concern – eventhough the plethora of discussion and analysis relating to the British advent in India, with its all-pervasive impact on the socio-cultural arena of the Indian milieu, has occupied multiple pages of history. However, the fact remains that with the migration of Scots to various parts of the world in the 18th and 19th centuries, India became a favourite abode and shelter of a huge number of Scots, irrespective of their occupation and status. Presumably this impression of India, providing peaceful shelter or refuge, enthused Sir Walter Scott to express his thoughts on India in a letter, addressed to Lord Montagu in 1821:

> India is the corn chest for Scotland where we poor gentry must send our younger sons as we send our black cattle to the south. (qtd. in Sassi 85)

One may recall in this context the much-quoted comment of Prime Minister Benjamin Disraeli:

> It has been my lot to have found myself in many distant lands. I have never been in one without finding a Scotchman and never found a Scotchman who was not at the head of the poll (Herman 331).

Indeed, since the 17th century, Scots migrated to India in quite sizable numbers, steered missionary activities, participated in governance, made an honest attempt to explore causes of various diseases, occasionally criticized the orthodox Indian civilization and somehow made an indelible impact on Indian life and psyche. But what is more significant in the historical and cultural perspective is how Scottish Enlightenment played a pivotal role in metamorphosis of Indian society and cultural set-up and paved the way of modern India with the passage of time.

To gauge and assess the impact of Scottish Enlightenment over India, steeped in the stupor of poverty, ignorance and caste-centric discrimination for centuries, let us have a cursory look at the nature of Scottish Enlightenment.

Etymologically Enlightenment means an exit, an escape from tutelage, from bondage. Accordingly, in his essay 'What is Enlightenment' (*Aufklarung*) 1784, Kant defined Enlightenment as liberation from dependence on others and the attainment of adequate maturity to assume responsibility for one's own action. Viewed from this perspective, Scottish Enlightenment, steered by a pair of Scots – Francis Hutcheson and Lord Kames – propounded that 'history' and 'human nature' are intertwined and it was finally envisaged that man is created by the environment – an idea considered to be the most significant revelation of the 'Scottish School'. Simultaneously, its emphasis on knowledge, permeated and manifested in various branches of social science vis. anthropology, ethnography, economics, psychology and many others – and backed by an emergence of Encyclopedia Britannica in Edinburgh in 1768 which was then considered as a compendium of scientific and human knowledge – shaped 'man' at the centre of all discussions, dethroning God and the Reformation Kirk. Arthur Herman put it very concisely:

> Human beings considered as individuals but also as the products, even the playthings, of historical and social change: in other words, human beings as we understand them today. (Herman 63)

India, reeling throughout the 17th and 18th centuries under the oppressive pressure of casteism leading to discrimination and disparity among the masses, religious orthodoxy, political strife, economic stagnation as an outcome of age-worn production system, unsympathetic governance by alien rulers, was looking forward to some drastic change or reformation which would relieve the masses from the clutches of desperation.

Scots, emboldened by their Enlightenment, came to India's rescue; they showed their concern for India, to say the least. In 1688, Scottish adventurer Captain Alexander Hamilton came to India and in his book, *New Account of the East Indies* (1727), he presented a detailed picture of late 17th century India. It is also a matter on record that in the 18th century, many Scots came to India as physicians and most famous of them was William Hamilton, who served at Madras and Calcutta between 1711 and 1714.

Indisputably, India was 'jewel in the crown' of the British Empire, dominated in the first phase by the East India Company and finally by the British monarchy. But Scots always sustained their interest in India. During the reign of James VI, there had been a tremendous effort to establish a Scottish East India Company, slated for trade and other auxiliary purposes, but the attempt had been crushed by the opposition of the English.

However, the most significant shift in attitude from an indifferent ruler to a benevolent master, bent on transforming the so-called wretched life of the Indians, happened through the medium of 33-year-old Scotsman James Mill, who was commissioned by East India Company in 1806 to write a history of the British presence in India. It is a fact that Mill never visited India but his much applauded book, *The History of British India*, highlighted the tyrannical attitude of the local rulers, the discriminatory caste system and demonstrated pathetic contempt for the prevalent laws which according to him, were comparable to those of Europe in the Dark Ages. He advocated British rule for India in the interest of the Indians themselves:

A simple form of arbitrary government, tempered by European honour and European intelligence, is the only form which is now fit for Hindusthan (Herman 337).

Taking clue from this message, appeared in the Indian scenario another illustrious Scot – Thomas Babington Macaulay – who, despite his arrogance, pressed hard to implement proposed reforms and advocated a national English-language school system for India. This move was indeed significant in view of the fact that the utility of the English language as a medium of instruction was recognized for the first time. It is indeed interesting that a plethora of Scottish administrators and intellectuals had initiated, on their own welfare, activities for uplift of the poor and oppressed Indian milieu. Thomas Munro, Governor of Madras, tried his level best to reduce tax burdens on ordinary farmers with a view to liberate them from the clutches of oppressive hierarchy. Arthur Herman in his book, *The Scottish Enlightenment*, has aptly mentioned how John Campbell, another Scot, spent 16 years in the remote hill country, rescuing potential victims of human sacrifice rituals. Thus, Scots were no longer mere strangers in India, they were in fact instrumental in implementing several reformist measures in Indian socio-economic scenario.

Equally fascinating is the impact exerted by Scottish missionaries and intellectuals in the spread of Western Education in Bengal, the hub of cultural activities in the then India. The initiation of the Charter Act in 1813, signalled two major changes in British policy in the form of assuming responsibility for educating the ruled and relaxing control over missionary activity in India, and was introduced by the Hindu College in 1817, spearheaded by David Hare and Rammohan, by Serampore College in 1818 by Carey, and by Marshman and Ward and School Book Society in 1817. English schools started in quite sizable numbers under the guidance of Calcutta Diocesan Committee, The Church Missionary Committee, London Missionary Committee etc. Against this background, arrived in Calcutta on the 27th May 1830, Dr Alexander Duff, an erudite Scot with his newly married wife and an assignment, offered by The

Committee of Foreign Missions in Scotland, to establish a College in Bengal which would be governed by Christian principles. He was the first overseas missionary of the Church of Scotland to India. It is indeed amazing how this young Scottish missionary took upon himself the cudgel of introducing English Education in an alien atmosphere prevailing in an unknown country. With the patronage and active assistance of Raja Rammohan Roy, he established, on 13th July 1830, the General Assembly's Institution and, in 1844, the Free Church Institution, later named Duff College. These two institutions amalgamated in 1908 in the form of Scottish Churches College, and was finally re-named the Scottish Church College after the union of Churches in Scotland in 1929. Admittedly, as a missionary, Duff encouraged moral and ethical education, backed by his evangelist predilection, as is evinced from the Minute Book of General Assembly School (1831):

> That it appears to the missionaries present and to several others with whose sentiments they are acquainted, that an Institution on the plan proposed by the Rev Mr Duff is admirably adapted in the present state of Hindus society in Calcutta, to secure progress of general science and true Christianity in India. (Basu, 'Voyage of Time', 175th year Commemoration Volume, 61)

Duff played a crucial role in the establishment of Calcutta University and a Medical College, first in India. Concerned about the pitiable condition of women in Bengal, he started a Hindu Girls School for the spread of education among Indian women. The commendable role of Duff and his luminous achievement, Scottish Church College, in the propagating of Western education had been highlighted by Calcutta Christian Observer:

> Christian education, a concentration and force which it had never possessed before in this country. Some missionaries have been distinguished for their labour in translations, other in composing and printing useful works, other in preaching and it has been the lot of our Scottish brethren to be eminent in providing an educational institution in every way worthy of the cause they desire to propagate. (Motilal, 'The Scottish Church College', 175th year Commemoration Volume, 20)

In this galaxy of academic stalwarts, mention may be made also in the context of David Hare, the Scottish founder of Hindu College and the bringer of renaissance in 19th century Bengal. As a matter of fact, Scottish Enlightenment, slated to liberate the human mind from the clutches of the Church, tyranny and oppressive socio-economic pressure through knowledge, carried to the Indian hemisphere by missionaries, administrators, doctors and many others, overwhelmed Indian minds too and subsequently laid to the rejuvenation of the Indian mind and thought process.

By the end of the 18th century, Scots were no longer strangers to India; on the contrary, they exercised their power in influencing and transforming Indian life and culture. This transformation, which would obviously trigger the emergence of an educated rational and enlightened group of people aspiring for self governance, signalled the fall of colonial regime in India. This had been predicted by Mount Stuart Elphinstone, one of the most trusted associates of Lord Minto, who felt that improvement of the so-called natives would mean disaster for the foreign rulers.

India will remember with both gratitude and apathy a Scottish Governor, General James Dalhousie Lord Ramsey, who, despite his imperialist inclination, dedicated himself to the upliftment of Indian milieu by implementing several welfare schemes – the construction of rail roads, schools, irrigation projects, telegraph lines, as well as his bold move to eradicate the so-called *thagi* robbers. Dalhousie's most significant contribution, however, was enactment of laws, banning child marriage, polygamy and murder of girl foetuses. The concept of women's emancipation, proclaimed by Scottish Enlightenment, presumably inspired this Scottish administrator to introduce girls' schools in India – under the impression that it would bring good to the country. Apparently, these are reformist measures no doubt, but at the same time, inspired by the tenets of Scottish Orientalism, these measures introduced by several Scotsmen, in whatever positions they might be, paved the way of the 19th century Bengal renaissance.

Scots made their impact felt in another arena too. That was in medicine. Despite their absolute lack of knowledge about Indian climatic conditions, flora and fauna and diseases, they tried to explore the root cause of various diseases and their plausible remedy. It was with this objective that Sir James Ranald Martin, a Scot, published his book titled *Influences of Tropical Climates on European Constitutions* in 1841. It is indeed amazing that the first compre-hensive account of poisonous snakes was composed in 1875 by Sir Joseph Fayrer, a Scot doctor and Professor of Surgery at Calcutta University. Another Scot, James Macnab Cunningham, wrote a book on cholera (1884), showing thereby Scottish involvement in Indian life and wellbeing.

The Scotland-India continuum of ideas, heralded by Scots under the impact of Scottish Enlightenment, found its most poignant expression in the binary relationship of two great stalwarts – Rabindranath Tagore of India and Patrick Geddes of Scotland.

With the passage of time, Scottish intellectuals became more inclined to India, characterized by its unity in diversity. At this stage, we encounter Patrick Geddes, a botanist and town planner, enamoured by India's cultural richness and beauty. So profound was his admiration for India that he composed a drama

Dramatizations of History, where, under the title head *The Masque by Ancient Learning*, he categorized sects viz. Hindus, Buddhists, Parsis and Persians. It is a fact that, by 1914, Geddes was enjoying considerable success with his Cities and Town Planning exhibition. However, he decided to visit India at the invitation of Lord Pentland, Governor of Madras. The alien cultural context of the East posed as an object of attraction to him. He came in contact with Andrews and fell upon re-interpreting the ancient Indian culture to the modern world. It is also an irony that Geddes came to India at a critical juncture in 1914 when the Nationalist movement was gaining a new vigour under Gandhi's leadership. Geddes was overwhelmed by the beauty of the old temples, and also appreciated the skyline and ground line of its towns. This was indeed amazing in the sense that an authority of European town planning had admiration for Indian towns, too. On 9 February 1915, he wrote a letter to his former Biology pupil, Annie Besant, a persistent fighter for Indian independence, eulogizing the planning of temple city of Conjevaram in most explicit terms.

Another luminary of 19th century Bengal, with whom Geddes had developed an intimate relationship, was Sir Jagadish Chandra Bose. The duo met at a Parisian exhibition in 1900. When they met again in India, Jagadish Chandra was about to start his own scientific institute and the speech he made on this occasion was masterminded by Geddes.

Geddes' planning model, Sympathy, Synthesis and Synergy, where Sympathy is the initial survey of a problem, always involved local people. His approach towards holistic education constituted the three Hs: Head, Heard and Hand. It may also be noted here that Sister Nivedita, his one-time secretary, wanted his help to understand the cause of famines in India and trace them to ecological problems.

Geddes had developed an intimate relationship with Tagore. What brought the duo together – emerging as they did from two different continents, belonging to a thoroughly different societal setup and markedly different in intellectual arena – one a professor of science and an architect, an environmentalist and another a poet, philosopher and fondly considered by Occident as a 'Sage'? Surprisingly, deep down they shared a strange affinity towards the respect of educational concepts, environmental predilections, architecture and several other arenas. Geddes shared Tagore's ideals of education in harmony with life, effected in close bond with nature – a system modelled after *Tapovana*-based education scenario of ancient India. This affinity of thought and concept brought them closer to each other. Both of them believed that educational activities must be designed to nurture creativity instead of killing it. On 9 May 1922, Tagore wrote to Geddes:

> I merely started with this one simple idea that education should never be dissociated from life... My first idea was to emancipate

children's minds from the dead grip of a mechanical method and a narrow purpose. This idea has gone on developing itself, comprehending all different branches of life's activities from Arts to Agriculture. (qtd. in Fraser 63-64)

Geddes wrote in reply on 17 May 1922:

The difference between us is that while I work out (the equivalents of) musical notations, the prosody of thought, you can make songs as well as poems! (Yet you know your musical notation, your verse notation too) (qtd. in Fraser 66).

Tagore wrote a satirical short story on current methods of education which is based on cramming and accorded the title *The Parrot's training*. Geddes was overjoyed to read it, as is evident from his congratulatory letter on 11 June 1918.

Dear Sir Rabindranath,

Admirable! The parrot is being avenged! And what is yet better, future parrots will be protected! Rescued… I am sure it will help the cause everywhere (qtd. in Fraser 52).

In a letter dated 15 June 1918, we hear for the first time Tagore's urge for an ideal university in the so-called native states:

What we need now in an ideal university in some of our Native States. A few months ago I received a letter from the Nizam state asking my opinion about the advisability of introducing Urdu to the medium of instruction in a new university they intend to start (qtd. in Fraser 53).

International University:
In 1921, Tagore conceptualized the idea of an International University in Santiniketan and wrote to Geddes:

I am arranging a conference of some representative men of the West and of Japan and China if possible… My scheme of the University has been well received in this country and I feel certain that I shall have volunteers who will join me from all parts of Europe (qtd. in Fraser 57).

Draft of the invitation letter:

You will know from the accompanying leaflet about the scheme of an International University in India with the object of paving the path to a future where both the East and West will work together for the general cause of human welfare... It will give the most welcome assurance to the Eastern people that the best intellectual minds of the world recognize the claims of a common human birthright overcoming the barriers of geography and race (qtd. in Fraser 58).

From a letter addressed to Rabindranath by Geddes, it is evident that Rabindranath was expected to visit Edinburgh as President of a first 'International Congress on University Progress', in which Geddes was the organizing secretary. Simultaneously he was invited to the World Conference in Education Equality and was invited to Jerusalem for the inauguration of the University to 'obtain your message on education as it should be and may be' What Geddes wrote to Tagore in this context on 12 February 1925 is significant:

I can safely assure you of an audience of the right sort not only of Zionists, and of Government etc (some of whom are accessible to ideas and even ideals) but also all sections of the Christian and Moslem communities also, of whom the best are not consumed by the mutual hatreds which are as exaggerated by the Press, but open to your message of mutual tolerance and even good will (qtd. in Fraser 103).

As to the offer related to the President's post in the Indian college of Montpellier, Tagore accepted it with some obvious reservations. On 7 December 1925, Tagore wrote to Geddes:

As for the President's post which you offer I do not have the heart to refuse although I have a profound dislike for taking any conspicuous place in a public function (qtd. in Fraser 107).

It is also interesting to note that, besides Rabindranath, three other illustrious Indians occupied key positions in that International university: Sir Jagadish Chandra Bose and Sri Brajendranath Seal as Vice Presidents and Dr GC Advani as Secretary. It may be recalled here that the entire planning of Visva-Bharati had been conceptualized and implemented by Rabindranath with active assistance from Rathindranath, Surendranath Kar and Patric Geddes despite their differences in opinion on certain issues. Needless to say, this was a conscious attempt to maintain environmental ethics and equilibrium. Arthur Geddes, who subsequently addressed Rabindranath as 'Gurudev' in his letter, made a compilation of 30 of Tagore's songs (15 from 'The King of Dark Chamber' and 15 Spring Tunes) about which Rabindranath wrote:

Do whatever you like with my songs; only do not ask me to do the impossible. To translate Bengali poems into English verse form reproducing the original rhythm so that the words may fit in with the theme would be foolish for one to attempt (qtd. in Fraser 115).

Arthur's thesis, *Soil and Civilization*, also speaks about his connection with Bengal. He also played a significant role in planning and execution of greenery in and around Santiniketan and Sriniketan, as well as the construction of houses in the Uttarayan complex and elsewhere.

Another Scot who we should not lose sight of in our discussion is Daniel Hamilton, who in fact steered cooperative movement in the remote place of Gosaba in the Sundarban area of Bengal. He was in favour of introducing cooperative commonwealth, where each individual will be rewarded for his physical and mental labour. He could convince British imperialism that farmers and labours could be appeased with the transfer of nominal power, backed by an incentive to become self sufficient with a small amount of funding. He was blessed by Rabindranath and Gandhiji in his untiring endeavour to elevate the wretched condition of villagers by making them self sufficient through cooperatives. In a conference inaugurated by Rabindranath on 9 February 1929, in Sriniketan, Hamilton, while chairing the session, remarked that the entirety of India in general, and Bengal in particular, was steeped in poverty and ignorance, and hardly six vessels in the forms of cooperation are there to save them; he sent a clarion call to British rulers to put an end to this oppressive tyranny. It is no wonder, therefore, that Rabindranath supported him unhesitatingly:

> I have my trust in individuals like yourself who are simple lovers of humanity, whose minds are free from race prejudice and the too loyal idolatry of the machine. I believe that the cooperative principle is the only civilized principle in commerce and also in politics (qtd. in Mandal, 'Daniel Hamilton O Rabindranath', *Rabindrabalaya Bidvajjan*, 109).

On the other hand, Indian influence on Scottish intelligentsia is none the less significant. Here we come across one of the stalwarts of the 19th century Bengal Renaissance, Prince Dwarakanath Tagore, who not only visited Scottish cities like Edinburgh and Glasgow but was also felicitated by the Queen and the Scottish public. Another illustrious Bengali Scientist, Acharya Prafulla Chandra Roy, who, in 1882, took admission in the University of Edinburgh had expressed his admiration of the University:

> It had then a time-honoured reputation as a seat of learning. Metaphysics and medicine, especially the latter, attracted pupils

from far and near. Physical Science as represented by chemistry and physics found also eminent exponents (*Acharya Prafulla Chandra Roy* 54).

At the commencement of the winter session, he enrolled himself as 'Civic academic Edinburgeris' and joined the classes in preparing for the First B.Sc examination, namely in Chemistry, Physics and Zoology. In his autobiography, Prafulla Chandra described his belief and then disillusionment in the British regime in quite explicit terms:

> I was a believer in those days in the doctrine of mendicancy and with child like simplicity held that if the wrongs and the grievances under which our country groaned could be brought home to the British people, they would be remedied. The disillusionment was not long in coming (*Acharya Prafulla Chandra Roy* 63).

He could realize that the powerful never yields power to the weak on their own. In his essay, which was considered as 'bearing marks of rare excellence' by Principal Muir, he made an appeal to the students of the university:

> The lamentable condition of India at present is due to England's culpable neglect of and gross apathy to the affairs of that empire. England has hitherto failed – grievously failed in the discharge of her sacred duties to India. It is to you, the rising generation of Great Britain and Ireland, that we look for the inauguration of a more just, generous and humane policy as to India – a policy which will not seek a justification in such platitudes as 'inevitable course', 'non-possums', 'eternal fitness of things', but one whose sole issue will be a closer union between India and England (*Acharya Prafulla Chandra Roy* 63).

It is difficult to assess the extent of the impact this had on Scot students, but that a young Bengali student positioned in a Scottish university could master the courage to denounce British rule was indeed amazing.

Thus, we find that Scottish impact – be it in the area of administration, or in the form of cultural rejuvenation or in the field of medicine, or in the issuance of environmental caution – had played a significant role in ushering in the 19th century Bengal Renaissance or in paving the path of modern India. The impact was indeed enormous, though little discussed.

Works Cited:

Basu, Monalisa. "Voyage of Time Seized in Pages: The Minutes Book, 1831." 175th *year Commemoration volume, Scottish Church College, Kolkata* 1830–2005, Kolkata, 2008. Print.

Defries, Amelia. *The Interpreter Geddes: The Man and his Gospel.* London: Routledge, 1927. Print.

Edinburgh Review Patrick Geddes volume Edinburgh, Scotland, 1992. Print.

Fraser, Bashabi ed. *The Tagore-Geddes Correspondence.* Kolkata: Visva-Bharati, 2004. Print.

Herman, Arthur. *The Scottish Enlightenment: The Scots' Invention of the Modern World.* London: Fourth Estate, 2003. Print.

Kripalani, Krishna. *Dwarkanath Tagore, A Forgotten Pioneer, A Life.* New Delhi: National Book Trust, 1981. Print.

M. Cain, Alex. *The Cornchest For Scotland: Scots in India.* Edinburgh: National Library of Scotland, 1986. Print.

Mandal, Sujitkumar. "Daniel Hamilton O Rabindranath Thakur: Samabay Bhavna O Ekti Biral Yogayog." *Rabindrabalaye Bidvajjan.* Eds. Tapati Mukhopadyay & Amrit Sen. Kolkata: Visva-Bharati, 2016. Print.

Motilal, Anup. "The Scottish Church College: A Brief Discourse on the Origin of an Institution." *175th year Commemoration volume, Scottish Church College, Kolkata 1830–2005*, Kolkata, 2008. Print.

Roy, Prafulla Chandra. *Life and Experiences of a Bengali Chemist.* Calcutta: The Asiatic Society, 1932. Print.

Sassi, Carla. *Why Scottish Literature Matters.* Edinburgh: Saltire Society, 2005. Print.

The Scotland-India Interaction: The Scottish Impact on a so-called Native Stalwart in India– Dwarakanath Tagore

Tapati Mukherjee

IT IS AN ACCEPTED fact that, since the 16th century, India had somehow captured the imagination of Scots – a fact substantiated by an abortive attempt to establish a Scottish East India Company in 1618. As a matter of fact, India was a favourite destination of Scots, who not only visited India in huge numbers, but also got entangled in Indian politics, practised medicine, tried zealously for the spread of western education in India and finally, in most cases, maintained a sympathetic attitude towards India, ignited by their association with the vast Indian milieu.

So profuse was the number of Scottish visitors to India by the middle of the 18th century – through a gradual but persistent mode of penetration in the army and administration, obviously by the grace of fast expanding East India Company – that in 1773, that a young Scot wrote in a letter that his countrymen 'grew so numerous that I am afraid I shall not be able to enumerate them with that exactness I have hitherto done.' (qtd. in Cain 13) Indeed, India was a merry-land for many Scots during that period.

Now the question arises: is this Scottish advent in India restricted to simple numerical terms ie by number only, or has it exerted an impact at least on a certain class ie the rich and the educated Indians, if not the entire mass? Or, to put it in other words, could the Indian intelligentsia assimilate Scottish influence in their culture and outlook? Was it a simple entry of an alien group of people in India or could it transform at least a few by influence, assimilation and impact? A passing reference may also be made to Scottish enlightenment, which believes that the only politics a modern society requires is a strong effective government. It was through Macaulay, his arrogance notwithstanding, and Lord Minto, the Edinburgh-educated Governor General who arrived in India in 1806, that the Scottish impact on Indian life was at least squarely felt. The Scottish impact, slated in the direction of education and other welfare activities designed for the betterment of Indian people, can be traced in the life and multifarious activities of a Bengali Zamindar cum industrialist, about whom HM Parker, a stalwart of the free press movement, said in an eloquent speech in February 1938:

> It (the name) is written in the hearts of thousands who have partaken of his inexhaustible charity; who have had cause to bless his boundless benevolence, confined to no caste, colour or creed. It shines brightly, surrounded with all that is urbane and kind and courteous, on the tablets of social hospitality. It is heard in the halls of our colleges, in the porticos of those literary and scientific institutions which he has supported and enriched. Gentlemen, need I say after this that it is the name of Dwarakanath Tagore (Kripalani 122).

Yes, he is Dwarakanath, an unsung hero in the intellectual arena, barely mentioned by his son Debendranath, despite the fact that he had inherited his father's legacy, and was largely ignored by his illustrious Nobel Prize-winning grandson Rabindranath. This almost ominous silence maintained about him by his illustrious successors notwithstanding, Dwarakanath stands unsurpassed not only in his contemporary perspective but in his colourful life and welfare activities in a colony under the siege of an imperialist superpower, remains a lesson for posterity. Not only did he imbibe Scottish enlightenment and benevolence for his own sake, but he utilized it for the uplift of his own folk, to whom he left the door ajar to higher education and carved a niche for himself and his country.

To gauge and assess Dwarakanath, it is imperative to take note of the socio-political perspective that shaped him. The entire 19th century in Bengal witnessed an intellectual upsurge that has been compared with the European Renaissance, which originated in Italy. The introduction of Western education, backed by colonial rule, ignited the Indian intelligentsia to challenge age-worn orthodoxies and initiated a new awakening in the Indian consciousness. Dwarakanath may be considered as one of the richest products of the East-West synthesis.

Born in 1794, Dwarkanath was in all respects much ahead of his time. It has been recorded that Sherbourne kept a school in the Jorasanko quarter where Dwarkanath Tagore learned the English alphabet and, having his first lessons from *Enfield's Spelling, Reading Book, Universal Letter Writer*, etc, Dwarakanath compensated his lack of preliminary training with academic help from Robert Cutler Fergusson, a renowned Scottish barrister and politician at the time. This Scottish impact was indeed significant in paving the future of young Dwarakanath, in view of the fact that the proficiency and knowledge he gained in legal and court matters helped him considerably in managing his estate and subsequently in running his enterprises. Guided and aided by Fergusson, Dwarakanath mastered the intricacies of legal jurisprudence, which not only helped him to expand the vista of his estate, but meant that he was also consulted by other landlords for sagacious advice in critical matters. While Scottish Fergusson was his mentor in the mundane issues of life, Raja Rammohan Roy, one of the stalwarts of the 19th century Bengal Renaissance, was his spiritual preceptor from whom he imbibed indomitable strength of character. As a matter of fact, there was a fusion of East and West in the character of Dwarakanath which enabled him to stand undeterred in the adversities of life. A member of Brahmo Samaj since its inception in 1828, he could hardly stay away from orthodox Hindu rites. It is indeed queer to note that, in some aspects, a strange affinity is discernable between Dwarakanath and his grandson Rabindranath. Like Dwarakanath, Rabindranath also had great faith in superb qualities of the alien dominating power while, on the other hand, he undertook several ventures to uplift his deprived countrymen. Backed by knowledge in legal and commercial enterprises derived from his Scottish mentor, Dwarakanath established Carr, Tagore and Co, and was felicitated by Lord William Bentinck on being the first native gentleman to set up a house of business in Calcutta on the European model. He was also credited with the innovative idea of establishing a banking system, with Union Bank flourishing under his tutelage, despite the fact that this Bank stopped functioning in 1847.

Another icon who had a lasting impact on the psyche and thought of Dwarakanath was David Hare, the Scottish founder of the Hindu College, with his notion of free thinking and secularism. Both Hare and Dwarakanath believed that western education must first be imparted to the rich and middle class, who, on account of their position in the social hierarchy, would be able to direct and control the instruction of the poorer classes. Indeed, the Scottish interaction had proved to be extremely fruitful for Dwarkanath in exercising his philanthropic missions of life.

This East-West confluence was indeed fruitful in paving Dwarakanath's several other memorable missionary-like activities. Since its inception on 1 June 1835, Dwarakanath associated himself with Medical College, where he instituted three prizes of Rs. 2000/- yearly simply to encourage medical students. On 24 March 1836, Dwarakanath wrote to Principal Bramlay:

> As an individual member of the native community, I feel it belongs to us as aid, as far as lies in our power, the promotion of your good cause. At present this can hardly be expected on any very great scale, but as example may be of service to you, I for one will not be backward to accept your invitation to my countrymen to support the college (Mitra 26).

It is indeed amazing that Dwarakanath had the courage and guts to take three Indian students with him to London in 1844 for medical education and their expenses were paid by him. In the end, they became the first FRCS and MDS of India.

One of the most illustrious acts in the public life of Dwarkanath is obviously the leading role he played with Raja Rammohan Roy for the abolition of widow burning, by promulgation of a law inevitably introduced by Lord William Bentinck.

An avowed aristocrat, Dwarkanath believed in good governance of the country and, with this view, established the Landholder's Society in April 1838. Subsequently, it culminated into the British Indian Association, which represented all classes and all interests.

Dwarkanath was instrumental in introducing steam communication between India and Europe, which necessarily elevated India through the medium of advanced western knowledge.

Another Scottish gentleman who had exerted profound impact on him was Mr Holecroft, the proprietor of the Calcutta Journal, who had succeeded James Silk Buckinghamand and who had been expelled from India for the scathing denunciation of his rival. Dwaarkanath's association with Holecroft helped him to believe that the press, free from the clutches of hegemonic power, would be machinery for progress and development of the country and, needless to say, Dwarakanath became an earnest champion for its emancipation.

Dwarakanath stood as firm as a rock against the 'Black Act' of 1836, by which British subjects were deprived of their right to appeal to English courts of law against the decision of the Mofussil tribunds. One is tempted to quote here how courageously Dwarakanath spoke against it and how he denounced the pitiable condition of the so-called native Indians:

> The Natives have hitherto been slaves; are the Englishmen therefore to be made slaves also? This is the kind of equality the Govt. are seeking to establish. They have taken all which the natives possessed, their lives, liberty, property and all were held at the mercy of Government, and now they wish to bring the English inhabitants of the country to the same state! They will not raise the Natives to the condition of the Europeans, but they degrade the Europeans by lowering them to the state of the natives (Hear, Hear!) (Kripalani 116).

However, his stance and advocacy for the British elicited much criticism in the Indian circle. The discrimination effected between British and Indian in the court of law no doubt violated all forms of natural justice and Dwarakanath's tacit support for such a draconian rule was thoroughly cricised by Indian intelligentsia.

Another benevolent act was perpetrated by Dwarakanath in the form of the establishment of a 'fever hospital'.

To eliminate the superstitious belief that crossing the *kalapani*, a sea voyage that could endanger life, the idea of visiting Europe dawned on Dwarakanath in 1841. It is indeed interesting to note that Dwarakanath was not content to visit England only; he also visited the Scottish cities of Edinburgh and Glasgow. It is also interesting that, after Raja Rammohan Roy, he was presumably the second Indian to make such extensive visits to European cities and suburbs.

On the eve of his journey, Dwarakanath was felicitated by the European and Indian community on 6 January 1842 at the Town Hall:

> Your unwearied benvolence, your upright conduct as a man in all the relations of life, claim and have received the need of public admiration in Calcutta, of which we trust the voice will be re-echoed in England (Mitra 76).

It is, indeed, interesting to note that Dwarakanath was not satisfied with visits to the so-called metropolises like London and other important stopovers; on the contrary, he ventured to visit parts of Scotland presumably because of his admiration for Scottish teachers and mentors. It may be mentioned in this context that his first biographer, Kissory Chand Mitra, quoted profusely from his diary in an attempt to present a lively picture of his voyage to Europe; unfortunately, the diary cannot be traced presently. His admiration for London is quite vibrant in his letter, addressed to Debendranath, his son:

> After seeing everything in the Continent, I did not expect that I should be so much taken by this little island; but really London is the wonderful city; the bustling of the city, the carriages, the shops and the people, quite bewildered me (Kripalani 156).

In his zeal to savour his appreciation of European advancement, Dwarakanath visited Scotland. He attended his first kirk service, which he found different from an Anglican service. From his diary, his biographer Mitra quoted: 'Thinking one sermon quite sufficient, I came away after the first, which was more of a lecture than of a sermon.'

On 29 August, Dwarakanath reached Edinburgh. The very next day, he was honoured by the Town Council of the city of Edinburgh:

> In Edinburgh, the 23rd day of August in the year one thousand eight hundred and forty two, on which day the Right Hon'ble Sir James Forrest of Comeston, Bart, Lord Provost, John Richardson, David Jugurtha Thomson, William Thomson and Andrew Wilkie, Esquires, Bailies, John Ramsay, Esquire, Dean of Guild, Sir William Drys dale of Pittenchar, Knight, Treasurer and the other Members of the Town Council of the City in Council assembled, admired and received

and do hereby admit and receive Baboo Dwarakanath Tagore of
Calcutta, Burgess and Guild Brother of this City, as a mark of their
esteem for his character as a Native Merchant in our Indian Empire.

(Extracted from the records of the city by Carlyle, Bell, Contingent
Clerk) (qtd. in Mitra 96).

The decolonised may feel humiliated at the expressions like 'native
merchant'and 'Indian Empire', but it may be remembered that, at that point
of time, it was nothing unnatural, but what was surprising was the admiration
and warmth with which the Scottish aristocracy honored Dwarkanath.
Incidentally, it may be mentioned here that on 1 September, the Queen reached
Edinburgh and it was indeed a feat of honour for Dwarakanath that Her
Majesty welcomed him – a so-called 'native subject' of her empire.

It is, indeed, encouraging to note that Dwarakanath was repeatedly
showered with felicitations from various quarters. On September 5th, the
Unitarian Association of Edinburgh honored him with an address and three
days later, on the 8th, he was honoured with another address:

We recognise in you a zealous advocate of just and equal laws for all
classes of the vast community to which you belong. Accept, then, the
only recompense we have it in our power to offer, the sincere tribute
of our admiration and esteem (Mitra 98-99).

As the outburst of emotion would spread over a few pages, a small portion
is quoted once again:

We recognize in you the fearless asserted to the rights of human
industry – at this moment striving to throw the shield of protection
over the humblest cultivator of the soil of your birth, and to secure
for honest toil a just participation in the fruits of the world... We
commend you to the care and keeping of the Maker and Preserver of
men. Farewell (Mitra 99).

Later, Dwarakanath visited Glasgow, the commercial capital of Scotland. He
visited the factories and warehouses and the monument built as a tribute to
Bell, the inventor of the steamboat. He also paid a visit to the tomb of 16th
century religious reformer, John Knox.

It may not be out of context to mention here that he received another
honour from the Cymregyddion Y Venni:

Most illustrious chieftain, Dwarakanath Tagore, in the name and on
behalf of the Cymreigyddion Y Vnni, I ask permission to address you

in the ancient and aboriginal language of this island and to express to you the high gratification (Mitra 102).

This article emphasizes Scotland-India interaction that prevailed right from 16th century. Initially, Scots came to India for various purposes and had a lasting impact on Indian society and culture. As an inevitable aftermath, backed by western education, Indians also reciprocated, and stalwarts like Dwarakanath could venture to visit Scotland. Not only did he get acquainted with Scottish culture but he was also showered with honour and appreciation under the legacy of the Scottish Enlightenment, which believed in the separate entity of 'Man'. Dwarakanath, despite his inclination to orthodoxy, tried to focus his attention on 'Man' and his welfare. He may be considered as an icon of the Scotland-India encounter and intercourse in the truest sense of the term.

Works Cited:

Bagal, Jogesh Chandra. *Unavimsa Satabdir Bangla*. Calcutta: Ranjan Publishing House, 1963. Print.

Cain, Alex M. *The Cornchest For Scotland: Scots In India*. Edinburgh: National Library of Scotland, 1986. Print.

Kling, Blair B. *Partner in Empire: Dwarkanath Tagore and the Age of Enterprise in Eastern India*. Calcutta: Firma Klm Pvt. Ltd., 1981. Print.

Kopf, David. *British Orientalism and the Bengal Rennaissance*. Berkeley: University of California Press, 1969. Print.

Kripalani Krishna. *Dwarakanath Tagore: A Forgotten Pioneer, A Life*. New Delhi: National Book Trust, 1981. Print.

Mitra, Kissory Chand. *Memoir of Dwarakanath Tagore*. Calcutta: Thacker, Spink and Co., 1870. Print.

*The Trio who turned the Clock of
Education in Bengal*

David Hare

Serampore Missionaries and David Hare: On the Penury of Education in Nineteenth Century Bengal

Saptarshi Mallick

Philanthropic hearts devoted to one generous end

RABINDRANATH TAGORE had once stated that the human mind 'has faculties which are universal' (Tagore, 'East and West' 530), as he believed *Esha devo visvakarma- maha-tma- sada- jana-nam hridaya sannivishatah* – 'This is the divine being, the world-worker, who is the Great Soul ever dwelling inherent in the hearts of all people' (Tagore, *The Religion of Man* 55). A true realisation of the divine being inherent in the hearts of the people can only occur:

> when a feeling is aroused in our hearts which is far in excess of the amount that can be completely absorbed by the object which has produced it, it comes back to us and makes us conscious of ourselves by its return waves (Tagore, *Personality* 9)

...enlightening us at once by transcending ourselves beyond constructed superstitious conventions and beliefs. The necessity of such a socio-cultural, psychological and intellectual realisation, along with a spirit of a reawakening, was ushered in the society of 19th century Bengal through 'the impact of the British rule, the bourgeois economy and modern western culture' (Tagore, *On The Bengal Renaissance* 13) involving an active participation of social thinkers, philosophers, humanitarians, educationists and missionaries, both from home as well as from the world, to address the factors responsible for the culturally and socially moribund society of Bengal (Mittra, *Bengal's Renaissance* 3). In such a social existence, the foundation of the city of Calcutta and its position as the capital of the British India (Ray, *Bengal Renaissance* 4), facilitated a cultural assimilation of the Hindu intelligentsia with the British officials, missionaries and citizens visiting Bengal on various political, humanitarian and trade pursuits (writer? *British Orientalism* 1). This socio-cultural process associated with modernization, revitalization and awakening (writer? *British Orientalism* 280) of the 19th-century has often been termed as the Bengal Renaissance. (Besides exposing the weaknesses inherent within the society, it was the 'new life' (Tagore, *On The Bengal Renaissance* 69) rich in possibilities through the gradual imagining of a nation which would be based on the amenable synthesis of manifold cultures (Raichaudhuri reference? 360) with 'the creative spirit in its most profuse richness and diversity' (*Awakening* 2) and an intense intellectual liveliness in literature and the arts which influenced religious, social and political thoughts ('The Nineteenth Century Indian') inspiring the Indian mind for a revolutionary awakening (*Awakening* 2).)

This awakening in Bengal was affected by an active participation of some enlightened foreigners and natives, who comprehensively took measures to address social vices and steered in reforms for common welfare. One of the major reforms was the necessity to spread education amongst the masses. In this context, the role of William Carey (1761–1834), Joshua Marshman (1768–1837), William Ward (1769–1823) and David Hare (1775–1842) towards one generous end ie to address the penury of education and initiate educational endeavours for the welfare of Indians, remains a turning point in the history of the 19th-century in Bengal. This study will give a full account of these dynamic individuals, to show how they set the scene for the advent of David Hare, who will be the focus of the latter part of the chapter.

William Carey, a humble, non-conformist Baptist minister (later a missionary) in Northamptonshire, volunteered to undertake missionary activities with a visionary zeal to spread the 'word' among the non-Christians in the world. He arrived in India in 1793, with his associates, Joshua Marshman and William Ward, joining him in 1799 at Serampore (Bengal), at a time when a strong conservatism grasped the entire society (Purkait 39) [where the loss of values led to socio-personal immorality at the cost of education and freedom] drawing the [generous] attention of the 'Serampore Trio' to spread education among the masses and develop their reading habit and reasoning power through several altruistic activities in translation, literature, journalism and printing. The Trio took the lead in promoting education based on western schooling [and not schooling *per se*,] and addressed 'ignorance' and 'immorality' (Potts 115). Carey emphasized the importance of education in Bengal by extending it towards the children of the Indians and the missionaries (*Periodical Accounts* I: IV 347). On 1 June 1800, a Free School with education in the vernaculars was established at Serampore ('Missionaries and the New' 60) under the efficient supervision and care of the Marshmans (Middlebrook 73) along with their boarding schools.[1]

After the baptism of Krishna Pal (Potts 116), the number of children at the Free Vernacular School (Drewery 114) began to decrease as parents feared their children would become Christians and be sent to England. The missionaries' assurance that they were concerned only to impart education for the welfare of the children subsequently increased the popularity of these institutions and the Missionaries overcame all obstacles and moved ahead with their educational endeavours, initiating a life bereft of the orthodox practices. The Marshmans also set up boarding schools in 1800 for European and Anglo-Indian boys and soon for the girls (Ibid. 113), a legacy carried ahead later by John Mack (Mack, *The Life of William Carey* 151). The Serampore Missionaries advocated the necessity for introducing the mother tongue as the medium of instruction (*Hints Relative* 11) to educate the children of the natives and the Indian converts on theology, history, geography, astronomy, English and Bengali languages. Their plan for establishing a different kind of school, ie a 'Free School at Calcutta for country-born children' ('Abstracts of Reports on' 107), materialised in 1809 with the establishment of the 'Benevolent Institution For The Instruction of Children of Indigent Christians' ('Missionaries and the New' 62) as an embodiment of active and indefatigable benevolence of the Trio (Lushington 208-228). Within a year, the numbers of students increased to a hundred and they were taught reading and writing in Bengali and English, arithmetic and accounts, along with the study of the Scriptures; girls were also a part of this institution and they were taught needle work and knitting (Ibid. 209-212). Though the two Scots, Dr Leyden and David Hare, were the co-sponsors of the institution, it was specifically through the efforts of Marshman that collection of funds was possible and the school was able to see the clear light of day. The First Report of the Institution (1812) proves that there were 310 boys and 102 girls admitted in the Institution ('Abstract Of Reports' 107). Branches of the 'Benevolent Institution' were opened at Serampore, Dhaka and Chittagong and, in December 1822, the total numbers of students was almost 500 (Lushington, 214). Subsequent reports of this institution show that, with time, the number of students, both boys and girls, increased.[2] The 'Benevolent Institution' gathered momentum and set a model for the indigenous schools and the Calcutta School Society in the later period with regard to the curriculum, class organisation, monitorial method and the examination system. It was estimated that, by 1816, the Trio were able to bring 103 schools under the care of the 'Benevolent Institution' with 6,703 students (Marshman, *The First Report of the Institution* 12) at Serampore and at Hooghly, Howrah, 24 Parganas, Dhaka, Jessore, Burdwan, Birbhum, Dinajpur, Murshidabad, and Ajmeer ('Missionaries and the New' 63-4), which has been considered a great blessing for the children of Bengal by Oussoren (208).

Carey requested the East India Company to devise a planned educational network by virtually dividing the country into circles with 150 miles diameter with an appointed superintendent residing in the middle of each circle, supervising and coordinating native school teachers in that district for better results (Laird, *Missionaries and Education* 71). According to him, the teachers of these schools could be chosen from the educated local people. The plan being costly, Carey suggested to the Government to concentrate its resources and facilitate the Indians to study European science at the College of Fort William – a wise proposal which went unheeded (Ibid.). Accordingly,

Joshua Marshman drew up a plan of action in 1813 for the introduction of the Lancastrian system into the vernacular schools where he emphasized three things: the requirement of books, adequate funding, and regular superintendence to reap positive results, thereby simplifying and organizing the work into a system (*Hints Relative* 21), and helping the mission to be self-supporting and self-propagating (Elliott 64) through common welfare. The curriculum emphasized the use of the mother-tongue to increase the effectiveness of the teaching-learning process for the students through the introduction of text books, periodical inspection (Marshman, *The Second Report of the Institution* 29) and following the 3 Rs – reading, writing and arithmetic – along with moral teaching based on Christianity through the use of printed books and widening the syllabus, which aimed at the sound education of students to be responsible individuals[3] through an upright life by being educated in ethics, the fourth 'R' in the curriculum (*Hints Relative* 36). Marshman's aim was to make the students familiar with 'an advantageous study of the Scriptures' (*The Third Report of the Institution* 35) to broaden their mind and perspectives (*The Life and Times* I: 160-1). To make their life useful, the Missionaries widened the curriculum by introducing history, geography, astronomy (Marshman, *The Third Report of the Institution* 10-19) and divinity (Oussoren 105) for their better understanding and reflection. Three full-time teachers were appointed, one each for teaching English and Bengali, and one for other subjects; importance was also given to prayer (Gine 42). The revised curriculum not only paid more attention to the individual students but was also fund-generating, along with Carey's salary at the College of Fort William (Drewery 132).

After Charles Grant's Charter Act (1813) proposed the idea of setting up schools for teaching English (Mittra, *Bengal's Renaissance* 7), Marshman presented the *Minute* of 1813, a systematic plan for elementary education through the vernaculars; a prototype of mass-education adopted later in Wood's Despatch of 1854 (*The Life and Times* I: 82, 83), which recommended the establishment of a well-coordinated system of secular education among all (Bhattacharya, *Bengal Renaissance* 28-9). In 1816–1817, girls were admitted in the schools set up by the missionaries and their room was separated by a mat-partition from the boys (Marshman, *The First Report of the Institution* 19). The fees collected from these schools were an important source of funds as they varied from 45 to 50 pounds every year, according to the number of languages studied.[4] This income[5] and, later, that from Serampore College, contributed a revenue to the Missionaries' common fund. Guided by Carey's *An Enquiry* and their 'Form of Agreement', the Missionaries emphasized the necessity of being self-sufficient, self-supporting and self-propagating among the masses (*Memoir* 374) in the field of education.

In 1814, the Missionaries issued the proposal for the establishment of 'Native Schools' to assist anyone who may undertake the measures to extend the benefits of knowledge at the least possible expense to the masses (*Hints Relative* 39-40). With considerable organisation and extensive plans, on 20 November 1816, the Trio published their ideas and arguments formally as a pamphlet entitled, *Hints Relative to Native Schools Together with the Outline of an Institution for their Extension and Management.*[6] Based on Lancaster's proposals (Potts 118), *Hints* proposed a strategic system of national education susceptible to great expansion, but the plan was never executed (*The Life and Times* II: 119-120). It stated the necessity of native free schools, the proper knowledge to be communicated, and the effectual means of accomplishing educational objectives, besides an account of the work undertaken towards the attainment of the plan along with the general support for their 'An Institution for Native Schools' which met with much encouragement (*Hints Relative* 39) as evident from *The First Report of the Institution* of October 1817. Therefore, *Hints* is an elaborate educational treatise suggesting vital reforms in the school curriculum (*Hints Relative* 1), emphasizing the students' ability to read, write and calculate, besides widening their understanding about God and man; initiating a modern and a scientific education (Marshman, *The Second Report of the Institution* 35). Though during July 1816 and October 1817, there were 103 schools with an average attendance of 6,703 pupils (Marshman, *The First Report of the Institution* 12), over 10,000 pupils' names were found on the school rolls; however, the lower figure was calculated by Marshman from a comparison of inspectors' and teachers' reports ('Patterns of Missionary Education' 300). The Missionaries, with support from Raja Radha Kanta Deb, Kalisankar Ghoshal, Rasamoy Dutta, established elementary schools for vernacular education between 1814 and 1820 (Purkait 41) and *Hints* was a part of this plan.

The Serampore missionaries realised that their educational endeavours would be futile without the availability of the teaching-learning aids (text books) for the students. Therefore, they concentrated on revising the school curriculum from the simple 3 Rs to complex modern education where subjects like Orthography, Bengali Grammar-Vocabulary, Arithmetic, Elementary Astronomy, Geography, Elementary Natural Philosophy, History and Chronology and Ethics and Morality were taught ('Missionaries and the New' 64). Hence, it became a huge responsibility of the Missionaries to publish books for the students, following a three-way approach: writing books afresh on each subject, translating the books made available in Bengali, and printing them through their press, which initiated a cultural revolution of 19th-century Bengal (Purkait 42, 43). As the Missionaries preferred the use of the Bengali language for education over the English language ('Missionaries and the New' 64), it became easy for the people to acquire education and this was conducive to social stability (Laird, 'William

Carey and the Education' 99). Though the Missionaries never opposed the learning of the English language by the rich, they believed that it would be 'a vain attempt to impart knowledge of this language to the masses in general' (Marshman, *The First Report of the Institution* 36-41), unlike the Orientalists and the Anglicists[7] of the time.

The Serampore Native Institution [free vernacular school] was instrumental in imparting education on the students and contributing to a comprehensive social transformation (Mukherjee, 'William Carey the Educationist' 115). The desire for higher education and a thirst for western knowledge among the people inspired the Trio to frame a plan for a college by 15 July 1816, for 'the spiritual and intellectual improvement of the country' (*The Life and Times* II: 168) through 'liberal education' (Davis 81). On 15 July 1818, the missionaries issued a prospectus entitled 'College For The Instruction of Asiatic Christian and Other Youth in Eastern Literature and European Science' leading to the foundation of the Serampore College (1818), where Christian theology, vernaculars, European sciences and information would be taught (*College For The Instruction Of Asiatic* 2, 6-10). In February 1827, King Frederick VI of Denmark granted the Royal Charter to the Serampore College, empowering it to confer degrees in all faculties, raising it to the rank of a university (Oussoren 209). The establishment of the School Book Society (1817) and the School Society (1818) helped the Missionaries to work vigorously in their educational ventures and promoted education among Indian women (Purkait 42) with great success (Gine 38), encouraging others to establish schools for girls.

The methodology of elementary education employed by the Trio was attractive and conducive to the pupils' environment. It was based on modern knowledge and Christian ethics which were emphasised in *Hints* (Laird, 'William Carey and the' 102), propitious towards the development of the body and the minds of the children (*Hints Relative* 15). The missionaries did not aim to convert the natives, but wanted to educate them properly from their childhood to enable them to see and understand things just as they are ('Abstract Of Reports' 111) as evident from some of their reports (Marshman, *The First Report of the Institution* 41-2). To address the problem of rote-learning (Laird, 'The Contribution of Missionaries' 341) and ensure effective teaching in the classes (*Hints Relative* 16), the Missionaries established a normal school for training teachers (*Hints Relative* 36) and, within a few months, several such schools were established near Serampore with the cooperation of the local people. Though the missionaries endeavoured to train the teachers (Oussoren 106), there were never enough and several of the schools had to be closed after a few years (Laird 'William Carey and the' 102). In November 1816, the 'Institution for the Encouragement of Native Schools in India' set up by the Serampore missionaries received more than 8,000 rupees in subscriptions and donations, enabling the institution to arrange proper supervision of the schools, printing of new and attractive books, charts for use in their schools along with the circulation of vernacular magazines like the monthly *Dig-Durshun* and the weekly *Samachar Darpan* among the students and the general masses, as well as popularizing the Christian doctrines, Mythology, Geography and Natural History.[8] The reports of this Institution vindicate the zeal of the Missionaries to promote uniform and efficient education among the natives in spite of encountering several problems.

The drilling method in teaching was substituted with the use of the black board, studying the printed books, writing, dictation, discussing orally the moral in fables and the monitor (Mukherjee, 'Missionaries and the New' 64) would be the steadiest of the class (*Hints Relative* 24). Periodical examinations were also conducted, facilitating a method of regular attention and evaluation towards each student (Gine 51-2). The Missionaries wanted to establish a sound educational foundation by imparting knowledge in orthography, a system of grammar, an extended vocabulary and arithmetic, including facts related to the solar system, a synopsis of geography, a collection of facts related to natural philosophy, history, along with a chronology of events and a compendium of ethics and morality (*Hints Relative* 11-8), similar to George Henry Loskiel's description of the *Delaware Reading and Spelling Book* compiled by David Zeisberger in 1776 and introduced in the schools at Schoenbrunn and Gnadenhuetten (*History of the Mission of the United* 113).

Through their arduous capacity for work, the Serampore Missionaries and the College of Fort William initiated the development in language, literature and education, affecting the cultural and literary life of Bengal and paving the foundation for the education in the English language (Purkait 44) through the introduction of the Charter Act. The distinct educational endeavours of these Missionaries ushered in a process of acculturation in Bengal which contributed to the renaissance, leaving an enduring mark in the history of Indian education.

While the philanthropist Serampore Missionaries worked together to spread education in the vernacular among the natives, a large-hearted Scotsman,[9] David Hare (1775–1842), a watch-maker by profession,[10] dedicated over four decades (1800–1842) of his life to Calcutta for the welfare of the people of Bengal. He was one of the main architects of the new education, initiated by the Charter Act, heralding the renaissance in 19th-century Bengal (*On The Bengal Renaissance* 97). Like the Missionaries, Hare was also a philanthropist who was not only pained to observe the socio-cultural degeneration of the Indians, but also pondered over its causes and the suitable remedies (Mittra, *David Hare* 2). Like Rammohan Roy,[11] he became a prominent figure in the Bengal Renaissance who helped to turn the clock of Bengal's education (Fraser np). His ardent conviction for propagating liberal Western education through the European Sciences and Literature among the natives led him to urge the necessity for introducing an English system of education of higher standards (Mittra, *David Hare* 2). He discovered that:

> nothing but education was requisite to render the Hindoos happy, and exerted [his] humble abilities to further the interest of India and... to promote the cause of education ('Asiatic Intelligence' 55)

...initiating modern Western system of scientific education in India (Mitra, Preface vii, viii).

> Being a philanthropist at heart, Hare was no intellectual scholar, though the Scottish contemporary intellect inspired him (*On The Bengal Renaissance* 97) to concentrate on 'the dynamics of humanity' (Mitra, Preface VII). Along with the enthusiastic natives, Hare carried the baton of progressive modern education in India – by proposing the idea and preparing a scheme for the establishment of Hindoo College in 1815 (Mitra, *David Hare* 3) that would facilitate modern, rational education for the native youths and enlighten their understanding and purge their minds from pernicious cants (Mitra, Preface XII). Therefore, on 14 May 1816, Hare, with Sir Edward Hyde East and several natives, planned the establishment of an English educational institution of the highest degree; the resolution being resolved on 21 May 1816 (Mitra, *David Hare* 3); the Hindoo College with the aim for 'the tuition of the sons of respectable Hindoos in the English and Indian languages and in the literature and science of Europe and Asia' ('A Sketch of the Origin, Rise' 72) was opened in Goranhata on 20 January 1817 (Mitra, *A Biographical Sketch* 7) with Hare being its originator and promoter (Mitra, Preface xiii), authenticated through the series of articles entitled, 'A Sketch of the Origin, Rise and Progress of the Hindoo College' published in the first three issues (June 1832) of *The Calcutta Christian Observer*, stating 'the merit of originating the Hindoo College must in justice be ascribed to Mr Hare ('A Sketch of the Origin, Rise' 17). Hare earned the distinction of being the 'Father of English Education in India', anticipating Macaulay's and Bentinck's policy of promoting English education in India (Mitra, *David Hare* 3). Imparting education on modern science and social philosophy, this college produced eminent students[12] who successfully produced 'cold tremors to hollow spines of the seasoned conservatives' (Mitra, Preface XIII, XIV), following an assimilation of cultures, realising Hare's ideals of modern English education within the cultural matrix and tradition of India.

Hare was also enthusiastically associated with the Calcutta School Book Society which was founded by several humane Europeans on 4 July 1817 for:

> the preparation, publication and cheap or gratuitous supply of works useful in schools and seminaries... suitable books of instruction for native schools in the English and Oriental Languages ('Calcutta School Book Society' 352).

This Society not only aided in the improvement of schools, but also helped to:

> establish and support any further schools and seminaries which may be requisite, with a view to the more general diffusion of useful knowledge amongst the inhabitants of India ('Asiatic Intelligence – Calcutta' 341).

Hare subscribed to the Society and was also an active member of it. He wrote to its Secretary on 6 October 1827 that:

> I believe there is no other institution in Calcutta that publishes books of the same description and I think the friends of education in this country are much indebted to your Society for the regular supply it has afforded (De 75).

The second report of this Society emphasized the proper distribution of the Society's publications among the needy and with Radhakanta Dev in charge, it was distributed as free books to school masters of the Bengali schools (Mitra, *A Biographical Sketch* 56). Periodical examinations were held at the house of Babu Radhakanta Dev ('Letter respecting the Calcutta School Society' 416) and prizes were offered to students and teachers (Mitra, *A Biographical Sketch* 56).The city was also divided into four districts for the efficient functioning and supervision of the schools ('Letter respecting the Calcutta School' 413). Hare, along with the other members of the Society, extended their unwearied attention to the promotion of education in this country and thereby prevent intellectual and moral education to appear tedious, but benevolent for the youths of Calcutta ('Letters illustrative of the utility' 95). The members of the Calcutta School Book Society established the Calcutta School Society on 1 September 1818 with the aim to improve existing schools and support the development of new schools.[13] The School Society, with which Hare was closely associated, played a pioneering role in establishing five regular vernacular schools and two English schools for all students without any discrimination. The first was at Arpooly,[14] where Rev Krishna Mohan Banerjea was a student before moving to Pataldanga school and then to the Hindu college (Mitra, *A Biographical Sketch* 57). From reports we observe that both the societies aimed at the education of the lower and higher classes. Hare also established and personally managed the schools at Simla, Pataldanga (called 'The Calcutta School Society's School' or 'Mr Hare's School' later 'Hare School') and at Arpooly for imparting free education to poor students (Mitra, Preface xviii), testifying to his solicitude and zeal for the promotion of vernacular and liberal western education, a cultural synthesis for a better India. The number of students increased with time and here they were taught by a pundit and four native teachers and were divided into eleven classes, occupied with

> different Bengali studies from the alphabet upwards... reading, writing, spelling, grammar, and arithmetic from the books published by the Calcutta School Book Society... nearly similar to an English school ('Asiatic Intelligence – Calcutta' 341).

The School Society appointed three sub-committees: (a) for the establishment and support of a limited number of regular schools for boys and girls, (b) for aiding and improving the indigenous schools and (c) for the education of a selected number of pupils in English and to groom them as future teachers (Mitra, *A Biographical Sketch* 54). Hare may have accepted the model of the Scot, Dr Alexander Bell, tried in the Military Orphan Asylum of Madras in 1791 ('Letter respecting the Calcutta School' 417), and the model of Robert May who established schools around Chinsurah. Classes were graded and meritorious students taught the juniors in this 'monitorial' method. The First Report of the School Society emphasized the necessity of educational opportunities in the country.[15]

Hare was never aloof from the socio-cultural movements of his time; he neither supported the Progressives – Conservatives nor the Anglicists – Orientalists,[16] but aimed at a comprehensive development of the masses through a sound education, becoming 'a champion for the cause of modern education at the dawn of the age of reason and renaissance' (Mitra, Preface xx). Having dedicated himself to the efficiency of the educational institutions for the enrichment of the students, as Dr Bramley stated (*Report of the General Committee of Public* 34-35), Hare regularly visited to inspect the Society's schools, the Hindoo College (Mitra, *David Hare* 11) and the Calcutta Medical College which was established on 1 February 1835 under his influence (Ibid.). Hare was not only desirous of serving the country as an educator, but he also ensured social and political upliftment of Bengal.[17] Though Hare had not actively undertaken any measure for the development of the education for the females, he was a subscriber to the Calcutta Female Juvenile Society whose name was changed into the Ladies' Society for Native Female Education.[18]

Bengal will always be indebted to David Hare for introducing a balanced education for the native children. His educational endeavours are embodiments of the Scottish influence upon the Bengal Renaissance which are evident even today. Hare introduced the liberal western education besides stressing the proficiency of education in the mother tongue, in this case, the Bengali language (Mitra, *A Biographical Sketch* 59, 60). The Report of the General Committee of Public Instruction (1835) praised this Scottish spirit by stating

> Few will be found, like Mr Hare, to bestow years of unremitting labour upon this object, noble and interesting as it is, without any expectation of reward except what is to be derived from the gratification of benevolent feeling ('Mode of Educating the Natives' 279).

Hare aimed at a subjective evolution as objectivity resting on creeds and dogmas were unimportant to him and his activities embodied his moral teaching as he was an inspiration for the age, benefitting youths in every manner, as he was ever ready to assist in various matters when approached.[19] Hare's generosity was equally felt through his philanthropic services as he emerged as 'the world-worker' (*The Religion of Man* 55). Hare dedicated his life towards one generous end and remained

> a heavy laden pilgrim looking for rest at the conclusion of his journey...the liberalizing effects of education which thousands had received through his instrumentality were being extended to several districts of Bengal – that culminated in the improvement of their moral tone – in the amelioration of their domestic and social relations and in the incipient evolution of their spiritual life evidenced by their earnest enquiry after religion (Mitra, *A Biographical Sketch* 149).

Hare's scientific temperament, free thinking and respect for human dignity were the pillars of his dynamic philanthropic activities which

> proved extremely effective in protecting and nursing the sapling of renaissance, so that it could, in time, grow into a mighty banyan tree, encompassing a whole sub-continent and inspiring subsequent generations (Chakravarti 118).

James Kerr's *A Review of Public Instruction in the Bengal Presidency, From 1835 to 1851* (1852) provides a heart-warming account of David Hare for being a great friend of education with a rational [he was an atheist][20] benevolent heart which Bengal cherishes with reverence and affectionate gratitude (Mitra, *David Hare* 24), inspiring us to draw from his life the invaluable lessons on enduring benevolence and philanthropy (Mitra, *A Biographical Sketch* 150), evident through Captain DL Richardson's tribute to him inscribed on a mural table at the Hare School erected on 1847, where he states,

Ah! warm philanthropist faithful friend!
Thy life devoted to one generous end,
To bless the Hindoo mind with British lore,
And truth's and nature's faded lights restore!
If for a day that lofty aim was crossed
You grieved like Titus that a day was lost!
Alas! it is not now a few brief honors
That withholds, a heavier grief o'er powers
A nation whom you love'd as if your own
A life that gave the life of life is gone.

William Carey and David Hare were sincere, dedicated and philanthropic individuals to whom Bengal remains indebted for their impetus to the Renaissance along with their associates, through their social, educational and humane endeavours. The 19th-century Bengal Renaissance not only ensured a new phase in the intellectual history of the people but also steadied the path for the unity and continuity of the Bengali culture (Dasgupta, Introduction XXII). Though Carey existed for his Lord and Hare was an atheist, their philanthropy, their far-reaching visions of the future, contributing to the common welfare through the spread of education which initiated an evolution from

> a luminous sphere of human mind from the nebula that has been rushing round ages to find in itself an eternal centre of unity ('Ideals of Education' 613).

Having never returned to England and being completely dedicated to their cause, Carey and Hare, through their ardent positive conviction in life, their enthusiastic decision, patience, persevering constancy and simplicity, ushered in the common welfare through the efficiency of education as Tagore believed. Towards the end of their life, William Carey and David Hare had no fears, no doubts, no wish left unsatisfied for being zealous towards the cause of human prosperity. They were men with

> no ordinary powers of mind, with prompt and acute apprehension, capable of vigorous and enduring application... perseveringly and zealously devoted all their faculties and acquirements to the intellectual and spiritual improvement of their fellow-creatures in the East (*Memoir* 610).

End Notes:

1. Fees were charged from the students who were studying in these boarding schools (Drewery 114).

2. By 1818 the mission cared 126 vernacular schools, with 10,000 pupils receiving elementary education, simple instruction on Christianity and the morals of life to the native's advantage (Ogilvie 317).

3. Education governs individual's character (Laird, *Missionaries and Education* 77).

4. Latin, Greek, Hebrew, Persian or Sanskrit languages (*The Life and Times* I: 80, 81).

5. Annual profit of £1000 contributed to the Serampore Mission's common stock (Drewery 113).

6. The 'first organised plan for the establishment of schools in India' (*The Life and Times* II: 82).

7. Orientalists stood for the revival and encouragement of learning Sanskrit and Persian languages; Anglicists stood for liberal education through an exclusive medium of the English language (*The Life and Times* II: 120, 121).

8. Joshua Marshman, *The First Report of the Institution*, Appendix; Joshua Marshman, *The Second Report of the Institution* 15-27; Joshua Marshman, *The Third Report of the Institution* 24-27.

9. Hare must have learnt the trade of watch-making from his father in London (Mitra, *David Hare* 1).

10. Aberdeen is supposed to be Hare's birth place (Ibid.).

11. Roy's and Hare's perspectives were different. Roy advocated religious reformation and the foundation of the 'Atmiya Sabha' for the teaching of Vedanta. Hare pleaded for the development of an 'English College for teaching European Science, Philosophy and Literature'. This however did not create any rift and they shared a cordial relationship until the end (Mitra, *David Hare* 28).

12. Young Bengals, Dakhinaranjan Mookherjee, Ram Gopal Ghose, Tarachand Chakravarty, Krishnamohan Banerjee (Mitra, Preface XIII).

13. The aim was to seek pupils of distinguished talents and merits from elementary and other schools and to provide for their instruction in seminaries of a higher degree with the view of forming a body of qualified Teachers and Translators who may be instrumental in enlightening their countrymen and improving the general system of education. When the funds of the institution may admit of it, the maintenance and tuition of such pupils in distinct seminaries will be an object of importance' ("Foreign Intelligence" 224).

14. Education through the Arpooly school, opposite to the Thanthania Kali Temple (Mitra, *David Hare* 8, 11), bore the best proof that can be offered of the estimation in which it is held by the native inhabitants of the neighbourhood is, the frequent and earnest solicitation from the most respectable natives to have their children educated in it ("Asiatic Intelligence – Calcutta" 341).

15. It concludes stating, nothing will be wanting to their successors in future years but funds and personal exertions to carry the benefits of the Society to an indefinite extent. Adult and female education, the extension and improvement of the indigenous system, and the education of a greater number of clever boys in English, as well as providing them with the means of acquiring scientific education, are all objects of great importance to be vigorously pursued in the metropolis and its vicinity; while the neglected state of the vast population under British dominion, and the means of improving them afforded by the application particularly of the indigenous system,

call loudly upon us to embrace every opportunity to extending our operations in the country ("Literary and Philosophical Intelligence" 368).

16. The Progressives were led by Raja Rammohan Roy and the Conservatives were led by Raja Radha Kanta Deb. The Anglicists were led by Macaulay; followed by Raja Rammohan Roy, Dwarkanath Tagore and others, while the Orientalists were led by Hastings, Minto, Munro and Elphinstone (Mitra, Preface XVIII, XIX).

17. Hare petitioned the Governor-General to repeal the press regulations of 1824 (Mitra, *A Biographical Sketch* 75).

18. It was established in 1824 and Hare attended the institution to evaluate the performance of Hindu girls at their examinations which were held at the residence of Raja Radha Kanta Deb. Hare believed that if he would have lived for ten years more then he would have surely endeavoured measures for active female education in Bengal (Mitra, *David Hare* 15).

19. Hare took care of those who were helpless and had not the means of subsistence, he educated at his own expense helping them with money for their food and raiment. Those who required occasional pecuniary support received it from him. Those who came to him without the means of buying books were assisted. Those who were sick received medicines and medical aid from him (Mitra, *ABiographical Sketch* 145).

20. As he was an atheist (anti-Christian) he could work for the welfare of the natives without any kind of inhibitions and this progressive perspective was looked down upon by the conservatives of his time. Therefore the whole of the Christian community of Calcutta were secretly hostile to him and they would not have permitted his interment in the cemeteries, besides Hare being an anti-Christian might have not liked to be buried in a Christian burial ground. Therefore he was laid to rest by his admirers in College Square in sight of the Hindoo College and his own School (Mitra, *David Hare* 29).

Works Cited:

"Abstract Of Reports On Native Education in India." *The Missionary Register for* MDCCCXIX. *Containing the Principal Transactions of the Various Institutions for Propagating the Gospel: With the Proceedings, At Large, Of The Church Missionary Society.* (March 1819): 103-121. Print.

"Asiatic Intelligence Calcutta." *The Asiatic Journal and Monthly Register For British India and its Dependencies* XXVIII. September (1829): 329-345. Print.

"Asiatic Intelligence." *The Asiatic Journal and Monthly Register For British and Foreign India, China and Australasia* VI. October (1831): 49-104. Print.

"A Sketch of the Origin, Rise, and Progress of the Hindoo College." *The Calcutta Christian Observer* I. June December (1832): 14-17, 68-76, 115-129. Print.

Balfour, Ian L. S. *Revival in Rose Street: Charlotte Baptist Chapel, Edinburgh 1808–2008.* Edinburgh: Rutherford House, 2007. Print.

Bhattacharya, Bijoy. *Bengal Renaissance: A Study in the Progress of English Education (1800–1858).* Calcutta: P. Sen and Company, 1963. Print.

"Calcutta School Book Society." *The Bengal and Agra Guide and Gazetteer for 1841.* I. 3 (1841): 352. Print.

Carey, Eustace. *Memoir of William Carey, late missionary to Bengal, Professor of Oriental Languages in the College of Fort William, Calcutta.* London: Jackson and Walford, 1836. Print.

Carey, William. *An Enquiry into the Obligations of Christians to use means for the Conversion of the Heathens.* 1792. Oxfordshire: Baptist Missionary Society, 1991. Print.

Carey, William, Joshua Marshman, William Ward, John Chamberlain, Richard Mardon, John Biss, William Moore, Joshua Rowe, and Felix Carey. "The Serampore Form of Agreement (1805)." *The Baptist Quarterly* 12.5 (January 1947): 125-138. Print.

Carey, William, Joshua Marshman, and William Ward, *Hints Relative to Native Schools, Together With the Outline of An Institution For Their Extension and Management.* Serampore: Serampore Mission Press, 1816. Print.

—. *College For The Instruction Of Asiatic Christian And Other Youth, In Eastern Literature And European Science, At Serampore, Bengal.* London: Cox and Baylls, 1819. Print.

Carey, S. Pearce, *William Carey.* London: The Wakeman Trust, 1923. Print.

Chakravarti, Hiralal. "Bengal Renaissance and David Hare." *David Hare Bicentenary Volume 1975–76.* Ed. Rakhal Bhattacharya. Calcutta: David Hare Bicentenary of Birth Celebration Committee, 1976. 109-118. Print.

Dasgupta, Rabindra Kumar. "The Nineteenth Century Indian Renaissance: Fact or Fiction." 1970 MS. Indian institute of Advanced Study, Simla.

—. Introduction. *Studies in the Bengal Renaissance.* 3rd Rev. ed. Kolkata: National Council of Education, 2002. xx - xxiv. Print.

Dasgupta, Subrata. *Awakening: The Story of The Bengal Renaissance.* United Kingdom: Random House, 2011. Print.

Davis, Walter Bruce. *William Carey: Father of Modern Missions.* Chicago: Moody Press, 1963. Print.

De, Amalendu. "Publication of Text-Books in Bengali: A Movement for Child Education in Nineteenth Century Bengal." *David Hare Bicentenary Volume 1975–76.* Ed. Rakhal Bhattacharya. Calcutta: David Hare Bicentenary of Birth Celebration Committee, 1976. 72-93. Print.

Drewery, Mary. *William Carey: Shoemaker and Missionary.* London: Hodder and Stoughton, 1978. Print.

Elliott, Kelly Rebecca Cross. "Baptist Missions In the British Empire: Jamaica and Serampore in the First Half of the Nineteenth Century." Diss. The Florida State University, 2007. Print.

"Foreign Intelligence." *The Missionary Register for MDCCC XIX. Containing the Principal Transactions of the Various Institutions for Propagating the Gospel: With The Proceedings, At Large, Of The Church Missionary Society* May (1819): 220-225. Print.

Fraser, Bashabi. *Scots Beneath The Banyan Tree: Stories From Bengal.* Edinburgh: Luarth Press, 2012. Print.

Gine, Pratap Chandra. *The System of Elementary Education of the Serampore Mission.* Assam: Eastern Theological College, 2001. Print.

Kopf, David. *British Orientalism and the Bengal Renaissance: The Dynamics of Indian Modernization 1773–1835.* Calcutta: Firma K. L. Mukhopadhyay, 1969. Print.

Laird, Michael Andrew. "William Carey and the Education of India." *Indian Journal of Theology* x (July 1961): 97-102. Print.

—. *Missionaries and Education in Bengal 1793–1837.* Oxford: Clarendon Press, 1972. Print.

—. "The Contribution of Missionaries to Education in Bengal, 1793–1837." *Preach and Heal: A History of the Christian Missionaries in India.* Ed. Sandeep Sinha. Kolkata: Readers Service, 2008. 340-348. Print.

"Letters illustrative of the utility and acceptableness of the School-Book Society's Publications." *The Second Report of the Calcutta School-Book Society's Proceedings. Second Year, 1818–19. With An Appendix, The Accounts of the Institution, &c. &c. Read the 21st September, 1819.* (1819): 80-96. Print.

"Letter respecting the Calcutta School Society." *The Friend of India, Containing Information Relative to the State of Religion and Literature in India, with occasional Intelligence from Europe and America for the Year 1819* II. (1819): 405-419. Print.

"Literary and Philosophical Intelligence." *The Asiatic Journal and Monthly Register for British India and its Dependencies* X. October (1820): 367-375. Print.

Loskiel, George Henry. *History of the Mission of the United Brethren: Among the Indians in North America, In Three Parts.* Trans. Christian Ignatius La Trobe. London: John Stockdale, 1794. Print.

Lushington, Charles. *The History Design and Present State of the Religious Benevolent and Charitable Institutions founded by the British in Calcutta and its Vicinity.* Calcutta: Hindostanee Press, 1824. Print.

Marshman, Joshua. *The First Report of the Institution For the Encouragement of Native Schools in India with A List of Subscribers and Benefactors.* Serampore: Serampore Mission Press, 1817. Print.

—. *The Second Report of the Institution For the Support and Encouragement of Native Schools, Begun at Serampore, November 1816: With A List of Subscribers and Benefactors.* Serampore: Serampore Mission Press, 1818. Print.

—. *The Third Report of the Institution For the Support and Encouragement of Native Schools, Begun at Serampore, November 1816.* Serampore: Serampore Mission Press, 1820. Print

Marshman, John Clark. *The Life and Times of Carey, Marshman and Ward: Embracing The History of the Serampore Mission.* 2 vols. 1859. Serampore: Council of Serampore College, 2005. Print.

Middlebrook, J. B. *William Carey.* London: The Carey Kingsgate Press Limited, 1961. Print.

Mitra, Radharaman. *David Hare: His Life and Work.* Calcutta: Manisha Granthalay, 1968. Print.

Mittra, Peary Chand. *A Biographical Sketch of David Hare.* Calcutta: W. Newman & Co., 1877. Print.

—. Preface. *A Biographical Sketch of David Hare.* By Peary Chand Mittra. Calcutta: W. Newman & Co., 1877. v - xxvi. Print.

Mittra, Sitansu Sekhar. *Bengal's Renaissance: An Era of Multi-Faceted Growth.* Kolkata: Academic Publishers, 2001. Print.

"Mode of Educating the Natives." *The Calcutta Monthly Journal* (November 1836): 271-315. Print.

Mukherjee, Amitabha. "Missionaries and the New Education in Bengal 1757–1823." *The Calcutta Review* 173.1 (October 1964). Print. 60-72. Print.

—. "William Carey the Educationist and Social Reformer." *Preach and Heal: A history of the Christian Missionaries in India*. Ed. Sandeep Sinha. Kolkata: Readers Service, 2008. 109-122. Print.

Ogilvie, J. N. *The Apostles of India: The Baird Lecture for 1915*. London, New York, Toronto: Hodder and Stoughton, 1915. Print.

Oussoren, Aalbertinus Hermen. *William Carey: Especially His Missionary Principles*. Leiden: A. W. Sithoff's Utigenermaatschappij N. V., 1945. Print.

Periodical Accounts Relative to the Baptist Missionary Society Vol. I: IV. Clipstone: J. W. Morris, 1800. Print.

Potts, E. Daniel. *British Baptist Missionaries in India 1793–1837: The History of Serampore and its Mission*. Cambridge: Cambridge University Press, 1967. Print.

Purkait, Biswa Ranjan. *Indian Renaissance and Education: From Rammohan to Vivekananda*. Calcutta: Firma K. L. M. Private Limited, 1992. Print.

Ray, Sibnarayan. *Bengal Renaissance: The First Phase*. Calcutta: Minerva Associates, 2000. Print.

Raychaudhuri, Tapan. *Europe Reconsidered: Perceptions of the West in Nineteenth-Century Bengal*. 2nd ed. New Delhi: Oxford University Press, 2002. Print.

Report of the General Committee of Public Instruction of the Presidency of Fort William in Bengal, For the Year 1836. Calcutta: Baptist Mission Press, 1837. Print.

Sarkar, Susobhan. *On The Bengal Renaissance*. Calcutta: Papyrus, 1979. Print.

Smith, G. E. "Patterns of Missionary Education: The Baptist India Mission 1794–1824." *The Baptist Quarterly* XX. 7 (July 1964): 293-312. Print.

Smith, George. *The Life of William Carey, D. D.: Shoemaker, and Missionary, Professor of Sanskrit, Bengali and Marathi in the College of Fort William*, London: John Murray, Albermarle Street, 1885. Print.

Tagore, Rabindranath. "East and West." *The English Writings of Rabindranath Tagore* Volume II. Ed. Sisir Kumar Das. New Delhi: Sahitya Akademi, 1996. 530-537. Print.

—. *The Religion of Man* (1930). New Delhi: Rupa Publications India Pvt. Ltd., 2005. Print.

—. "Ideals of Education." *The English Writings of Rabindranath Tagore* Volume III. Ed. by Sisir Kumar Das. New Delhi: Sahitya Akademi, 2006. 611-614. Print.

—. *Personality* (September 1916-January 1917). New Delhi: Rupa Publications India Pvt. Ltd., 2007. Print.

Understanding the Renaissance in Nineteenth Century Bengal

Kathryn Simpson

THIS PAPER IS a reflection on the discourse between Scotland and the Bengali Renaissance, and the profoundly dynamic socio-cultural site of colonial interaction in Bengal in the early 19th century, with particular reference to Scottish missionaries and the Hindu elite.

The Bengal Renaissance began within, and in direct opposition to, the British colonisation of India. The commodities of knowledge, religion, and art were, however, exchanged between the two nations as they sought to identify themselves within the larger colonial world. This paper focuses on the interchange of ideas by concentrating on the lives and writings of Alexander Duff (1806–1878) and Raja Rammohan Roy (1772–1833). Duff is remembered primarily as a missionary but his reputation lies in his educational legacy in Bengal. Roy's legacy lies in his fashioning of a cultural self-image that pulled from both Eastern and Western thought. He helped to create a composite cultural synthesis which re-appropriated ideas from the ambiguous mid 19th century colonial interactions in ways not predicated on Western superiority.

Is it possible to expand upon our understanding of the colonial encounter, the site of which has often, if not always, created a new historiography? JS Mill said that the 'whole government of India is carried out in writing,' those seated at the Imperial metropole presided over, organised, and dictated the colonial sphere, but far more interesting are those who physically encountered each other (Bhabha 133). It is in this geo-cultural site of the colonial encounter that a new historiography is formed, or in which the influence of people can be seen and the effectiveness of their agency measured. This way of analysing the socio-political encounter follows from the work of Clifford Geertz, who explained that to understand the structure of meaning within cultures, how something–be it gesture, behaviour, action, signal or practice–can have any number of responses; yet it is how it is produced, perceived and interpreted that defines its meaning, its Thick Description. He wrote in his seminal collection of essays, *The Interpretation of Cultures*: 'believing, with Max Weber, that man is an animal suspended in webs of significance he himself has spun, I take culture to be those webs, and the analysis of it to be therefore one in search of meaning' (Geertz 5). Max Weber put the question: 'which motives led and continue to lead individual functionaries and members of this 'community' to behave in such a way that it comes into being and continues to exist?' (Weber 21). In a similar vein to Geertz and Weber, what are the 'motives' or 'webs of significance' that are produced by a community, in this case the Scottish missionaries, at once removed and yet constrained by the Imperial metropole.

History has taught that it is impossible to undo the colonial encounter. No matter how benign the interloper, the socio-cultural and geo-political exchange and influence will always be profound. This leads back to missionaries and specifically Alexander Duff. There are some standard tropes one expects when studying missionaries: the nature of their work often meant they were some of the first external people to arrive in a place; they often had difficulty communicating with the indigenous people they met; and finally they often turned up unannounced. Yet none of these were issues that Alexander Duff encountered. This then suggests that what was happening in India was a unique site of socio-cultural colonial interaction.

In understanding the colonial interaction the researcher is not a passive consumer, nor does a focus on history mean the researcher is 'distracted from real political engagement'. It is in fact what makes these discourses so interesting, that they involve real people, and people are political and cannot be reduced or homogenised; moreover, the researcher cannot presume to know absolutely what another person has thought. As David Bunn states, by the acknowledgement of 'the political implications of the scholarly decision to engage in research and teaching on colonial (or post-colonial) discourse' academics ensure the work being done continues to destabilise the Western academic colonisation of an-'others' history or culture (Bunn, 'Embodying Africa' 4).

Monological assumptions abound in colonial research, particularly when it comes to histories ascribed from the Imperial metropole. In 1839, prior to being made Under Secretary of State for India, Sir Herman Merivale said, that '[t]he modern colonizing imagination conceives of its dependencies as a territory, never as a people' (Bhabha 133). This is clearly falling into the same category as the above mentioned assumptions regarding missionaries. Duff never went out to proselytize to India; he went to preach to the Hindu people (the emphasis on people). There is no doubt that he never refers to the people of India as anything other than a group of people. Emphatically his colonial encounter was human in its character. Already it is clear that what happened in colonial India, specifically Bengal up to and including the Renaissance, was a distinct and complex interaction. At first glance the basic power structures suggest that the agency of the colonised was far greater than it was in any other site of colonial encounter. This ultimately leads to the research question: is it possible to identify strands of interaction that are contra-narratives to the primary hegemonic Western scribed Imperial history through the micro-narratives of the colonial encounter, and leading from that, is the perceived Scottish Bengali comradeship a response to their shared English subjugation?

For is this not in essence what a renaissance is, not solely an ideology but that which inspires many within a geo-political and socio-cultural group to welcome and engender change? The term renaissance would be problematic as the idea of free spirited enlightened thinking under the yoke of colonialism should be a non sequitur, yet that is what makes the Bengali renaissance all the more interesting. Niyogi posits that 'although there was no fundamental socio-economic change characteristic of the 18th century European one, the Bengali renaissance fostered a long period of universalism, humanism and rationalism' (Niyogi 2). To take this a little further and return to Geertz, the researcher must look at:

> [The] historically transmitted pattern of meanings embodied in symbols, a system of inherited conceptions expressed in symbolic forms by means of which men communicate, perpetuate, and develop their knowledge about and attitudes towards life (Geertz 89).

What then can the research be grounded upon, what could be more symbolic and expressive of person's 'inherited conceptions' than how they choose to educate their children? To draw on the words and logic of Sudhir Chandra, it is to the 'aspects of man-in-society that reflect movement' (Chandra 287, 288). Many small movements engender a change, it is not just those who are willing to talk, but those who are willing to listen, those willing to do and most strikingly those who are willing to put their children on the front line of that change. The machinations of a renaissance enable the main protagonists to enact their ideas. In Bengal the lyricism that came from the instigators of the change and the younger English language-educated generation could only happen in an environment of flux, providing an arena to ruminate and debate on both the changing religious impetus and the aspects of colonialism that could be reengineered or crafted for the good of the indigenous population.

There is a further question which emerges from the above point, which is whether the renaissance was in part due to not being able to get rid of the British physically, as evidenced by the first significant struggle for independence, the Indian revolt. As has become evident to the researcher, the revival of Bengali culture had been happening since the 18th century. It was a renascent identity, an oppositional response to the moribund stasis of a previously vibrant and varied culture, embodied in a shoring up of nationalist feeling and identity. As the Scots did not wish the State to be integral to their religion, so Bengalis pushed against the overwhelming wave of imperial socio-cultural ideology, so rigidly written into governance by the East India Company. Ultimately it is possible to suggest that an iconoclastic approach by the British stimulated stronger opposition to the Interlopers.

Alexander Duff came to India with an attitude similar to that of the fictional Marlow in Joseph Conrad's *Heart of Darkness* (1899). As Marlow was drawn to the spaces 'of delightful mystery' in South America, Africa and Australia, so Duff as a child was drawn to India. He writes: it was 'in perusing the article on India in Sir David Brewster's Edinburgh Encyclopaedia that my soul was first drawn out as by a spell-like fascination towards India' (Smith 43, 44). Duff sailed with his wife, Anne Scott Drysdale on the Lady Holland, an East Indiaman, for India in 1829. They arrived in Calcutta, after two shipwrecks which left them with a most inconveniently slender wardrobe, on the 27 May 1830. Duff instantly set to work absorbing all he could about the religion and education of the city of Calcutta and its surroundings; he went to every school, every mission and made a detailed study of all the current forms of education, and found them lacking.

Duff's interest in education was long founded; he was from the tiny village of Moulin near Pitlochry in Scotland, and it was a place of dual language, the indigenous Gaelic which had been dying out since the Highlands Clearances (which caused massive population movement and emigration) of the 18th century, and the English language of learning and commerce. Many people in the vicinity spoke Gaelic and from his father's time it was considered a hindrance to the spread of the Christian gospel, as most ministers spoke English and thus a large percentage of the population could not be ministered to because of this language gap. Part of the solution was to send children to school when they were young, to enable them to learn English. The idea was that they would be able to hear the word of God from all preachers, not just those who could speak Gaelic. The importance of duality of language was evident in Duff's own beliefs. Whilst Duff was adamant about English being the language of instruction, he also believed strongly in the independence of Scotland and its people as a nation distinct from England. He said:

> [T]he genuine spirit of liberty and independence could outlive the wear and tear of whole centuries of oppression; and ever and anon, rallying into fresh vigour, could humble in the dust the pride and flower of all her chivalry. Thus roughly cradled amid the storms, and nurtured amid the tempests of troubled life, the character of the Scottish people grew up into a robustness and hardihood, and their principles of action into a tenacity of sinewy strength, that could not brook the touch of foreign tyranny (*The Sole and Supreme Headship* 4).

Duff's understanding of a dual language culture, alongside his early fascination with the India as evidenced in the encyclopaedia quotation, gives an insight into the way Duff thought, and begins to show why Roy took to him as he did.

Duff was a reformer, educationist, and nationalist. His work suggests a kind of egalitarianism which mirrors the early constructs of the Bengal Renaissance. Duff took the earliest opportunity to meet Roy, and in fact, had been told to see him by his Church superiors. He was thoroughly pleased by the conversation they had and it appears Roy was also taken with the young Scotsman. It is quoted that they both believed that theology helped develop and regulate the powers of the mind, heart and conscious. Roy was part of a group of men, many of whom spoke English, who were the vanguard of educational and to some degree social reform in Calcutta. The group included men such as Dwarakanath Tagore, Ram Komul Sen and Raja Radhakanta Deb. They were men who not only spoke English but were erudite and had influence due to their social status and wealth which enabled them to enact change. Sumanta Niyogi notes that:

> [T]he first half of the nineteenth century, which can be termed as the age of Rammohan Roy, witnessed the advent of rationalistic and scientific spirit, the endless endeavour for the acquisition and dissemination of knowledge, the tireless struggle for the emancipation of women and continuous battle against the time honoured orthodoxy, backwardness and superstition (Niyogi 1).

The early 19th century was recognised as the spirit of a new age, a chance to instigate socio-cultural transformation. These men were prima facie in the colonial discourse, a chance to change or reform colonial ways, and push for an enlightened colonial discourse around education. As Mignolo emphasises the use of:

> ... colonial discourse in my vocabulary particularly when talking 'of the humanities and the social sciences with a literary bent' as it offers, in my view, an alternative approach to a field of study dominated by notions such as 'colonial literature' or 'colonial history.' As defined by Peter Hulme... colonial discourse embraces all kinds of discursive production related to and arising out of colonial situations, from the Capitulations of 1492 to William Shakespeare's *The Tempest*, from royal orders and edicts to the most carefully written prose ('Colonial and Postcolonial Discourse' 124).

Roy had been helping Scots and English set up schools in and around Calcutta. Duff's personal colonial discourse was primarily influenced by Roy at the initial stages as his arrival in India was facilitated by Roy's recommendation. Roy had even sent a letter in support of James Bryce, first chaplain of the kirk in Calcutta's petition to the Scottish General Assembly for missionaries. In the *Life and Letters of Raja Rammohan Roy*, Collett writes that,

> Scotsmen will doubtless regard it as a compliment to their national type of religion that while this cultured theist was horrified by the overtures of the Anglican Bishop and was antagonised by the Baptist editors, he was induced to beg for the presence in his country of Scottish Presbyterian missionaries (*The Life and Letters* 151).

Whether or not Roy was quite so keen on the Scottish presbytery or whether it was a canny awareness on his part that what the Scots offered was much more in line with his own ideas than that of the absolutist English orthodoxies remains to be uncovered. As to what Duff offered, as Reverend Day notes that whilst Duff was impressed with the sheer domineering character of the English colleges already in place in Calcutta, he 'saw with regret that, though the English education was mighty in pulling down the strongholds of error, it constructed nothing in their room' (Day 24). He noted that the English Colleges offered a doctrine heavy on pedagogy that was rather light on the theory of knowledge. What Roy wanted, and Duff was suggesting, was a holistic pedagogical environment.

Duff wanted to facilitate a form of education that at the time was very modern; based on three principles that were remarkably similar to Derozio's concept of a free interchange of thought between professor and pupil. Firstly, he pushed for an Interrogatory method: students should be able to question what they learn, pull it apart and analyse it. This then leads on to the second premise: that students should have a clear conception of the subject in their mind, rote learning would not produce nimble brains. And thirdly, students should be able to then express the subject in their own words. He was also adamant that education was transmitted in English, as DH Emmott notes, Duff had to instruct in the English language.

As a native of the Scottish Highlands, he had early realized that among Gaelic-speaking people the demands of higher education could only be met by English. Duff placed Gaelic and Bengali in the same category. English was necessary for the education of people who spoke either (Emmott 161).

To return to the quotation from Day, it is clear from Duff's concept of pedagogy that the current system did not fulfil his ideal. Emmott expands on this when he notes that 'whereas elsewhere as in the Hindu College, western knowledge was being taught divorced from Christianity, Duff, in his college did show that western knowledge did not necessarily mean materialistic knowledge' (Ibid.). It is this separation of education from 'materialistic knowledge' that binds Duff and Roy. Provantasu Maiti says 'the connection between society and education is very deep and intimate.

The education people receive exercises a deep and far reaching influence on the moulding of society' (Maiti 'English Education in Bengal' 4). Roy and Duff used each other to mould their society, for Duff saw his role as an inherent part of his Scottish-ness: '[I]t is not the nature of the genuine sons of Scotia to refuse aid, or sympathy, or gratulations, the weal or the woe, the joys or the sorrows of their fellow creatures' (Duff 149). He saw it as his duty to provide an education that was appropriate for the colonial population and not one that suited the Imperial metropole. Rabindranath Tagore writes of Roy that

> Rammohan was the only person in his time, in the whole world of man, to realise completely the significance of the modern age. He knew that the ideal of human civilisation does not lie in the isolation of independence but in the brotherhood of interdependence of individuals as well as of nations in all spheres of thought and activity' (Tagore 668).

This new design for creative education in this site of cultural interaction, facilitated a profound exchange of beliefs and ideologies, creating a new concomitant culture, neither one nor the other but a new transient and malleable culture subject to intervention on both sides. The educational establishment these two men set up forced a dialogue, a socio-cultural site of colonial ambiguity. When one creates a new pedagogy and asks for input many people have ideas and suggestions but few have concrete conceptions. What Roy and Duff created was a structure, a beginning, which though not ideal, created a concept that could be built on and refashioned. Although the Hindu College in theory was Roy's attempt at a syncretic binding of modern educational policies with traditional Indian Spiritual concepts and literature, it was a project he had to step away from to prevent antagonising a section of the Hindu orthodoxy, 'who were a bit suspicious of the Christian foreigners and of those who like Rammohan, held views far more advanced than what could be appreciated by them' (Chattopadhyaya 12). With Roy, it seems that others mistook his ideas of education to be a duplicitous subterfuge. As Bhabha writes in *The Location of Culture*:

> They [the paranoid], too, cannot regard anything in other people as indifferent, and they, too, take up minute indications with which these other, unknown, people present them, and use them in their 'delusions of reference' (Bhabha 132).

Ultimately, the reifying of the place of Indian literary historiography in education owes much more to the later work of Debendranath Tagore and the Tagores in general. What the researcher is trying to show is that Duff and

Roy's school was allowed to develop because at that particular moment, in that particular time, they created a new colonial discourse. Using education they opened the doors to both Western and Eastern pedagogies, and, essentially, religion was just another medium to engender dialogue, bearing in mind Roy's truism, 'no one ever became a Christian by reading the bible', but education in English would give greater agency to the indigenous population (Collet 151). The only way to respond to colonial ideology is to furnish oneself with the tools of the interloper, write in his language, and use his own words to reflect his own folly. There is a parity of thought between Rammohan Roy and Alexander Duff, that, while often oppositional, the inherent similarities between their aims – knowledge acquisition, creation, and expansion – were great enough to override their fundamental differences.

Works Cited:

Bhabha, Homi K. *The Location of Culture.* Abingdon: Routledge, 2004. Print.

Bunn, David. "Embodying Africa: Woman and Romance in Colonial Fiction." *English in Africa* 15. 1 (1966): 1-26. Print.

Chandra, Sudhir. "The Oppressive Present - Literature and Social Consciousness in colonial India." *Between Tradition and Modernity: India's Search for Identity.* Ed. Fred Dallmayr and G. N. Devy. New Delhi: Sage Publications, 1998. 287-288. Print.

Chattopadhyaya, Bankim Chandra. *Renaissance & Reaction in Nineteenth Century Bengal.* Bengal: South Asia Books, 1977. Print.

Collet, Sophia Dobson. Alexander Duff and the Foundation of Modern Education in India. India: Classic Press, 1914. Print.

Day, Lal Behari. *Recollections of Alexander Duff: And of the Mission College Which He Founded in Calcutta.* India: Nelson, 1879. Print.

Duff, Rev. Alexander. *The Sole and Supreme Headship of the Lord Jesus Christ over His Own Church; a Voice from the Ganges, Relative to the Cases Which Led to the Recent Disruption of the Established Church of Scotland and the Consequent Formation of the Free Church of Scotland.* Calcutta: W. Rushton, 1840. Print.

Emmott, D. H. "Alexander Duff and the Foundation of Modern Education in India." *British Journal of Education Studies* 13. 2 (1965): 160-169. Print.

Geertz, Clifford. *The Interpretation of Cultures: Selected Essays.* New York: Perseus Books Group, 2000. Print.

Maiti, Provantansu. "English Education in Bengal: From Class Education to Mass Education." *Commemoration Volume Published on the Occasion of the 150th Year's Celebration of the Scottish Church College.* Ed. Aparesh Bhattacharjee. Kolkata: Principal Aparesh Bhattacharjee, 1980. 2-20. Print.

Mignolo, Walter D. "Colonial and Postcolonial Discourse: Cultural Critique or Academic Colonialism?" *Latin American Research Review* 28. 3 (1993): 120-134. Print.

Niyogi, Sumanta. *The Brahmo Samaj Movement and Development of Education 1872–1911.* Patna: Janaki Prakashan, 1986. Print.

Smith, George. *The Life of Alexander Duff, D.D., Ll.D.* London: Hodder and Stoughton, 1879. Print.

Tagore, Rabindranath. "Rammohan Roy." *The English Writings of Rabindranath Tagore* Volume III. Ed. Sisir Das. New Delhi: Sahitya Academy, 2012. 667-669. Print.

Weber, Max. "The Nature of Social Action in Wirtschaft Und Gesellschaft." *Max Weber: Selections in Translation*. Ed. by W. E. Runciman. Cambridge: Cambridge University Press, 1956.

Alexander Duff

The Caledonian Legacy: Of the Scottish Church College in Kolkata

Kaberi Chatterjee

The new hath come and now the old retires:
And so the past becomes a mountain cell,
Where lone, apart, old hermit-memories dwell
in consecrated calm... (Naidu 65)

THE SCOTTISH CHURCH COLLEGE in Kolkata (erstwhile Calcutta) has undergone many nomenclature changes right from the time of its founding by Rev Dr Alexander Duff, the first overseas missionary sent by the Church of Scotland, in July 1830. Unlike such changes elsewhere these do not signify local socio-political currents. These changes reflect important shifts in the dynamics of an organisation many miles away, namely the Church of Scotland. Even today, when postcolonial considerations would make it entirely appropriate to re-name this august institution, the administration continues to use the name Scottish Church College. Hence it is not an exaggeration to conclude that the umbilical link, however remote, still binds the institution to its parent in Scotland. So I begin deliberately with a reference from Sarojini Naidu's poem 'Past and Future' to foreground the importance of memory in a continuum when speaking of the Scottish Church College.

It was called the General Assembly's Institution when it was first founded by Duff as it was directly under the control of the General Assembly of the Church of Scotland. The Great Disruption of 1843 saw the first separation when those who wanted to continue with the Established Church stayed back with the original seminary while those accepting the spirit of the Free Church, including Rev Dr Duff, had to move out and begin the Free Church Institution in *Nimtollah*, a new neighbourhood. The two institutes ran parallel until the two churches decided to unite the two colleges in Calcutta. In 1908, when the colleges came together, it was named as the Scottish Churches College. In 1929, with the re-union of the churches in Scotland, the plural ending was dropped and thus began a new phase of the college as it continues until today.

Mitchell William Numark in his dissertation *Translating Religion: British Missions and the politics of Religious knowledge in Colonial India and Bombay* (2006) speaks of the 'conquest of knowledge', referring to the establishment of Western education, as an 'intentional goal of British colonial administrators and Christian Missionaries' (Numark 1). In this conflation of the role of the administrator and the missionary there seems to be a deliberate side-stepping of the evangelical and developmental orientation of the missionary. He also calls Alexander Duff and Charles Trevelyan the most 'vulgar missionary and colonial official advocates of India's Christianization and Anglicization' (Ibid.). While he may have reasons to support his views, it seems precipitate to reject the positive role played by Alexander Duff as an educationist in the spread of higher education in Calcutta as we will see in the evolution of the General Assembly's Institution into the modern day avatar of the Scottish Church College.

The impact of the introduction of English as a medium of instruction post Macaulay's Minutes has been variously interpreted, but usually viewed as creating 'white minds' in a 'brown body'. At this juncture of history it would be correct to re-assess the contribution not only of the founding fathers of these English medium missionary institutions of colonial times, but also of those who followed after them and continued the developmental enterprise with a zeal that went beyond their sectarian call of duty. My endeavour is to view the work of the missionaries of the Church of Scotland at the General Assembly's Institution, Calcutta, apropos its founding and later growth in order to isolate what made it distinctive from the rest of the institutions set up concurrently.

I would readily accept Mr RS Trivedi's opinion, as quoted by S Subrahmanyan, that the 'importation of English University education was an urgent necessity of the time suddenly created by the introduction of new conditions of life with a new order of political situation' (Subrahmanyan 'Education in India' 374) as a backdrop to the establishment of the many schools and colleges set up by the colonial government and the missionaries. But to critique the contribution of all missionaries on the ground of conversion and numbers and to debunk any achievement for their sectarian ideology is to view it myopically. Today, 186 years later, when we see that Scottish Church College, through the various name-changes, has emerged as a seat of higher education in India, we realise how the missionary ideology established by Rev Alexander Duff and taken forward by people like Rev Mackay, Rev Hastie, Dr Urquhart and others went beyond the purely evangelical interest to the developmental .

According to Parna Sengupta 'although not many Bengalis converted to Christianity through schools, the impact of the evangelical schooling on modern Indian schooling' (Sengupta 'The Molding of the Native' 2) is clearly visible as it is related to the crucial questions that the missionaries controlled, namely who should be educated? Who deserved to be educated? What that education should look like? (Ibid). Since the missionaries decided on both curriculum and pedagogic methodology, it was but expected that they would be prompted by the thought of conversions and spread of the knowledge of the Bible. The question of education, whether Western/modern or vernacular/traditional, has always been a part of the mainstream political and administrative narrative and never treated as a separate entity and to expect otherwise, especially during colonial times, would be extremely naive. Since the avowed purpose of the emphasis on missionary work was to spread the 'Lord's message', again, it would be simplistic to expect a foregrounding of 'secular' education. Within the given parameters, the work of the Scottish missionaries in Calcutta in the early 19th-century were definitely tilted towards a spread of 'quality' education, so it is not wrong to see them as both evangelists and educators.

Today if we continue to evaluate the outcome of western education during colonial times as only to produce 'Macaulay's minutemen' (Rushdie 165) then we will be guilty of what Nayanjot Lahiri discusses in her lecture, recently, on 'what imperils India's heritage' and cites the example of an earlier proposal to remove the text and inscriptions from the Mutiny Memorial that described the mutineers as the 'enemy' (Lahiri, Presidency Bicentenary). The importance of the English language in modern India has gone beyond any nationalist rhetoric and can be viewed as necessary along economic, pragmatic and literary trajectories. This is not a new concept and both writers and critics have accepted the prevalence of English in the social fabric of India. To think otherwise may, again, be myopic in the long run. In spite of Partha Chatterjee's observation about the predicament of the bilingual intellectual of India 'who is sometimes on one discursive terrain, sometimes on another' (Chatterjee, *A Possible India* 284), the presence of the bilingual in India cannot be either dismissed or ignored; we can argue about the effectiveness only. After all we do have Kamala Das announcing to her detractors:

> Why not let me speak in
> Any language I like? (Das, 'Introduction' 141)

It would be incorrect to assume that the introduction of English education post Macaulay's *Minutes* (1835) and Wood's *Despatch* (1854) led to a gradual decline of the 'vernacular' as a language of literary expression, posits Meenakshi Mukherjee (*The Perishable Empire* 22-24). On the contrary, she states that, 'even in the heyday of imperial rule, despite the overwhelming presence of English literature in the curriculum of higher education, the English language remained quite peripheral in the literary agenda of the country' (Ibid. 24). Though English became the language of the elite classes and connoted a power equation, the 'vernaculars', a term made popular by the colonial administrators/educators, continued a quiet 'writing back' as has been pointed out by Mukherjee. *This is, definitely, not to approve of the colonial education policy but to view the work of some in an/'other' light* (italics my own).

Alexander Duff arrived in Calcutta on 27 May, 1830 after suffering two ship-wrecks and undergoing a rather perilous journey which had left him physically devastated but buoyant in spirit as he saw in these adversities God's plan of testing the strength of his belief and commitment to religion (Watson 22, 23). These reactions to the adversities that he faced proved his overt spirituality and made him best suited to the purpose of the General Assembly of the National Church of Scotland. On reaching Calcutta he made extensive investigations in and around Calcutta (Smith 87, 105) to know about the existing schools and came to the conclusion that he would set up the institution in Calcutta itself. This was a major deviation from the brief he had received from the Church, which was to set up the institution in the rural belt around Calcutta (Ibid. 63, 86). In this deviation one can see a glimpse of the educator rather than a proselytizer because he was interested in the spread of quality education rather than just popularizing the reading of the Bible.

While Bible reading was a daily activity in the General Assembly's Institution [as it was called then] established by Duff, his vision also included the teaching of every variety of useful knowledge, first in elementary forms, and, as the pupils advanced, in the higher branches, which might ultimately embrace the most advanced and improved studies in history, civil and sacred, sound literature, logic, mental and moral philosophy after Baconian method, mathematics in all department with natural history, natural philosophy and other sciences (Ibid. 109, 110).

This clearly indicates his broad vision which includes all branches of knowledge to be taught in this institute. Duff had started the school in 1830 and had left India in 1834 due to ill health. When he came back after a long sojourn in 1840, his first act was to organise the institution into a college and preparatory school. Prior to this, in 1831, after the resounding success of the general examination of the school at the Freemason's Hall where the students had performed with great ease and fluency, a series of meetings had been held in Calcutta where the decision was taken for the foundation of a central Institution or College for higher education.[1] In June 1831, one year after the General Assembly's Institution had been established, in a meeting held in the Union Chapel House and with Rev Yates in the chair,

> it was unanimously resolved that an Institution, in Calcutta, adapted to carry on the literary and Christian education of promising Natives to a higher degree than has been hitherto attempted is highly important to the propagation of Christianity in India (Minutes 1831, 1).

This was followed by a meeting on 5 July 1831 where they deliberated on the plan for a higher education unit proposed by Rev Alexander Duff which they felt was the best for the *progress of general science* and *true Christianity in India* [ital. mine] (Ibid. 2). We must not overlook the twin objectives and appreciate that the religious imperative was accompanied by a secular one. So plans were already afoot for the expansion and extension of the preparatory seminary to a seat of higher education. But the final division of the school and college happened in 1840. What these minutes reveal is the fact that the missionaries with Duff at the helm, were interested in 'teaching and preaching' each augmenting and enriching the other.

In this context it is important to go back to the observation in the *Friend of India* that 'no one will dispute the claim to the appellation of a collegiate Institution of a seminary where Brown's Philosophy and Laplace's Mecanique Celeste are textbooks in Mental and Physical Science' (Day 113). With such a curriculum no one could deny that it was a place for the spread of education among the youth of Calcutta. Critics may point out that this curriculum was a part of the institutions of Christian Europe and not necessarily required for or necessary for the youth of Calcutta. But it definitely bears testimony to Duff's efforts at educating the young of Calcutta in diverse branches of knowledge rather than to merely count the number of converts to Christianity. What the Committee in Edinburgh had wanted in their first overseas missionary was

> nothing less than a combination of the distinguished talents requisite for that office [head of a college] with such disinterested zeal for the propagation of the gospel (Smith 51, 52)

and by appointing Alexander Duff they had definitely made the most appropriate choice, a fact that would be validated by later developments.

At the outset Duff was helped in his endeavour by none other than Raja Rammohun Roy, social reformer and one of the early modernists of India. In fact Duff, himself, acknowledges his indebtedness in a letter he wrote to his mentors at the General Assembly at Edinburgh on the help he received from 'Ram Mohun Roy' (Watson 21).[2] In this letter he also mentions how 'RR and myself differ in our religious creed' (Duff's letter from 'Hindoo College Square' dated November 15/18(?), 1830) but at the same time speaks of the common ground they share on the question of 'moral' education. While scouring the city for accommodation for his institution he was grateful to be offered Firinghi Kamal Bose's house on upper Chitpore Road which was previously being used by the Brahmo Sabha, for £4 per month through the intervention of Rammohun (Smith 112, 118). While handing over possession of this hall to Duff, he had also offered the 'punkah hanging from the roof' (Ibid. 120) as his 'legacy', to the fledgling institute. Rammohun's personal reputation and persuasive powers helped in getting students from the elite families to join the new institution. These families were willing to send their wards for the liberal education but were afraid of forcible conversions. Though conversions took place and were appreciated by the Home Office of the Church Headquarters it was not the sole criterion for evaluation of performance of the institution even in the initial stages.

It is interesting to note that the biography written by Duff's grandson is entitled *Self Lost In Service: Alexander Duff of India.* When viewed against Duff's words this description does seem entirely appropriate. 'By profession a missionary, by his life and labours, the true and constant friend of India,' these were the words Duff desired to have as his epitaph (Watson 124). Every utterance, thus viewed, reiterates his 'sacred' commitment as well as his interest in the general improvement of India. For four years *The Calcutta Review,* which was neither a missionary nor a Free Church organ and never used for denominational purposes, was under his stewardship and had a great role in the dissemination of scholarship in Calcutta. His support of the Ilbert Bill and the Indigo peasants match this 'friend of India' image. The only sound of discord is in Duff's trenchant criticism of the Indian point of view in his presentation of the history of 1857. In this, in an uncharacteristic manner, he is seen to be subscribing to an overt imperialism. One can only assume, but never justify, that there must have been political/administrative/pragmatic compulsions which had prompted this *volte face* in a missionary.[3]

That he was aware of the exploitation inherent in the colonial situation and that he considered India as a 'fellow-subject' of Britain, equal to the 'natives of the Hebrides or the Catholics of Ireland', is made manifest in the answer he gave when defending the Church Of Scotland's India Mission in a speech in 1835 (which was later published) followed by a riposte he had formulated to answer criticism of the same in 1837 (Smith 107, 108). In this connection he had also referred to reparation of wrongful appropriation through the transfer of 'useful knowledge' and 'Gospel grace'. In this colonial self-consciousness, what surfaces is the image of the evangelist and the educator and not the imperialist per se.

The Disruption of 1843 led to the separation of the two institutions–one run by the missionaries of the Established Church and the other by the followers of the Free Church. Since Duff had elected to join the Free Church he was forced to leave the institution that he had built up with such great care. The great educationist that Duff was, he managed to set up the Free Church Institution and was at the helm of affairs until 1863 when he finally left India owing to ill-health. The Free Church Institution was later renamed the Duff College in a fitting tribute to its founding father. An important reason for the success of Duff's institution/s was 'his concern for good educational method: indeed he adopted a very professional approach to his work' observes Michael Laird ('Legacy of Alexander Duff' 146). This evaluation is clearly an approbation of Duff's educational policy from the modern point of view.

To revert to the narrative of the earlier institution one may go back to 1851. The report of the Annual Examination for the year 1851, as published in the *Calcutta Christian Advocate*[4], speaks of a positive response to the education imparted by General Assembly's Institution. It was conducted by Rev Messrs Ogilvie, Herdman, Henderson, and by Drs Grant and Boaz. The examination was held in the Town Hall and 'it is observed that the attendance of native visitors is larger than they could recollect' (Mission Report 100), so interest in this institution was definitely on the rise. The report further states that 'the conductors of the Institution have laboured to diffuse as widely as possible the blessings of an *enlightened* education, both literary and scientific' as well as 'that knowledge which alone maketh wise unto salvation' [ital. mine] (Ibid.). This once again re-iterates the dual focus of the education imparted in the General Assembly's Institution in Calcutta.

That education at this institute was neither circumscribed by nor confined to racial or religious constraints is amply borne out by an anecdote from the life of Swami Vivekananda, an alumnus, 'who turned from being a social reformer to a social revolutionary' (Datta 88) and is regarded as an architect of modern India.

Narendranath Datta, as he was known then, had initially taken admission in Presidency College in 1880. But he 'contracted malarial fever in the second year, his percentage of class attendance fell short of the requisite number' (Datta 87) and he was not allowed to appear at the F. A. Examination. It was then that he had taken admission in the General Assembly's Institution and was allowed to take the Exam in 1881. We have an account from his classmate Haramohan, recounted by his brother, where it is described how Rev Hastie, the then Principal of the college, mentioned 'a man living in Dakshineswar who often experienced a state of bliss through the kind of trance referred to by Wordsworth', and the boys were advised 'to go and meet him' (Ibid. 89). Such openness in any European institution in the colonial times would have been rare indeed; especially in one run by the evangelical orders it was totally unexpected and unique. The transformation of Narendranath to Swamiji was as much due to his historic meeting with Ramkrishna Paramhansadeb as to the advice by his teacher and so it would not be inappropriate to say that in some way his Scots teacher had acted as a catalyst.

An incident from the life of another famous alumnus of the college, Netaji Subhas Chandra Bose, also highlights this broad vision of education that was nurtured by Scottish Church College (as it was called between 1908–1929) as well as brings to light the work of a great educationist from the Church of Scotland who had worked tirelessly for the development of higher education in India. WS Urquhart had the rare distinction of having served as the Principal of Scottish Church College as well as the Vice-Chancellor of the University of Calcutta simultaneously. Urquhart was instrumental in Subhas Chandra Bose's admission into Scottish Church College after his expulsion from Presidency College following the famous Oaten incident.[5] When the University relented, after Sir Ashutosh Mookerjee's intervention, to allow Subhas to study from a different college, he chose this institution that had a formidable reputation in Philosophy honours, a subject he wanted to study. He took admission in the third year in 1917 and graduated from the college in 1919. During this time, apart from teaching Philosophy, Dr Urquhart also gave Bible lessons that this particular student enjoyed very much.

During the turmoil years when the country witnessed many protests against colonial excesses by students, Dr Urquhart, very often, did not toe the colonialist line. In 1930 when the college was celebrating its centenary he invited Subhas as a successful former student. Subhas, then the Mayor of Calcutta, was asked to read the address on behalf of the former students. He, in eloquent language, expressed his gratitude for the education that he had received in this college and made a special mention of Dr Urquhart as a teacher who had inspired him the most.

But in 1938 when the students wanted to felicitate Subhas Chandra Bose, then President of the Indian National Congress, permission was initially denied to them. It was only after vehement protests by the students that the authorities changed their stance. When Subhas came for the meeting he divulged that on the previous occasion when Dr Urquhart had invited him in 1930 he had laid down two conditions for his acceptance of the invite (Maiti 134-149).[6] The first was that the Governor-General (Lord Irwin) would not be invited to share the dais and that the Union Jack would not be hoisted on that occasion. The assembled students were then amazed to hear that Dr Urquhart had kept both promises. This is also corroborated by the report on the Centenary Celebrations of the arrival of Alexander Duff in India and the establishment of the institution ('The Duff Centenary In Calcutta'). Kamala Mukherjee, a former student, in an interesting article, writes how during this period when Government Colleges were expectedly restrictive and hostile about student participation in anti-colonial acts, Scottish Church College was not averse to accepting students involved in the nationalist struggle ('Amar Abhigatai' 535, 536). This shows how Scottish Church College struck out on its own at all times and made education its first goal.

In conclusion I would refer to David Punter who discusses Elspeth Barker's *O Caledonia* as a postcolonial text as he forwards the view that 'now there is a commonly recognised assumption that these two [Scotland and Ireland] are cultures that have, at least in the British context, a post colonial dimension' (*Post Colonial Imaginings* 7). In a similar vein I would argue that it was this idea of being 'fellow subjects' as declared by Alexander Duff himself, rather than being 'empire' and 'subject' that led to the success of this evangelical-educational relationship. The founding of the General Assembly's Institution was more of an *interaction* between the Scottish missionaries and the local population rather than an *encounter* between *imperial* forces and the *native* population.

End Notes:

1. I have referred to the General Assembly's Institution Minute Book of 1831, Calcutta in MS which is at the Library at Scottish Church College. In this context one may also see Professor Monalisa Basu's essay "Voyage of Time Seized in Pages: The Minute Book, 1831" in the *Scottish Church College 175th Year Commemoration Volume.*

2. Watson observes that before Duff came to India he had already heard of Ram Mohun Roy. "Dr John MacWhirter had given him [Duff] a letter of introduction where he had mentioned Ram Mohun Roy".

3. For Duff's opinion on the events of 1857 see his *The Indian Rebellion: A Series of Letters.* Manilal C. Parekh's "Reverend Alexander Duff's Imperialism" provides an in-depth discussion of Duff as an imperialist.

4. Full text of the article on General Assembly's Institution included in The Home and Foreign Missionary Record for the Church of Scotland, vol. VII, Jan-Dec.1852, p.100

5. This incident resulted in Subhas Bose's expulsion from the Presidency College.

6. Girish Chandra Maiti refers to newspaper articles in the *Hindustan Standard* and *Dainik Basumati* of April 17, 1938 to substantiate his observation.

Works Cited:

Basu, Pradip, et al. eds. *Scottish Church College 175th Year Commemoration Volume.* Kolkata: Scottish Church College Teachers' Council, 2008. Print.

Basu, Monalisa. "Voyage of Time Seized in Pages: The Minute Book, 1831." *Scottish Church College 175th Year Commemoration Volume.* Ed. Pradip Basu et al. Kolkata: Scottish Church College Teachers' Council, 2008. 56-71. Print.

Chatterjee, Partha. *A Possible India: Essays in Political Criticism.* New Delhi: Oxford University Press, 1997. Print.

Das, Kamala. "Introduction." *Indian Poetry in English.* Ed. Makarand Paranjape. Rev. ed. Delhi: Macmillan, 2009. 141, 142. Print.

Datta, Bhupendra Nath. *Swami Vivekananda: Patriot-Prophet: A Study.* 2nd rev. ed. Calcutta: Nababharat Publishers, 1993. Print.

Day, Lal Behari. *Recollections of Alexander Duff.* London: T. Nelson & Sons, 1879. Print.

Duff, Alexander. *Letters.* November 15 or 18? 1830. MS 7530 no. 44. National Library, George IV Bridge, Edinburgh, Scotland.

—. *The Indian Rebellion: Its Causes and Results.* New York: Robert Carter & Brothers, 1858. Print.

Home & Foreign Missionary Records For the Church of Scotland VII (Jan Dec 1852). Edinburgh: Paton & Ritchie. Print

Laird, Michael. "Legacy of Alexander Duff." *A Occasional Bulletin of Missionary Research* 3.4 (October 1, 1979): 146-149. Print.

Lahiri, Nayanjot. "Archaeological Heritage at the Crossroads of Politics and People." Presidency Bicentenary Celebrations, Kolkata, 22 Jan. 2017. Lecture.

Minutes, 1831, MS, Scottish Church College, Kolkata.

Mukherjee, Kamala. "Amar Abhigatai Scottish Church College" (1999).Rept. *Scottish Church College 175th Year Commemoration Volume*. Ed. Pradip Basu et al. Kolkata: Scottish Church College Teachers' Council, 2008. 535-536. Print.

Mukherjee, Meenakshi. *The Perishable Empire: Essays on Indian Writing In English*. New Delhi: Oxford University Press, 2000. Print.

Naidu, Sarojini. *The Golden Threshold*. London: William Heinemann, 1905. Print.

Numark, Mitchell William. *Translating Religion: British Missions and the Politics of Religious Knowledge in Colonial India and Bombay*. Diss. University of California, Los Angeles: ProQuest Dissertation Publishing, 2006. Print.

Parekh, Manilal C. "Reverend Alexander Duff's Imperialism." *Modern Review* LXI.5 (1937): 529-532. Print.

Paton, William. *Alexander Duff: Pioneer of Missionary Education*. London: Student Christian Movement, 1923. Print.

Punter, David. *Post Colonial Imaginings: Fiction of a New World Order*. Edinburgh: Edinburgh University Press, 2000. Print.

Ray, Alok. *Alexander Duff O Anugami Kayekjan*. Calcutta: Papyrus, 1980. Print.

Rushdie, Salman. *The Moor's Last Sigh*. London: Vintage, 1995. Print.

Sengupta, Parna. "The Molding of the Native Character: Missionary Education in Bengal, 1854–1906." Diss. University of Michigan, 2000. Print.

Smith, George. *The Life of Alexander Duff, D.D., LL.D.* 2 vols. London: Hodder and Stoughton, 1879. Print.

Smith, Thomas. *Alexander Duff, D.D. LL.D.* London: Hodder and Stoughton, 1883. Print.

Subrahmanyan, S. "Education In India." *The Calcutta Review* 302 (October, 1920): 369-379. Print.

"The Duff Centenary In Calcutta." *Bharater Sadhana* XXI. III (1931): 181-186. Print.

Watson, Alexander Duff. *Self Lost In Service: Alexander Duff of India*. Edinburgh: Marshall Brother's Ltd. 1926. Print.

The Poet and the East-West Encounter

Robert Burns

A Complex Interface: Rabindranath and Burns

Amrit Sen

WHILE MOST OF US are aware of Rabindranath Tagore's debt to Romantic poetry, especially Wordsworth and Shelley, his interface with the Scottish national poet Robert Burns remains unexplored. The reputation of Robert Burns in the circle of Tagore largely resides in the awareness that two of the Tagore's major songs *Phule Phule Dhole Dhole* and *Purono Shei Diner Katha* were based on Scottish melodies collected and published by Burns. Yet, a closer inspection suggests that Robert Burns may have had a significant presence in colonial Bengal and could have shaped Rabindranath's consciousness and creativity quite deeply. Accordingly, this paper will attempt to trace this interface by asking three questions – what was the presence of Burns in 19th century Bengal, the context in which the young Tagore was honing his creative skills? Why did Tagore translate and adapt Burns and what were the dynamics of these translations? Beyond such translations, how did Burns affect the creative and political dimension of Rabindranath's horizon of ideas?

Robert Burns (1759–1796) is widely known as the national poet of Scotland, writing in the Scots language, and acknowledged as one of the pioneers of the Romantic Movement. Burns collected folk songs from across Scotland, often revising or adapting them. His poem and song 'Auld Lang Syne' and 'Scots What Hae' served for a long time as the Scottish national anthem. Burn's songs often tap into the Scottish folk tunes, represent natural topographical details and refer to the local population and customs. Indeed, Burns is credited for having carved a distinct Scottish cultural identity in the aftermath of the Act of Union of 1707 that overwhelmingly brought the hegemony of British mainstream culture to Scotland.

Robert Burns in 19th Century India

As Mary Ellis Gibson has pointed out British culture, as we know it in the early and mid 19th century, was a melting pot of regional British identities including Irish and Scottish (Gibson 5). Due to its Protestant sympathies, Scotland received a lion's share of the East India Company's disbursements of the employments in India. Nigel Leask points out that in the decade after 1774 a staggering 50 per cent of the East Indian Company's writers were Scots. The same proportion was applicable to the recruitment of officers and surgeon recruits in the Company's army. Sixty per cent of the merchants awarded the Company's prized 'country trade' permits were Scottish and, by 1813, 14 of the 38 prominent merchant houses in Kolkata were dominated by Scots (Leask 179). Scotsmen, like John Gilchrist, David Hare, Alexander Duff and John Grant, also dominated the educational and journalistic establishment in British Bengal. Given the superior technical and scientific education in Scotland, Scots medical men, religions preachers and school teachers exercised a significant influence on Indian students who studied English (Gibson 6). Indeed, in 1808, Walter Scott described India as 'the cornchest for Scotland, where we poor gentry must send our young sons as we send our black cattle to the South' (quoted in Sassi 85). The colonisation of India played an important part in the economic transformation of Enlightenment Scotland. As Devine points out 'the profits from the colonial trades were pumped into schemes of land improvement, the coal mining ventures and factory villages... it is now apparent that the colonial empire may have played a more important role in Scotland's economic growth than in other parts of Britain' (Devine 256).

It is through the travelling Scots that Burns must have been a live presence in 18th century Bengal. *The Asiatic Journal* in 1816, for example, printed a song written for the 'Celebration of the Feast of St. Andrew' at Calcutta on November 30, 1815:

> What cheers us' mid the sultry toils
> O' India's schorch'in clime?
> Its' nae the rupees' witchin smiles,
> Its thoughts of O' lang Syne (quoted in Gibson 18)

Associations of regional affiliations within the imperial structure were quite powerful. The Burns monument in Edinburgh was largely built with contributions from India in 1817, the initiative taken by J Forbes Mitchell who had just returned from India. The fundraising was done chiefly by Governor General Hastings (1812–23). There are records of one of the earliest Burns suppers that had been held in Calcutta in 1812. Two of Burns' own sons also served in the East India Company army and both served in the third Maratha War. Nigel Leask has thus suggested that Burns' poetry proved a symbolic focus for Scottish identity in the colonial diaspora, an identity that often proved more durable than Britishness (Leask 173).

Steve Newman argues that

> ...this system of patronage illustrates how Burns becomes a figure in the well of affiliations that constitute the British imperial system and how his multiform representations complicate politics understood in terms of party allegiance, Scottish identity within Great Britain, or a disposition towards reaction, reform or revolution (Newman 76).

Thus the presence of Burns percolated from the Scottish consciousness in Bengal to the Indian consciousness. Prominent administrators and soldiers like Sir Thomas Munro, Sir John Malcolm, Mounstuart Elphinstone as well as two Scottish Governor Generals, Lord Minto and Lord Dalhousie too played their parts.

The chief trigger for Burns' popularity in 19th century Bengal was probably the rise of Henry Derozio (1809–1830). Derozio located within Burns a tradition of 'bardic nationalism' and the inculcation of a distinct cultural nationalism that could resist imperial impositions. Alexander Duff recollected that the Bengali students in Derozio's discussion group of the 1820s would be introduced to Burns: 'More than once were my ears greeted with the sounds of Scottish rhymes from the poems of Robert Burns' (quoted in Chaudhuri 25).

Burns' stance of literary and equality (man to man the would o'er/ shall brothers be an' that) must have influenced Derozio's critique of both imperial and indigenous practices. In *The Slaves Lament*, Burns talks about the slaves' transfer from 'sweet Senegal' to 'This Burden I must bear, while the cruel scourge I fear / In the lands of Virginia O/And I think on friends most dear, with the bitter bitter tear/And alas! I am weary, weary O!' (quoted in Leask 179). In a later letter dated August 1789 to Helen Maria Williams, Burns refers to 'the infecting selfishness of the oppressor... the misery of the captive and the wrongs of the poor African (quoted in Leask 178)'. Clearly the radical sympathies of Burns would have appealed to the young Derozio and his Indian students.

Derozio's first volume of poetry included a poem 'Her's a health to thee, lassie!' written in imitation of David Drumond. Derozio also adapted the meter of Burns' poetry in his short lyric poem 'To my Brother in Scotland'. But the most important use of metaphor is Derozio's use of the harp of the rustic societies as a symbol of national culture. In his poems the rustic harp becomes a point of entry to the idea of a bardic nationalism that then has strong political intonations. As discussed later, the mature Rabindranath would also respond to this feature of Burns' poetry. Burns thus arrived to the late 19th century as a symbol in a number of ways – he was a representative of British Romanticism, a symbol of a provincial nationalism attempting to create a cultural past, an archivist of local language and music and at the same time a sympathizer of radicalism and equality. It is this multifaceted Burns that Tagore's interface took place with.

Tagore and the Translations of Robert Burns

The young Rabindranath's introduction to Burns seems to have been through family members, acquaintances and tutors, namely Akshay Mazumdar, Jyotirindranath Tagore and Akshay Chowdhury. The multicultural atmosphere of the Tagore household of Jorasanko also vibrated with exposure to western music. As Tagore was to later recollect in *Jibansmriti* (*My Reminiscences*):

> While we were growing to boyhood music was largely cultivated in our family. This had the advantage of making it possible for me to imbibe it, without an effort, into my whole being (43).

Akshay Mazumdar's influence in familiarizing the young Rabindranath to Moore's Irish Melodies is mentioned in *Jibansmriti* (*My Reminiscences*) (1912) and Rabindranath makes an interesting point here:

> I longed to hear the real tunes. Some longings unfortunately do get fulfilled in this life and die in the process... they somehow did not fit in with the silent melody of the harp which filled the old Ireland of my dreams (43).

Accordingly Rabindranath engaged in a creative experimentation with the tunes with his brother Jyotiridranath:

> My brother Jyotirindra, was engaged the live-long day at his piano, refashioning the classic melodic forms at his pleasure. And, at every turn of his instrument, the old modes took on unthought of shapes and expressed new shades of feeling... Akshay Babu and I sat on either side fitting words to them as they grew out of my brother's nimble fingers (43).

Although Rabindranath's first interactions with English literature were through the translation of sections of *Macbeth* in 1873, he turned to Irish and Scottish poetry in 1877. He published his first translations of Burns' verse 'Biday Chumban' (Final Kiss) based on the poem 'Ae fond kiss' and 'Lalit Nalini' based on Burns' 'O Philly' in the periodical *Bharati* in Magh 1284. The next two translations came two years later in 1879 when he translated '*Rupashi amar, Preyoshi amar*' ('Beautiful woman, beloved mine') based on Burns' poem 'The Birks of Aberfeldy' and 'Sushila Amar Janalar Pare' ('Sushila by the Window side') on Burns' text 'Mary Morison'. In these issues of the *Bharati* he also translated segments from Moore, Byron, Amelia Opie, Tennyson and Shelley. The first translation, 'Biday Chumban' (Farewell Kiss) seems to be a straightforward attempt to render the feelings of the source text in exact terms. Thus the text of Burns:

> Ae fond kiss and the we sever
> Ae fareweel, and then for ever
> Deep in heart-wrung tears I'll pledge thee

Warring sighs and groans I'll wage thee

is translated as:

> *Ekti chumban dao Promoda Amar*
> *Janomer Moto dekha hobe nako aar*
> *Marmobhed Asru Diye, pujibo tomai priye*
> *Dukher niswas ami dibo upohar.*

> One kiss for me oh my Promoda
> We will never probably meet again
> With deepest tears will I worship thee
> My deepest sighs are my gifts to thee.
> (*Rachanavali*, Vol. 30, 60, translations mine)

While the use of the name Promoda is interesting (the girl in Burns' name is called Nancy), what is more curious is Rabindranath's use of a stylized Bengali that has no resonance of the immediacy and colloquial flavour of the Scottish tune. The passion and the dramatic fervour of the moment of separation is highlighted in that refrain *Ekti Chumban dao Promoda Amar*, a distinctly Western influence in a predominantly conservative Indian society. The same stylization is observed in the translation of the poem:

> O Philly Happy be that day,
> When roving thro' the gather'd hay,
> My youthfu' heart was stown away,
> And by thy charms my Philly.

In Rabindranath's poem titled 'Lalit Nalini: Krishaker Premalap' (*Lalit Nalini: The Love of a Farmer*) the lines become

> *Ha Nalini geche aha ki sukher din*
> *Dohe jabe ek sathe! Beratam hathe hathe*
> *Nalin hriday churi karili nalin*
> *Ha nalini kato sukhe geche se din!*

> O Nalini! How happy were those days
> When we were together holding hands
> You stole my heart Nalini
> Oh Nalini how happy were those days.
> (*Rachanavali*, Vol. 30, 61, translations mine)

Although the intensity of the feeling is preserved, it is inconceivable that a Bengali farmer would make love in the ornate and polished language of the translated text! The rustic immediacy of the Scottish dialect is completely diluted in what once again proves to be a stylised rendering. Take another stanza of Burns

> As songsters of the early year,
> Are ilka day to mair sweet to hear,
> So ilka day to mair dear
> And charming is my Philly.

That is rendered as:

> *Mridutara Ratikar sunil akashe*
> *Herile sasyer ashe, hridoy karoshe bhashe*
> *Tar cheye a hridoye bare go ullas*
> *Herile Nalini to mridu has.*
> In the clear sky of midnight
> When I look at the sight my heart wanders
> But my heart fills with glee
> When I see the smile on Nalini's face.
> (*Rachanavali*, Vol. 30, 61, translations mine)

The only difference here seems to be in the more familiar *tui* (the intimate form of you in Bengali) used in the relationship. But the language fails to render the locale, the dialect or the urgency of the sentiment. Kalisadhan Mukhopdahyay in *Paschatyo Kobitar Anubade Rabindranath* suggests that the name Nalini was used frequently in these translations even for poems of Moore and Tennyson and might have referred to the adolescent poet's deep attachment to the Marathi girl Anna Tadkha,d whom the poet encountered in Ahmedabad. Tagore had renamed Anna as Nalini. Is Burns' poem of love then transposed and indigenized as the young Rabi's expression of love for Anna in a language in which he would have been familiar? My point here is in these early translations there is no recognition of either the dialect, the Scottishness (or Irishness) or the location/class identities that the poet talks about. They are more amateurish renderings into a language that the poet was familiar with. The same is true of the fate of 'Rupashi Amar Preyoshi Amar'. The 'bonnie lassie' of Burns' poem is now the 'Rupashi and Preyoshi' (beautiful and beloved), the birks of Aberfeldy are the rather anonymous Girikanane (mountain forests) while the 'burnie pours' is rendered as 'Nijhar dhara' (spring waters). 'Sushila Amar Janalar Dhare' seems even more inadequate. 'O Mary, at thy window be,' becomes 'Sushila Amar Janalar Pore darao ektibar' ('Sushila stand by the window once') while the more urgent

'O Mary, canst thou wreck his peace/Wha for thy shake wad gladly die?'
becomes the rather dull 'Sushila Kemone bhango tar mon/Horoshe Morite
Chahe jei jan' (How do you break that heart/That seeks to die in joy). The
Bengali that all these poems uses is the more polished metropolitan, upper
class version, entirely obliterating the more local reverberations of a particular
dialect and topography. What is clear is that the young Rabindranath was
translating Burns as a Romantic English poet without tracing his Scottish
dialect or identity. The range of vocabulary or the awareness of the Scots
language was lost on Rabindranath.

His next efforts at adaptation would occur with two of Burns' famous
songs. The young Rabindranath had been rather disappointed with Western
music in his first sojourn to England, but saw the dramatic quality of
western music as suitable for his operatic text *Kalmrigaya* (composed 1882)
embellished by the experimentations and indigeneity of Jyotirindranath.
Thus Burns' song 'Ye Banks and Braes o' Bonny Doon' are translated as
'Fule Fule Dhole Dhole'. Bonny Doon, the river that flows from Loch Doon
to the Firth of Clyde in Aryshire, Scotland is mentioned by Burns in 'Sam
'O Shanter' as well. In Rabindranath the Bonny Doon becomes the more
generic 'Tatini' (river); while the 'bloom so fresh and air' is translated as
'mridu bai' (gentle breeze) while the 'ilka bird sang o' its love' becomes
'piku kiba kunje kunje / Kuhu kuhu kuhu gai' (the cuckoo sings in the
branches). However in Rabindranath the song is one of desire and longing,
while Burns' song is one of heartbreak and grief – 'But my false lover stole
my rose / But ah! She left the thorn wi' me.' with 'departed joys / Never
to return'. This is different from a more simple tone of longing in 'ki jani
kisero lagi / Prano kore hai hai' ('Who knows why my heart aches so'). The
next song 'Auld Lang Syne' is even more interesting. Rabindranath's initial
translation in *Kalmrigaya* was

Kal Sakale Uthbo Mora Jabo Nodir Kule
Shib Goriye Korbo Puja Anbo Kusum Tule
Mora Bhorer Bela Gathbo Mala Dulbo Se Dolai
Bajiye Banshi Gan Gahibo Bokuler Tolai

Tomorrow at dawn will we go to the river
Worship the *sivalinga* with the flowers
We will weave garlands and swing together
Playing the flute and singing beneath the Bakul trees.
                                (*Rachanavali, Acahlita Sangraha*, Vol. 1 320)

This was entirely in consoance with the dramatic continuity of his text,
but entirely out of sync with Burns' original lyric. In the first instance then,

Rabindranath was just transferring the tune rather than the lyric. In the second translation published later in *Rabichhaya,* the song is in greater proximity to the original. Thus:

> Should auld acquaintance be forgot
> And never brought to mind
> Should auld acquaintance be forgot
> And days o' auld lang syne

becomes

> *Purono shei diner kotha bhulbi kire hai*
> *O shei Chokher Dekha, praner kotha she ki bhola jai*

> Can you ever forget those old memories
> The acquaintances and the heartfelt exchanges can
> never be forgotten. (*Rachanavali*, Vol. 30, 65).

The Scottish 'taking a cup of kindness yet' becomes the more sedate 'ful tulechi' (plucking of flowers) to suit his milieu, but the rhetorical question is in consonance with the original. We thus have two translations – one that uses the tune in an entirely different dramatic context, the other a freer translation that fits the original sentiment into a more localized milieu. Once again there is no attempt to indicate the Scottishness of the song or the deliberate cultural nationalism latent within it. For the younger Tagore then, Burns's specific Scottish identity did not provoke any special experimentation – he was content to incorporate him within the broader canon of British Romanticism and western music.

The Later Rabindranath and Burns

Interestingly Burns seems to crop up later in Rabindranath's later writings. In the *Parisisto* (Afterword) to *Samaj (Society)* Rabindranath draws upon the archetype of the uneducated poet and uses Burns as an example:

> I do not think a poet needs to be highly educated... Burns was not greatly educated. Many poets have originated from lower classes and uneducated background (*Rachanavali*, Vol. 13, 872).

One wonders whether Rabindranath's post 1890's career and his familiarity with the poetry and songs of Lalan, Dadu and Kabir were at the root of such a statement. Like Burns, Rabindranath had collected the popular songs of Lalan Fakir and the itinerant bauls (wandering minstrels) of rural India as seers of wisdom and aesthetic merit as his writings in *The Religion of Man* articulate. It is useful to recollect the term bardic nationalism that has often been associated with Burns. The short-circuiting of metropolitan knowledge to admire a more rooted and spontaneous indigeneous culture, was part of the Burns' image. Rabindranath, one notes, was employing the local Baul tradition aggressively in his nationalist collection of poems. His poem *Amar Shonar Bangla* ('My beautiful Bengal') is closest to Burns' poetry with its use of a Baul tune and its intimate detailed references to the Deltaic landscape of Bengal. My point here is that Rabindranath's awareness of the cultural nationalism of Burns deepened with his own prolonged interface with nationalism. This is evident in the reference to Burns in an essay on *Kobi Yeats* (*The Poet Yeats*):

> Yeats can never be one of the crowd, his uniqueness is obvious to all... certain individuals are born with a need for direct experience, and they do not permit any barrier to come between that experience and its inner realization... Burns was free from any trace of literary artifice His feelings sprang straight from the heart could express them in words. And so he was able to pierce through the bonds of literary usage and give unrestrained expression to the soul of Scotland. In our time, the poetry of Yeats has been received more warmly for the same basic reason. His poetry does not echo contemporary poetry, it is an expression of his own soul... In Yeats's poetry the soul of Ireland is manifest (*Rachanavali* Vol. 26, 521).

The passage is interesting because Rabindranath places Burns together with Yeats as giving expression to the intrinsic and immediate spirit of their respective nations. Quite clearly Rabindranath was almost replicating part of Yeats's introduction in the *Gitanjali*:

> These lyrics... appear as much as the growth of the common soil as the grass and the rushes... a whole people, a whole civilization seems to have been taken up into this imagination (*Gitanjali* 4).

Ironically, the Burns-Yeats comparison was probably a mistaken one since Burns based his poetry quite clearly on an ethnic dialect and identity while the mature Yeats was quite clearly reluctant to restrict himself to it. What is important is that Burns' poetry seems to have impressed the adult Rabindranath in far more important ways.

The other important passage on Burns can be traced in the essay *Sahityer Pathe* in *Adhunik Kavya* where Rabindranath articulates his own aesthetic stance as a subjective Romantic poet, as opposed to the more modernist tendencies. Interestingly he sees this Romantic age as 'initiated by Burns. In this turn a number of major poets had emerged like Wordsworth, Shelley, Keats, Coleridge... After Burns, a new age in English poetry was initiated, where the individual human will (*marji*, will) was present... literature had acknowledged the experimental individual imagination.' (*Rachanavali* Vol. 13, 872). In *Kobi Yeats* Rabindranath distinguishes between the poets of the world (as Yeats and Burns and he himself were) and the poets of the world of letters (an example he draws is that of Swinburne). For Rabindranath, Swinburne is the 'poet of poetry as opposed to life' who is 'adroit at verbal music' (*Rachanavali* Vol. 26, 526), Rabindranath thus sees himself in the 'republic of poets' (a term that he uses to include Hafez in *Journey to Persia*) that includes Burns as a precursor.

Interestingly Rabindranath's engagement with the cultural nationalism of Burns did not extend to any rigorous examination of Burns' own political position or the Scottish position vis-à-vis colonialism. Burns himself talked repeatedly about British rapacity taken from his intellectual mentor Henry Mackenzie 'when shall I see a commander return from India in the pride of honourable poetry' (quoted in Leask 172). His radical position on individual freedom endeared him in America but in his more desperate years he was ready to work in a slave plantation in Jamaica. Curiously Burns was caught in his bardic vis-à-vis his poetic reputation too. While he thrived and drew his reputation from his Scottish poetry, he was subsequently eager to be accepted within British canonical poetry. Rabindranath too was caught in this dual identity – a voice for freedom and cultural indigeneity, yet a simultaneous metropolitan engagement as part of a republic of poets.

Rabindranath's interface with the Scottish Burns raises a number of interesting issues. The popularity of Burns in India indicates the desire of the Scots participating in the colonial process to retain a certain sense of nationalist identity while sharing the economic and political spoils of empire. For the young Rabindranath translating the poetry and music of Burns was an exercise in finding a Romantic lyrical voice without any major engagement with issues of national identity. As Rabindranath matured in his responses to national identity and the poetic craft, Burns appeared to him in a newer light. He saw within his poetry and his attempts to collect indigenous literature and transform it, a replication of many of his endeavours. There were two sides of the poet here – one who sang the soul of his country and the other who carved out a space in the republic of poets through his imagination and craft. Rabindranath's reception of Burns in the context of the colonial situation was thus a process of complex aesthetic maturing.

Works Cited:

Chaudhuri, Rosinka. *Gentlemen Poets in Colonial Bengal: Emergent Nationalism and the Orientalist Project*. Calcutta: Seagull Books, 2002. Print.

Devine, John. *Scotland in Europe 1600–1815*. London: Allen lane, 2003.

Gibson, Mary Ellis, *Anglophone Poetry in Colonial India 1780–1913: A Critical Anthology*. Ohio: Ohio University Press, 2011. Print.

Mukhopadhyay, Kalisadhan. *Paschatyo Kabitar Aloke Rabindranath*. Kolkata: Tuli Kalam. 1987. Print.

Leask, Nigel. " "Their Groves o' Sweet Myrtles": Robert Burns and the Scottish Colonial Experience" in *Robert Burns in Global Culture*, ed. Murray Pittock. Plymouth: Bucknell University Press, 2011: 172-189 Print.

Newman, Steve. "Localizing and Globalizing Burns' Songs From Ayshire to Calcutta", in *Global Romanticism: Origins, Orientations and Engagement 1760–1820*, ed. Evan Gottlieb. London: Bucknell University Press, 2015: 57-80. Print.

Sassi, Carla. *Why Scottish Literature Matters*. Edinburgh: Saltire Society, 2005. Print.

Tagore, Rabindranath. *Rabindra Rachanavali*. Kolkata: Visva-Bharati, 1998. Print. This is the standard Bengali edition for the Collected Works of Rabindranath Tagore. Referred to in the article as Rachanavali.

—. *My Reminiscences*. Kolkata: Visva-Bharati, 1917. Print.

—. *Gitanjali. A Centenary Edition*. Kolkata: Visva-Bharati, 2014.

Daniel Hamilton (Front) with Rabindranath Tagore

An Assessment of Sir Daniel Hamilton's Political Philosophy: The Panacea of Scottish Capitalism and Utilitarianism

Thomas Crosby

Preface

ACADEMIC STUDY into the life and work of Sir Daniel Hamilton is hampered by the lack of records and written literature surrounding his accomplishments. Fortunately, the 'utopia' that he sought to create in the Sundarbans region of West Bengal, still stands. It now encompasses more than 40 districts which are still, to some degree, under the co-operative wing of the original experiment in Gosaba.

However, regardless of how revered a figure Daniel Hamilton is by the Indians in that region, academic study of the man, especially in English, is disappointingly sparse. The main compendium of his writing and speeches, *The Philosopher's Stone* edited by Alapan Bandyopadhyay and Anup Matilal, inevitably forms the bulk of any academic exploration of his life. This collection is of course the main source when seeking to understand the thoughts and motivations that led him to set up a co-operative in India.

Therefore, the following paper will use these writings and speeches as a base for study into his personal political philosophy of the Scotsman. It will also make use of the *Report on the working of the co-operative credit societies* in Bengal found in the National Library of Scotland as well as scattered references to him and Gosaba in the *Annual report of the Bengal Veterinary College and of the Civil Veterinary Department, Bengal* and contemporary primary sources that provide an essential wider context together with a few pieces of relevant academic work which reference Hamilton's thoughts and ideas.

Despite Hamilton's remarkable achievements and consistent good intentions, the philosophical basis for his experiment is rarely explored or criticised. The fact that his often anti-democratic or anti-English sentiments are glossed over, does demand further exploration, as does his willingness to include in speeches the words of fascist political figures such as Adolf Hitler.

Ultimately this paper will deal with the context of Hamilton's political and social thought, seeking to define a clear message from the context of the time during which Hamilton lived and worked. A wider contextual look is vital to understand how he viewed both the economic Scottish reality he had grown up in and subsequently left, contrasted against/with the Indian future that he sought to create.

Economic Reform in Scotland

So deep had been the poverty of Scotland during the first half of the eighteenth century, and so small the amount of accumulated wealth, that even the celebrated honesty of the Scotsman could scarcely have ameliorated their economic condition, had the note issue not stepped in for occupying the place of capital (Graham 117).

The economic mire which Scotland had clawed itself out of in the 18th century formed the backdrop to Hamilton's particularly Scottish perception of capitalism and reinforced, in his mind, the need for a Caledonian solution to the problems of India.

If there is any fallacy in my finances let Sir George [Schuster, financial minister of the council of India] say where. It is, however, not my finance but the finance of Adam Smith and the Scottish banking system undiluted with English Blood (Hamilton, 1929).

It is clear that Hamilton draws a distinction between English and Scottish colonialism in India: 'His critique of colonialism in India often became a Scotsman's rejection of an English project' (Bandyopadhyay xix).

However, Scottish agriculture, so saved by the Scottish banking system, was spurred into a 'revolution' due to the need to catch up with the more incremental agricultural change in England and France. This was a leap forced by the Scottish bourgeois who, as a result of the Union of 1707, 'had been able to call on a British army to destroy the internal counter-revolution, but the very fact is that this had been necessary indicated how weak the indigenous forces of Scottish capitalism remained, compared with those of England. And it was in agriculture that this weakness was most keenly felt' (Davidson 412). Therefore, Hamilton's contentions of Scottish 18th century capitalist weakness are founded, but the idea that the English had no hand in Scotland's agricultural revival is clearly false. Ultimately, for Hamilton, it was the capitalist process that brought prosperity to the nation, and thus it must be mirrored in Bengal.

Scotland was undergoing a process of modernisation, which of course could not ignore the modern agricultural nation just across its own border. However, the weakness of Scottish Agriculture at the point is often overplayed: 'Widespread evidence [can] be found of an agriculture in Scotland which was not as backward as was painted by many 19th century commentators' (Wittington 205). The agricultural practices of the nation were fit to feed it, providing that famines such as that of 1690 did not occur. Those criticising Scottish agriculture were locked into the industrial mind-set, 'their point was that mere adequacy was no longer sufficient' (Davidson 414). India simply required agriculture to sustain itself, as the current conditions were very poor as opposed to Scotland previous sustainability, devoid of the surplus output desired in Scotland.

Hamilton's Scottish exceptionalism, although undoubtedly a great source of inspiration, was tainted with scorned English blood from the outset. From him India would get Scottish agricultural capitalism based on an English paradigm.

Paper Currency

For Hamilton, the Scottish solution to its agricultural stagnation was to create capital from essentially thin air. The printing of money by private or state banks, the creation of pound notes, was, as far as Hamilton was concerned, the panacea that put the idle back to work and helped to transform Scotland into one of Europe's more progressive cultural and agricultural powerhouses. Hamilton quotes from Dunning MacLeod's *Elements of Banking* in his writing *Man or Mammon*: 'There were immense quantities of reclaimable land, and abundance of unemployed people, but no capital or money to set the industry in motion' (Dunning Macleod in. Bandyopadhay and Matilal 69). Macleod's quotation could just as easily be talking of the turn of the century in India as of 18th century Scotland. It was the new paper notation, the new form of credit, which had inspired the changes in Scotland's agriculture: 'All these marvellous results, which have raised Scotland from the lowest state of barbarism up to her present proud position in the space of 150 years are the children of pure credit' (Dunning Macleod in. Bandyopadhay and Matilal 69).

The adoption of bank notes in Scotland was seen at the time as having 'produced such remarkable changes... upon the whole of our money dealings' (Maxwell 585). The 18th century magazine, *The Critical Review,* voiced a fear that 'an immediate abolition of small paper credit in Scotland might be attended with very dangerous consequences for that country' (1765, 239). Maxwell is still cautious when selling the successes of the scheme, spelling out the dangers that a dishonest private banking sector may bring: 'It is liable to abuse... paper money may grow beyond the due proportion it ought to bear to the specie of a country, and it may be difficult to find gold and silver to give in payment for it' (Maxwell 586). Regarding the need to anchor the capital to precious metals, Hamilton often quotes from the opening of Smith's *Wealth of Nations*: 'The annual labour of every nation is the fund which originally supplies it with all the necessaries and conveniences of life which it annually consumes, and which consist always either in the immediate produce of that labour, or in what is purchased with that produce from other nations' (Smith 1) It is men, not gold or silver, that would form the basis of Hamilton's Gosaba co-operative, backed throughout by a supply of paper credit. He was aware that 'hard cash starves a nation, because there is not enough to go around; and what there is, is in the wrong hands. The hands of the moneylender or the non-producer' (Hamilton 2003, 64) and concluded 'money is only the instrument which sets the men a going, the real capital being the man himself' (Hamilton 2003, 71). Hamilton, with help of the British authorities and their resources, could become the honest figure that anchored the new currency, providing a Scottish tonic for the Indian malaise of the early 20th century, 'to chain young India to a dying gold mine would be like marrying a girl bride to a dying man' (Hamilton 2003, 71).

Reliable Men

Everything hinges on 'men of conscience', the reliable and trustworthy that keep a system based on promises to pay the bearer on demand in working order. From Gosaba's inception Jamini Mohan Mitra, Registrar of Co-operative Societies, Bengal, could see this need as clearly as Hamilton himself,

> The scheme has limitless possibilities, but to begin with the society will confine its attention strictly to zamindary business. It is a practical and business-like proposition and cannot fail of success granted the two conditions of a very active and energetic Managing Committee, and, above all thoroughly reliable members. Slackness or half-heartedness in either will be fatal (Co-operative Societies: Bengal, 1909).

Throughout the annual *Report on the working of the co-operative credit societies in Bengal*, references to Hamilton's co-operative become fewer and fewer as it became increasingly established and the risk of its failure diminished. Subsequently the reports are mainly confined to the tiny government controlled section of his estate. 'The Bengal Young Men's Zamindary Co-operative Urban Society, Limited, constitutes a new venture in co-operation. It aims at applying the principles of co-operation in acquiring Zamindary through the collective credit of the members' (Co-operative Societies: Bengal, 1909). Hamilton needed the central government to be the issuer of credit, but not to support the co-operatives themselves. Gosaba became somewhere for the government to experiment – a safe environment, backed by a reliable man.

It is clear that this reliability is the cornerstone of Hamilton's co-operative philosophy, 'No credit can be issued if trustworthiness is non-existent in the would be borrower' (Hamilton 2003, 151). 'The one rupee note... will do for India what the one pound note, based not on gold or silver but on the labour of poor reliable working men, did for Scotland' (Hamilton 2003, 73). As the population of the Sunderbans was spare at the start of the Gosaba project, many immigrants were essentially 'shipped in'. These new raiyats (peasants or agricultural labourers) in Gosaba were quite reliable, (enough to) follow Hamilton's orders, although during an anthrax outbreak in 1917–18 the task of disposing of animal carcasses wasn't fulfilled, especially in the neighbouring settlement of Basanti as 'little or no attention was paid to this instruction' (Bengal Veterinary College 2-3). For Hamilton to create reliability in the raiyats, he would require more than simply their trust in his economic system. That outbreak alone killed 1,600 individual pieces of livestock, (Bengal Veterinary College 2-3), so clearly faith in Hamilton's dictates themselves, and in him as a man, would also be required from the new 'reliable class'.

In order for Hamilton to create these reliable men, he required that they would be free from their shackles of debt. Many of these new citizens of Gosaba were in debt to local Maharajas or other money lenders, debts, which at a special court, Hamilton settled in an afternoon (Matilal 10). Through his philanthropy Hamilton solved a problem endemic in the Indian co-operative movements up to 1970s and beyond, the problem of 'old debt' that still needed scaling down across India (Madan 118).

Hamilton, although a staunch Christian, does not require conversion to produce his ideal man, nor does he demand even freedom via democracy, instead freedom from cancerous debts and a man with the will to work are all that are needed. The application of debt free loans and hard work wouldn't however generate the general freedom that was becoming an increasing requirement for the Indians to stand on their own. Those in Gosaba relied in many ways on him, even as a benevolent lord he was still a foreign power, above them in the hierarchy. Hamilton's approach was practical and crucially utilitarian but as the century wore on and Indian freedom becomes ever more likely, his ideas shifted away from pure financial freedom towards wider political suffrage.

Christian Philosopher and Anti-Socialist

'Trust is faith. Faith is the power which removes mountains, and is the only power which will remove India's Himalayas of debt, and ignorance, and ill-health, and usher in a healthy Swaraj [home rule]' (Hamilton 2003, 81). Hamilton had a Christian outlook that permeated all he did. His faith in God was mirrored by his 'subjects' faith in him: 'It is not by gold or silver that men live, but by labour and bread, and the word of God' (Ibid. 71). His representations of the problems in rural India that he hoped to rectify, were steeped in Christian imagery: 'unorganised and disunited as they are now, the great masses of the people are like sheep without a shepherd, and they fall prey to the wolves, whose chief is the mahajan' (Hamilton 1929, 103).

Potentially, it is the case that he saw himself as a Jesus figure, their shepherd. More likely he just used religious imagery to frame his understanding of their plight. In fact, regardless of his biblical language, Hamilton was often more concerned with the indigenous leaders of Indian antiquity, Asoka and Akbar, then by Christ. Hamilton was especially taken with Asoka, a man ruling in India 2,300 years ago, hence not too far from the time of Christ, so revered by external powers looking inwardly at India, as the gentle hand, the spreader of Buddhism. HG Wells regularly quotes describing Asoka in gushing language, 'amidst the tens of thousands of names of monarchs that crowd the columns of history... the name Asoka shines and shines almost alone, like a star' (Wells 175). Comparatively, Akbar is the religious pragmatist, promoting a form of top down tolerance in India, a macrocosm of the cultural and caste composition of Gosaba, 'it is Akbar's religious tolerance that marks him – a fierce autocrat in politics – for his special place in history' (*The Economist* 1999, 63). It was in the need for unity of his new people at Gosaba that Hamilton found historical justification for co-operative projects: 'India's 700,000 villages and the people who dwell therein are the foundation-stones of the temple of Akbar's dream; but the dream will remain only a dream: until the people have been organised co-operatively into One' (Hamilton 2003, 275): 'Hindu, Moslem, Christian, touchable and untouchable, must stand or fall together' (Hamilton 1930, 138). There was a conscious effort to link the desire for his project to succeed with how he perceived an Indian would traditionally live, and Indian society traditionally function, in the form of co-operative village unity.

So it is with unity, not division that there would be a road to freedom, and crucially a return to ground-up government and the co-operative salvation of the village unit (Hamilton 2003, 228). The desire to ameliorate the poor of their conditions would also generate their freedom. It is not through democracy as such that this would be achieved. Hamilton, at points, shows a complete distain for democracy as a means of attaining this freedom, 'but the fruits of democracy are neither freedom from self, nor abundance of good deeds. Its gospel is the gospel of grab, its fruits the apples of Sodom, and taxation which sinks the state' (Hamilton 1929, 85).

He, too, is no blanket supporter of voting, or of enfranchisement, 'votes are well enough in their own place, and the proper place for many of them is the waste paper basket; but votes do not fill empty stomachs' (Hamilton, 101). In many ways Hamilton was being astute, judging that a Democracy without freedom from the conditions of poverty, and taking place in an intellectual vacuum of limited education, would not be a democracy in any serious sense, 'Votes without money are like curry without spice... without the flavour they may sell it to the highest bidder for what it is worth, and that is not much' (Hamilton 1929, 98).

What is shocking about this political attitude, outside of its Indian pragmatism, is that it is clearly incongruous with the political reality of the United Kingdom, somewhere Hamilton cannot be that dramatically out of touch with as is exemplified by him, 'the people of Great Britain have now more votes than they ever had before, and there is now more unemployment in Great Britain than there ever was before' (Hamilton 1929, 101).

Founded in 1917, the Co-operative Party has existed almost unknown in UK politics for as long as the Labour Party, and since 1927 fielded joint candidates with them in general elections. A year previous to Hamilton's strong statements on enfranchisement, Britain had arguably achieved full suffrage with the inclusion of women over 21 in the voting process through the Equal Franchise Act 1928. The Co-operative party were keen to canvass this new voter in the subsequent 'flapper election'.

The co-operative and enfranchisement movement were working in tandem in the UK to such an extent that Lord Rothermere, the dedicated 'Anti-Socialist' head of the *The Daily Mail*, held a distinct fear that these young women would vote overwhelmingly with Labour (Bingham 17). Enfranchisement was seen as promoting the Socialist cause, something Hamilton was, of course, opposed to. Labour managed to form a brief minority government in 1924 and then formed another only a few months after Hamilton's anti-voting statements were made in late January 1929-about governments that were arguably more representative of ordinary people than any that had come before.

Hamilton didn't see these new British remedies as panaceas for India's problems. The handing out of the vote to 1920s Indians would not have enabled them to increase crop yield or to reverse the frightening medical reality of their existence, a fact Hamilton was all too aware of. According to the All-India Conference of Medical Research Workers in India in 1929, around 5-6 million people a year were dying of preventable disease (Hamilton 1929, 101-2). Literacy rates too were exceedingly low. Hamilton opened schools at all levels, including night schools. Agriculture and weaving were compulsory in all of them. By 1941 25 per cent of Gosaba's 15,000 residents were literate (Matilal 14-15), compared to an estimate 16.1 per cent for all India. It would take 20 years for India's general literacy rate to equal that which Hamilton had managed in Gosaba (Premi, 2002).

Despite Hamilton's deep connection with the co-operative movement, a movement that is often associated with the left-wing, Hamilton is clearly no lover of Communism or even Socialist theory: 'The Lenin Road is the road travelled by the anti-God Society the way of the anti-Christ, and it leads to the field of blood, with hell beyond' (Hamilton 2003, 80).

In *Fertile Currency and its Crop*, among the incredible list of benefits paper currency is meant to bring, alongside doctors, teachers and the preservation of individualism is 'the destruction of Communism' (Hamilton 2003, 112-3). The bringing of 'Scottish' capitalism to rural India could well destroy its feudal system but to offer it as a panacea for the rise of global left wing movements, is at best naïve.

On Indian Independence

Towards the end of Hamilton's life he was faced with an ever more confident independence-minded India. As the viability of India leaving the Empire grew, so did his support for it: 'While Hindu and Moslem stand facing each other with no love between them, the British soldier must stand between' (Hamilton 2003, 115). Hamilton had too grand a concept of the perfect conditions needed for Indian independence. On caste Hamilton also had lofty ambitions, 'whilst hand will not touch hand, India will never march hand in hand' (Hamilton 2003, 115). Crucially he vastly underestimates the required conditions to bring about Indian independence. His vision of that independence was also somewhat regressive, often a justification for his co-operative principles via a return to Asoka's India, 'group life, which is co-operative life, is, therefore, the indigenous form of political system' (Hamilton 2003, 228). Hamilton also quoted from a speech given by Adolf Hitler about how he put the jobless to work and used that work to underpin a German mark based on man power (Hamilton 2003, 230-31). There is not a political figure, ideology or concept that cannot be crowbarred into Hamilton desire to reform the flow of capital on the Indian sub-continent, and thus secure for them practical freedom: 'Germany is now finding financial salvation in the Gosaba currency system the Man Standard' (Hamilton 2003, 231). He advocates a Panchayat (council of chosen village elders) 'chosen by the people from all castes and creeds' forming an 'Aristocracy of Democracy' (Hamilton 2003, 239).

However, Hamilton's assertion that India wasn't ready for her independence is one that was mirrored across the political spectrum at the time. Nicholas Owen explains how, at the Labour conference in 1930, Fenner Brockway, once suspended in parliament for demanding a debate on India at PMQs, is able, like Hamilton, to predict the bloodshed of Partition.

> Hindus and the Mohammedans had not sunk their differences of creed. Caste had not been wiped out... Did they want India to go through all the... bitterness and civil war that had characterised China in the last ten years? That was what was likely to happen if there was a hasty ill considered departure from Idia' (Brockway 1930, 217-8).

There is a clear level of practical astuteness about Hamilton's thinking. He has little time for the grander concepts if they do not improve things at the base level for the ordinary Indian, 'For, while the British Government may give India a status on parchment, it is our business to give her a status in life' (Hamilton 1930, 114). He wants 'Scottish' capitalist reform and poverty elevation beyond all other concerns; theories and political figures can be utilised as long as at least a tiny portion of their activity justifies his own.

Conclusion

Hamilton is never truly out of step with either the thinking of the left or right at home, nor with the accepted ideas of when and how India should become independent. As Mishra suggests, most of all Hamilton is a utilitarian who 'got attracted with this land of Sundarban to cherish his dream of ameliorating the sufferings of the poverty stricken people and to develop a community undivided by caste and religion' (Mishra 101). He is concerned with the immediate: healing the sick, feeding the poor and dragging the Indian village back to the power he once felt it had under Asoka, or to at least the power it was clearly capable of. Hamilton's Christianity is a basis for his theory, as is his capitalism, but democracy or larger political freedom isn't required if the people aren't even free from debt or the crippling conditions of poverty. It is in the need to solve the problems of the now that Hamilton implements his 'Scottish' brand of compassionate co-operative capitalism, a Scottish capitalism that was truly based on compassion but intrinsically tainted by 'English blood'.

Works Cited:

Annual Report of the Bengal Veterinary College and the Civil Veterinary Department, Bengal, for the year 1917–18. Calcutta: The Bengal Secretariat Book Depot, 1918. Print.

Bandyopadhay, A., & Matilal, A. *The Philosopher's Stone: Speeches & Writings of Sir Daniel Hamilton.* Gosaba: Sir Daniel Hamilton Estate Trust. 2003. Print.

Bingham, A., 2002. "'Stop the Flapper Vote Folly': Lord Rothermere, the Daily Mail, and the Equalization of the Franchise 1927–28" in. *Twentieth Century Brit History.* Vol. 13, No. 1, pp. 17-37, doi:10.1093/tcbh/13.1.17 available at: http://tcbh.oxfordjournals.org. ezproxy.napier.ac.uk/content/13/1/17.full.pdf+html accessed 28 September 2015.

Brockway, F., 1930. In. Labour Party, Report of Annual Conference, 1930, p. 217-18. Quoted in: Owen, N., 2007. *The British Left and India: Metropolitan Anti-Imperialism, 1885–1947* [e-book]. Oxford Scholarship Online, doi: 10.1093/acpro f:oso/9780199233014.001.0001 available at: http://www.oxfordscholarship.com. ezproxy.napier.ac.uk/view/10.1093/acprof:oso/9780199233014.001.0001/acprof-9780199233014-chapter-7#acprof-9780199233014-note-781 accessed 29 September 2015.

Co-operative Societies: Bengal. *Report on the working of the co-operative credit societies in Bengal for the year 1908–1909.* Calcutta: The Bengal Secretariat Book Depot, 1909. Print.

Davidson, N., 2004, The Scottish Path to Capitalist Agriculture 2: The Capitalist Offensive (1747–1815). *Journal of Agrarian Change*, 4: 411-460. doi: 10.1111/j.1471-0366.2004.00087.x accessed 27 September 2015.

Graham, W., 1911. *The one pound note in the history of banking in Great Britain*, James Thin: Edinburgh. Available through the California Digital Library [Online] available at: https://archive.org/details/onepoundnoteinhioograh accessed 26 September 2015.

Hamilton, D., 1929. "Asoka's Political System: Address by Sir Daniel Hamilton to the second Presidency Divisional Co-operative Conference held at Jiagunj, District Murshedabad, on the 26th and 27th January, 1929." *The Philosopher's Stone: Speeches & Writings of Sir Daniel Hamilton*. Eds. A. Bandyopadhay & A. Matilal. Gosaba: Sir Daniel Hamilton Estate Trust, 2003. pp. 82-9. Print.

Hamilton, D., 1929. "Bardoli or Bira: Closing address by Sir Daniel Hamilton at the Burdwan Divisional Co-operative Conference held at Bolpur on 9th, 10th and 11th February, 1929." *The Philosopher's Stone: Speeches & Writings of Sir Daniel Hamilton*. Eds. A. Bandyopadhay & A. Matilal. Gosaba: Sir Daniel Hamilton Estate Trust, 2003. pp. 97-100. Print.

Hamilton, D., 1929. "India's Best Hope: Address by Daniel Hamilton to the Burdwan Divisional Co-operative Conference held at Bolpur District Birdhum." *The Philosopher's Stone: Speeches & Writings of Sir Daniel Hamilton*. Eds. A. Bandyopadhay & A. Matilal. Gosaba: Sir Daniel Hamilton Estate Trust, 2003. pp. 90-96. Print.

Hamilton, D., 1929. "The Capitalisation of Labour: Paper read by Sir Daniel Hamilton at a social gathering held at Calcutta University under the auspices of the Bengal Economic Society on 31st January, 1929." *The Philosopher's Stone: Speeches & Writings of Sir Daniel Hamilton*. Eds. A. Bandyopadhay & A. Matilal. Gosaba: Sir Daniel Hamilton Estate Trust, 2003. pp. 101-6. Print.

Hamilton, D., 1930. "The Nation Builders: Address given by Sir Daniel Hamilton to the students of the Scottish Church College, Calcutta, on 14th February, 1930." *The Philosopher's Stone: Speeches & Writings of Sir Daniel Hamilton*. Eds. A. Bandyopadhay & A. Matilal. Gosaba: Sir Daniel Hamilton Estate Trust, 2003. pp. 136-143. Print.

Hamilton, D., 2002. "Fertile Currency and its Crop." *The Philosopher's Stone: Speeches & Writings of Sir Daniel Hamilton*. Eds. A. Bandyopadhay & A. Matilal. Gosaba: Sir Daniel Hamilton Estate Trust, 2003. pp. 107-113. Print.

Hamilton, D., 2003. "Man or Mammon: The True Capital and the False." *The Philosopher's Stone: Speeches & Writings of Sir Daniel Hamilton*. Eds. A. Bandyopadhay & A. Matilal. Gosaba: Sir Daniel Hamilton Estate Trust, 2003. pp. 61-76. Print.

Hamilton, D., 2003. "India and the Empire: Akbar's Dream." *The Philosopher's Stone: Speeches & Writings of Sir Daniel Hamilton*. Eds. A. Bandyopadhay & A. Matilal. Gosaba: Sir Daniel Hamilton Estate Trust, 2003. pp. 273-283. Print.

Hamilton, D., 2003. "The Banking Enquiry." *The Philosopher's Stone: Speeches & Writings of Sir Daniel Hamilton*. Eds. A. Bandyopadhay & A. Matilal. Gosaba: Sir Daniel Hamilton Estate Trust, 2003. pp. 148-153. Print.

Hamilton, D., 2003. "The Swaraj Road: Capitalism or Communism." *The Philosopher's Stone: Speeches & Writings of Sir Daniel Hamilton*. Eds. A. Bandyopadhay & A. Matilal. Gosaba: Sir Daniel Hamilton Estate Trust, 2003. pp. 77-81. Print.

Hamilton, D., 2003. "The Road to Independence: A Constructive Programme for Congress and All-India." *The Philosopher's Stone: Speeches & Writings of Sir Daniel Hamilton*.

Eds. A. Bandyopadhay & A. Matilal. Gosaba: Sir Daniel Hamilton Estate Trust, 2003. pp. 226-241. Print.

Madan, G, R. *Co-Operative Movement in India.* 2nd Edition. New Delhi: Mittal Publications, 2007. Print.

Maxwell, J., 1763. "Thoughts concerning Banks, and the Paper-Currency of Scotland." *The Scots Magazine* 1739-1803: 585-588. Print.

Mishra, S, S. "Identity Crisis among the tribes of Jharkhand settled in Sundarban." *The Lagoons of The Gangetic Delta.* Eds. G, K. Bera & V. S. Sahay. New Delhi: Mittal Publications, 2010. Print.

Premi, M, K., 2002. "Seminar on Progress of Literacy in India: What the Census 2001 Preveals, Neipa, New Delhi, October 05 2002." Available at: http://www. educationforallinindia.com/page172.html accessed 28 September 2015.

Smith, A., 1904. *An Inquiry into the Nature and Causes of the Wealth of Nations,* [e-book] London: Methuen & Co., Ltd. Available through: Library of Economics and Liberty [Online] http://www.econlib.org/library/Smith/smWN1.html accessed 26 September 2015.

The Critical Review, 1765. "38. Remarks on the Proposed Plan for regulating the Paper Currency of Scotland", In. *The Critical Review, or, Annals of Literature,* issue 19. pp. 239.

The Economist, 1999. "Muslims and Hindus: Multicultural Akbar", *The Economist* [Online]. 25 December 1999: 63. Expanded Academic ASAP. Available at: http://go.galegroup.com/ps/i.do?id=GALE%7CA584086 42&v= 2.1&u= napier&it= r&p= EAIM&sw=w&asid= 4163b385bd2074c9865236ff2c8f1dd5 accessed 28 September 2015.

Wells, H, G., 1920. *Outline of History: Being a Plain History of Life of Mankind,* [e-book]. Garden City: New York. Available at: http://www.archive.org/details/OutlineOfHistory accessed 28 September 2015.

Whittington, G., 1975. "Was There a Scottish Agricultural Revolution?", *Royal Geographical Society* (with the Institute of British Geographers). Vol. 7, No. 3, pp. 204-206, available at: http://www.jstor.org/stable/20001011 accessed 27 September 2015

A Scotsman in Sriniketan

Neil Fraser

THIS PAPER EXPLORES one Scotsman's contribution to Rabindranath's project at Santiniketan. This is Arthur Geddes, Patrick Geddes' son, who worked at Sriniketan (the Institute for Rural Reconstruction) from March 1923 to late 1924. I begin by looking at the vision shared by Rabindranath Tagore, Leonard Elmhirst, and Patrick Geddes for Sriniketan, the setting up of the Institute for Rural Reconstruction (Sriniketan) in 1922, and then at Arthur Geddes' considerable contribution a year later.

An initial puzzle concerns Arthur Geddes' dates at Sriniketan. I am inclined to believe evidence from letters that he went there in March 1923. Rabindranath sent an invitation to Patrick Geddes in December 1922 (Fraser 83) and Arthur sent two letters to his father in March 1923 (File Number 129 i). He also referred to going to Santiniketan in summer 1923 as mentioned in his essay 'Two Friends: Rabindranath Tagore and Patrick Geddes'. In addition Leonard Elmhirst's *Poet and Plowman* which gives the story of Sriniketan up to July 1922, makes no mention of Arthur Geddes. The main argument for a longer period in Sriniketan is the amount Arthur Geddes did there, particularly the considerable research work.

Rabindranath's vision

Rabindranath set up a School in Santiniketan in 1901 and a university, Visva Bharati, in Santiniketanin 1921.Though both were tremendous achievements, Tagore recognised their incompleteness unless they also addressed the problems in the surrounding rural area. He was thinking about this for a long time, probably from the time of his interaction with his own tenants in Shelidah (1891–1901). For example, Rabindranath, in his speech *Swadeshi Samaj* in 1905 (Tagore, *On the Edges* 60), expressed his wish to see rural Bengal re-organised on the basis of self-help and the revival of indigenous industries. Rabindranath bought the farm at Surul a long time in advance of the setting up of the Institute.

A further indication of his interest in the future of Indian agriculture is his sending of his son, Rathindranath to an American agricultural college, after which Rathindranath was very involved in the Sriniketan experiment and became a friend of Arthur Geddes.

Rabindranath saw Santiniketan 'surrounded by villages which were decaying and dying' (Kar xiii). 'For the past thirty years Tagore had himself been looking for someone who would be ready to live in an Indian village in order to try and find solutions for some of the problems Rabindranath realized that villagers seemed to have lost all ability to help themselves and that both research and technical assistance would be needed to rescue themselves' (Elmhirst 1).

In his Introduction to Elmhirst's 'The Robbery of the Soil', Rabindranath attributed the decay of villages to the growth of greed and individual ambition in cities, leading to a breakdown of the traditional family system, which particularly affects villages. The bond of harmony gives way and brothers become enemies. We have to relearn not to exhaust the soil of life, to bond with nature and the environment. To help the villages, 'the scholars, the poets, the musicians, the artists as well as the scientists have to collaborate' (Tagore, Introduction 21, 24).

He argued that boys at the school could help with support of self-help (e.g. as Boy Scout leaders) and then the University should take up the needs of the villages, both by teaching agriculture and by giving training in 'rural reconstruction'. For Rabindranath the two experiments (Santiniketan and Sriniketan) pedagogic and agricultural, cultural and rural, were vitally linked' (Kripalani viii). He wanted not merely agricultural development but total regeneration of social, cultural and economic life (Sinha, 'Rabindranath and Elmhirst' 57). Rabindranath had a vision of the university helping to build a more co-operative village life.

Elmhirst and Tagore

Rabindranath deliberately sought out Leonard Elmhirst when he was in America, as he heard he had a background which suggested he might be able to lead the effort to revive the villages and teach agriculture. He was English and a student of agriculture at Cornell University. Elmhirst was very willing to come. 'My dearest ambition was to get back to India and to work there in some Indian village, preferably for Rabindranath Tagore' (Elmhirst 1). He was twenty-nine when he came to Sriniketan.

Rabindranath invited Elmhirst to come and lead Sriniketan in 1921. He had found a true kindred spirit in him (Sinha 58). Elmhirst settled on the farm in January 1922 with a keen team of workers training students and then villagers and their children towards new ways of living together. The aim was 'restoring fertility, growing better crops, improving crafts and achieving co-operation'. Tagore asked Leonard Elmhirst, Rathindranath Tagore (the poet's son), Santosh Majumdar, Kalimohan Ghosh and Gour Gopal Ghosh to draw up plans for Sriniketan (Elmhirst 3). Their first students – ten college students – took up residence in Sriniketan in February 1922.

Elmhirst's thinking is also displayed in his lecture 'The Robbery of the Soil' (Ibid. 26). He argues that the soil needs to be tended to avoid erosion: 'Men succeed insofar as they repay the soil generously for that which they have taken from it.' The production of food [used to be] a community enterprise and the proper treatment of the soil with irrigation and manure was a community responsibility. But with the insatiable demand of the modern city, with the coming of easy means of communication, all that is gone.' (Ibid. 26) But we cannot go backwards to a 'golden age'. Rather the community life of villages should be rebuilt with the tools of the modern world. Without good soil, villagers will not maintain a healthy diet, which was needed to prevent diseases like malaria, a major factor in the lethargy of villagers. There should be trained village workers. Tenant farming is particularly bad for the long term health of the soil. Remedies are various but they all require mutual trust.

In the Arthur Geddes files in the Rabindra Bhavana Archives is a paper described as Elmhirst's principles for the work of Sriniketan (File Number 129 iii).

1. Win friendship of villagers by assisting in solving pressing problems
2. Train young men as good farmers, craftsmen and rural leaders
3. Give practical training by a) raising food, vegetables and milk, b) by village work such as scouting and gardening.
4. Meet expenses by profitable farming

Elmhirst stresses healing feuds (a major problem in the villages at that time), encouraging co-operation, setting an example of good practice, attention to health needs, animal breeding, and restoration of crafts.

Patrick Geddes and Tagore

Arthur Geddes' father, Patrick Geddes, the Scottish polymath, worked in India for 9 years. He came to India in 1914 and became a correspondent with Tagore in 1918. Geddes and Tagore particularly shared interests in education: 'Both sought universal education in harmony with life, effected in close bonds with nature, conscious... of man's environment... They agreed on village reconstruction and land regeneration, which could be facilitated through the initiative of universities' (Fraser 25). Geddes became Professor in Sociology and Civics in the University of Bombay. He was a man of great energy (like Rabindranath), particularly spending time on plans for some 50 Indian cities. But his interests still included rural planning, as evident in his article 'The Condition and Prospects of Deccan villages'.

Being a planner and architect, Patrick Geddes was involved in plans for buildings at Santiniketan and Sriniketan. However the people on the spot were too slow reporting to Geddes, reducing what he could do. Geddes was quite angry, particularly in a letter, dated 26.02.1923, to the Secretary of Visva-Bharati, Mahalanobis (Fraser 91).

Geddes was a scientist, which appealed to the modernist in Rabindranath – though his humanity was the real basis of his appeal (Ibid. 34). Rabindranath wanted a scientific approach to agriculture, such as might be analysed with Patrick Geddes' graphical methods, so he asked Arthur Geddes to introduce these methods to the students.

Institute for Rural Reconstruction

The early days of Sriniketan are represented in Elmhirst's book *Poet and Plowman* and also in the Rabindra Bhavana Archives by a *Prospectus of the Training Camps and Apprenticeships,* including a progress report for the first year and a report *'Health Programme for a Rural Village.'* Sinha speculates that Arthur Geddes was responsible for this Training Prospectus, given that it is in his file in the Archive.[1]

One group of young men went to the farm at Surul before Elmhirst arrived to try Gandhi's ideas of non-co-operation with the British (Elmhirst 5-12). Elmhirst says 'they had difficulties in adapting a somewhat rigid political programme to local village conditions'. They abandoned the attempt after several of them were ill with malaria. Non-co-operation with the British was being interpreted as meaning, for example, burning foreign – made cloth, having no dealings with the British authorities in relation to road improvement or making no collection of donations from Britain. This was opposed by Tagore and Elmhirst. This illustrates the rather fevered politics at the time. The nationalist programme had impact from time to time in Sriniketan, but the rural reconstruction proceeded notwithstanding (in spite of having an English director and later a Scottish deputy).

I will use the *Prospectus of Training Camp and Apprenticeships* which is dated in pencil, 1924, to describe the Sriniketan courses in the first year or so of the Institute for Rural Reconstruction (File Number 129 ii). *Training Camps* for 15-18 year olds, lasting 3-4 weeks each, were to introduce boys to a 'wider conception of the art of living' e.g. housecraft, handicrafts, the art of thinking, the art of expression through games, songs and drama. It is stressed that especially the camps are to learn welfare work. Then there were *Apprenticeships* for two years, available to those successful in the training camps. Initially there were apprentices in farming, gardening and weaving. The courses had a practical bent, with academic subjects coming in only when the need arose. All students were given a garden plot to cultivate. The aim was not only to train young men to earn their own livelihood but also to be equipped to initiate village welfare and reconstruction work and stimulate a spirit of self-help among villagers.

Included in the Prospectus is a *Progress report from first year of Sriniketan 1922/23,* which reports on

1. A night school for children
2. Two troops of scouts organized
3. The provision of First Aid which brought villagers in – 'breaking down walls of suspicion'
4. Classes progressing in carpentry, smithy, tannery, weaving, poultry-keeping, and dairying
5. All the students and staff members of the Surul Farmers Union

According to Arthur Geddes initial students were 10+ from the Santiniketan School. It is clear that initial efforts were in winning over villagers and getting classes started.

Also of interest is the report: *Health programme for a rural village* (File Number 129 ii).

In the beginning (from February 1922) First Aid was given by untrained staff of the Department. With health being a big problem – especially malaria – it is argued in the report that the spirit of hostility gradually disappeared. In October 1922 a health worker, Gretchen Green, arrived from USA, who set up a dispensary. This led to 3000 cases in the first four months and 10, 330 patients in the first full year. After providing lectures failed to win over villagers, they decided to 'put the tools in the hands of children'. They aimed at getting children to set an example in hygiene by cleaning up their homes – to win over the parents. Diet, poor parental care and unclean drinking water were blamed for many ailments. Birbhum District had a dreadful infant mortality rate of nearly 400 per 1000 live births and a lot of mothers dying in childbirth.

The norm amongst local villages was 80 per cent of the population having malaria after the rainy season. But one village, Moadpur, was found which defied the malaria norm with no malaria cases at all. This was attributed to local boy scouts opening a 300 yard drain, the cleaning of tanks, and regular quinine treatment.

The report echos Rabindranath in arguing there used to be a sense of co-operative unity in villages with public opinion enforcing standards of hygiene, but 'with the coming of the competitive spirit all that was gone and with it any sense of co-operative responsibility'. It was concluded that they had to win the friendship of villages e.g. by training for farming, co-operation for common needs. The mutual mistrust which was leading to feuding had to be overcome. The report includes a plea for skills to be taught to village people (especially girls). It also included a plea for the use of a lady doctor and domestic science expert for a group of villages.

Arthur Geddes (1895–1968)

Both Patrick Geddes and Arthur Geddes were at the Department of Sociology and Civics, Bombay University until March 1923, when Arthur came to

Sriniketan (aged 28). This was preceded by letters, dated, 28 December 1922, to Patrick Geddes from Rabindranath urging him to send Arthur to Santiniketan (Fraser 83). In addition, Patrick and Arthur Geddes both visit Santiniketan and Sural for two days in November 1922, evident through Geddes's letter to Tagore on November 10, 1922 (Ibid. 72). Arthur was in Sriniketan from March 1923 until late 1924.

There are four main areas of his contribution: 1. Transcribing Tagore's songs (he played the violin for Rabindranath); 2. His geographical thesis on Bengal, exploring the causes of the malaise in the villages in the Santiniketan area; 3. Work on rural development, including teaching in the Institute; 4. Representing his father in relation to architectural planning. One can say that Arthur was a conduit for Patrick Geddes' ideas, which were extensive.

He taught Sociology, including introducing graphical methods and Nature Study. He appears also to have been organizing Training, as Dikshit Sinha discusses in his essay 'Arthur Geddes and Sriniketan: Explaining Underdevelopment' published in this volume. He did village studies as part of his thesis but also as part of understanding rural needs.

Rabindranath recognized that he could have a special role with extra responsibilities when Elmhirst was away (Elmhirst accompanied Rabindranath on a number of his trips abroad).

Arthur wrote a short article entitled, 'An Adventure in Reconstruction and Re-education' in the September 1923 issue of *Welfare* about Sriniketan. Here he argued that people could 'find themselves' through service. He took the example of scouting as a way of reaching the villagers, e.g. when scouts helped put out a fire which was threatening thatched houses. He mentioned 'rural re-education' – the value of a good farm for its example to the district and he advocated 'efficiency socialized through the prime human purpose.' He wanted careers in social leadership, e.g. within co-operative organizations' and argued there was a need for mediators and humane and disinterested organizers and managers. Teachers too needed to be re-educated.

Village studies and the link between geography and culture
An important contribution to the work of the Institute for Rural Reconstruction, done by Arthur Geddes with his students, were village studies. Arthur went on to use these in his PhD thesis[2] entitled, *Au Pays de Tagore: La Civilisation rural du Bengal occidental et ses facteurs geographique*, and a number of them are in the Rabindra Bhavan archives. One chapter of his thesis entitled, 'The Villages of Birbhum', analysed six Hindu villages and three Moslem villages. He drew maps, noting rivers and tanks, and the placement of buildings and areas by their social composition e.g. castes. He noted that better off villages kept their tanks and water supply cleaner. He collected data on the incidence of malaria. He also found out about the history of villages e.g. where population

was in decline, where industries were in decline e.g. oil-crushing industry, silk industry. He described the state of homes and whether crafts existed. Arthur said he appreciated the value of survey work in rural reconstruction after spending time with the regional and national survey teams set up in preparation for National Planning under Mahalanobis, who was later a central figure in the Planning Commission of India (File Number 129 iv). Village surveys continued to be organized by Sriniketan long after Arthur left.

Arthur Geddes' exploration of the links between geography and culture can be found in his thesis; his academic papers 'The Population of Bengal, its Distribution and Changes: A Contribution to Geographical Method', 'The Regions of Bengal' and in his posthumously published *Man and Land in South Asia*.[3] In 'The Regions of Bengal' Arthur contrasts west and east Bengal. Flood water was carried to the east in monsoon time, depositing silt in the fields there and benefiting agriculture there. But in the west of Bengal there was no such silting, the soil was impoverished by each successive cropping and the economic return was ever-diminishing. 'The population of the west [including the Santiniketan area] though not subject to famine, is chronically underfed.' And it affected not only agriculture through soil exhaustion but also health because malaria-causing mosquitoes bred in the small puddles and stretches of stagnant water that were prevalent in western Bengal. Endemic malaria took its toll in lessening the vitality of its victims. As Arthur notes 'it affects all classes including the leaders of the community, endangering the intellectual heritage of Bengal.'

There had been changes in the course of the great rivers (distributaries of the Ganga). One of the causes was road and railway building, creating embankments which altered irrigation and drainage. The result was dead rivers (e.g. ox-bow lakes), dead streams and dead tanks. Deforestation, e.g. for railway sleepers, and over-cultivation, were further factors.

Arthur Geddes traced the changes in population density in the sub-regions of the western part of Bengal. In some cases there had been a population fall of as much as 12 per cent a decade. There had been emigration from the area of Bengalis, partly replaced by Santals, the local tribal people. He notes the area in the west known as the Rarh from the 14th to the 19th century [it] produced so much of the ability and genius of Bengal and almost all the poets and religious men of Bengali Hinduism. Its decadence is thus a disaster, not only in itself but to the culture of the whole province and of India and a real loss to the English speaking world (Geddes 'The Regions of Bengal' 194, 195).

If the Rarh area could be irrigated and made healthy again the potentiality of its administrators and craftsmen could be realised again. What happened in the preceding century 'lends special significance to the initiative of Tagore' (Ibid. 197). A further factor Arthur Geddes notes is competition from Britain and a crushing tariff on the local crafts of muslin and silk weaving (Ibid.). In 'The population of Bengal, its Distribution and Changes', Arthur Geddes argued that the precise mapping of population density and changes was a vital service human geography could provide, e.g., in showing the effect of malaria on demography.

Conclusion on Arthur Geddes' contribution to Sriniketan

Sriniketan was fortunate to have Arthur Geddes on the staff at Sriniketan at an important period when its work was being established, and when Arthur could stand in for Leonard Elmhirst when he was away. In particular Arthur developed the analysis of what could be done made by Rabindranath and Elmhirst (and his father Patrick Geddes). They all reached conclusions of an environmental nature (as in Elmhirst's 'The Robbery of the Soil') but Arthur's research went further, giving a scientific basis to their thinking in terms of the geography of Bengal, with an explanation of areas with high prevalence of malaria. He showed why the energy of workers was declining. He shared their belief that communities had to be revived and that self-help rather than government help was essential. He also saw irrigation as a way out, though whether 'self-help' could enable this is open to question. He sought to use the energy of youth (like boy-scouts) to educate their elders.

Rabindranath, Elmhirst and Arthur Geddes all had a faith in co-operative institutions, though their efforts were not really born out something which Arthur might have pointed out from his knowledge of the crofters (subsistence farmers) of Scotland. As Sinha states in his essay in this volume that co-operatives depend on building mutual trust, which was a difficult task in the villages around Sriniketan. Arthur in the chapter 7 of his thesis tries to assess the effect of the first five years of Sriniketan, and claims a 'new solidarity' was evident in five or six villages.

There is a strong realization of the importance of health for the success of villages. In fact winning the friendship of villagers tended to come through the provision of health resources in terms of First Aid and the teaching of basic cleanliness to start with. The paper 'Health Programme for a Bengal village' goes further, e.g. arguing for a lady doctor and for domestic science teaching (File Number 129 ii).

Another feature they all had in common was a belief in the positive impact the arts could play in village regeneration. Arthur was a musician and knew the power of folk-art from his native Scotland. He wrote a drama, 'A Masque of Earth and Man' to illustrate his environmental ideas (Ibid. 129). Rabindranath and Arthur wanted to revive the *Jatra* folk-art of Bengal. Arthur pursued the link between geographical features and culture in his doctoral thesis for Montpellier. Comparing west and east Bengal, he saw how changes in the environment impinged on civilization, cultural and material, in each part of the province.

Arthur stressed in the chapter 7 of his thesis the complimentarily of Sriniketan with Visva Bharati (as did Rabindranath). The music and painting Departments at the university were encouraged to work with the villages. Scientific studies such as ecology, soil studies, public health and social anthropology could contribute to their prosperity.

The teachers at Sriniketan were keen on the teaching of crafts as a supplementary source of income to agriculture for the villages. This is one area where Sriniketan continues to thrive to this day. There are now workshops for a large range of crafts and NGOs organize the production and selling of craft goods (e.g. the famous range of Santiniketan bags).

Another real contribution of Arthur Geddes was in representing his father in the building work at Sriniketan. Arthur himself drew up a plan for Sriniketan, according to chapter 7 of his thesis. CF Andrews, writing to Patrick Geddes on 30 September, 1925 writes 'will you tell Arthur, if he is with you, that his plan of what we call 'Tata Building' has been a very great success. It crowns the slight rise of ground beautifully and is wonderfully breezy and cool. The design is almost perfect and we are all delighted with it' (Fraser 112). Further, in support of his father, Arthur says he persuaded Rabindranath that a true architect was a master builder and not merely a draughtsman.

Although Arthur Geddes and LK Elmhirst were in Sriniketan for only a relatively short time they both kept up their interest for many years, writing letters to those there and visiting when the opportunity arose (Geddes went in 1938 and 1956). They both incorporated their Sriniketan experience in later work – Elmhirst at Dartington Trust and Arthur Geddes in his academic career at Edinburgh University's Geography Department.

Notes:

1. Diksit Sinha speculates in his essay, "Arthur Geddes and Sriniketan: Explaining Underdevelopment" in this volume.

2. Geddes' unpublished thesis is available at the Rabindra Bhavan Archives.

3. Arthur Geddes' exploration of the links between geography and culture can be found in the chapter 7 of his *Man and Land in South Asia*.

Works Cited:

Elmhirst, Leonard K. *Poet and Plowman*. Rev. ed. Kolkata: Visva-Bharati Publishing Department, 2008. Print.

Fraser, Bashabi. *A Meeting of Two Minds: Geddes Tagore Letters*. Edinburgh: Word Power Books, 2005. Print.

Geddes, Arthur. "File Number 129." MS. Rabindra Bhawan Archives, Visva-Bharati.

—. "An Adventure in Reconstruction and Re-education." *Welfare* (September 1923). Print.

—. *Au Pays de Tagore: La Civilisation rural du Bengal occidental et ses facteurs geographique*. Diss. University of Montpellier, 1927. Paris: Armand Colin, 1927. Print.

—. "The Regions of Bengal." *Geography* 15. 3 (September 1929): 186-198. Print.

—. "The Population of Bengal, its Distribution and Changes: A Contribution to Geographical Method." *The Geographical Journal* 89. 4 (1939 April 1937): 344-361. Print.

—. "Two Friends: Rabindranath Tagore and Patrick Geddes." *Annual Journal of Architecture, Structure and Planning* (1961). Print.

—. *Man and Land in South Asia*. New Delhi: Concept Publishing Company. 1982. Print.

Geddes, Patrick. "The Condition and Prospects of Deccan Villages." *Bombay Co-operative Quarterly* VI. 1 (June 1922). Print.

Kar, Surendranath. Introduction. *Poet and Plowman*. By Leonard K. Elmhirst. Kolkata: Visva-Bharati Publishing Department, 2008. xiii - xiv. Print.

Kripalani, Krishna. Foreword. *Poet and Plowman*. By Leonard K. Elmhirst. Kolkata: Visva-Bharati Publishing Department, 2008. viii - xi. Print.

Sinha, Dikshit. "Rabindranath and Elmhirst: When Two Kindred Souls Met." *Rabindranath Tagore and His Circle*. Ed. Tapati Mukhopadhyay and Amrit Sen. Santiniketan: Visva Bharati, 2015. 51-68. Print.

Tagore, Rathindranath. *On the Edges of Time*. 2nd ed. Calcutta: Visva-Bharati, 1981. Print.

Tagore, Rabindranath. Introduction. "The Robbery of the Soil." By Leonard K. Elmhirst. *Poet and Plowman*. By Leonard K. Elmhirst. Kolkata: Visva-Bharati Publishing Department, 2008. 17-25. Print.

Arthur Geddes

Arthur Geddes and Sriniketan: Explaining Underdevelopment

Dikshit Sinha

ARTHUR GEDDES' PRESENCE in Sriniketan was brief but his contribution to the development of the institution was no less significant, although most of the time he remained at the background. He was overshadowed by the presence of Leonard Knight Elmhirst who played a key role in establishing the institution. But both contributed immensely in making it possible for Rabindranath Tagore's ideas of rural reconstruction come to fruition. Both contributed from their individual spheres of competence; both were concerned life-long about the way Sriniketan was taking shape. Geddes' effort to present poet's musical creations to Western audience perhaps drew more attention than his contributions to Sriniketan's attempt to initiate developmental measures. To a lesser extent, his architectural planning of Shantiniketan and Sriniketan also left a lasting impression on the then fledgling university. He straddled effortlessly across various disciplines and left his mark in several areas, such as, geography, sociology, folklore, and town planning. An accomplished violinist, he had the unique knack of versification and rendered Hebridean folk songs to English. He left for posterity critical contributions to each of the areas. In this paper, however, I shall restrict myself on his work at Sriniketan when the institution was just trying to find its feet and encountering social and cultural behaviours that put hindrance to development work.

Translating the poet's ideas of development on the ground and building the institution from scratch so that it could carry out the plan of rural development in a land dissimilar in every aspect from Western society was a no mean task. Both LK Elmhirst and Arthur Geddes were party to the idea of sovereignty and freedom of reason no matter how much people differ in their structure and pattern of civilization. Elmhirst left behind a rich account of how Sriniketan went about instituting the rural reconstruction work at Sriniketan. It has interesting comments about Scottish district administrators of the time, but Geddes finds no place in it (Elmhirst, *Poet and Plowman* 92). Perhaps this was due to the fact that Geddes did not reach Sriniketan during the period covered by Elmhirst's Diary, *Poet and Plowman* (21 November

1921 to 26 July 1922) or it might have been due to the fact that he was not directly involved in day-to-day village work.

From the meagre evidence, and that too indirect one, it seems that his role was complementary to village development work, helping in putting in place the modalities of training of village workers, the village scouts (*bratidal*) and the students of Sriniketan in consonance with the aims and objectives of rural reconstruction work, constructing the architectural structure in harmony with its environment, people and work and providing sociological and economic explanations of the prevailing ground situation. If one compares Elmhirst's account of how he along with other members went about implementing rural reconstruction work with the letters that Arthur Geddes left behind or preserved at Sriniketan, one finds unanimity of views about the problems that affected village life of the area and methods to be followed to overcome these (*Poet and Plowman* 92). Both Elmhirst and Geddes played important roles in giving shape to the institutional structure of Sriniketan. There is no doubt that the former's role in establishing and giving orientation to Sriniketan's rural reconstruction work was pre-eminent. But Arthur also put in significant effort in giving shape to Sriniketan as an institution.

Apart from helping in the construction of the institutional edifice of Sriniketan, both were also part of Tagore's effort to create a universal reach of reason and knowledge system that would help the rural people to define their own learning needs, be self-reflexive, learn in collaboration with each other and build a better future for themselves. In doing so, both helped to build the institutional structure of Sriniketan where many strands of knowledge were moulded together so that not only education could be imparted – not by bits and pieces but holistically – in terms of life as lived by the people, so that they could utilize knowledge creatively and be part of the universal whole. Elmhirst did it in helping to set up the *Siksha-Satra* school, Geddes by constructing the broader academic environment. In many ways Arthur Geddes was a worthy inheritor of his father Patrick Geddes' ideas of 'life in environment'. In his effort to understand the development of civilization and the causes of its decay he focussed attention on the nature and structure of society and culture, its interaction with the environment, both man-made and natural.

Arthur Geddes helped Sriniketan to understand the behaviour of the people as they reacted to its attempt to organize developmental measures in the area and, secondly, his effort to explain the geographical causes of decay and underdevelopment of rural areas of western part of Bengal within which Sriniketan was located. Unlike many Europeans of his period he maintained a neutral approach to the problems under scrutiny befitting the canons of science. Underlining his approach he wrote in one of his letters to Tagore that it was necessary to approach the problem from the point of view of people as they see their own 'life and country' and try to make a better one out of it and not impose a category on them from outside (Geddes, Letter to Tagore). Tagore was concerned about the decadence in culture along with sense of hopelessness and lack of efforts that had set in among the rural population of Bengal. Arthur Geddes tried to find out how an area that witnessed cultural resilience lapsed into decadence. It was not only cultural decadence that drew his attention but also the intricately related nature of the local problems drew his attention that included agriculture, education, health, cottage industries, co-operation and self-governance.

Work at Sriniketan and explaining behaviour of the rural people
If the university that the poet built was an attempt at practising the unitary concept of humanity and establishing sovereignty of reason beyond any particularism, then Geddes was one of the prime examples of such interaction on the ground between the Western culture and the orient. Geddes, as pointed out above, did not restrict his interaction within the limited sphere of implementing developmental paradigm but also tried to find how music and literature connect the two cultures. He provided sociological and cultural explanation, utilizing concepts from geography or sociology wherever necessary, regarding the way rural people around Sriniketan behaved and interacted with the field-workers, their perceptions and needs, the rationale of accepting or rejecting the hand of 'friendship' that Sriniketan offered and thus helped to understand the field-situation better and channelize the life of the people along the path of progress. For the students and staff of Sriniketan, along with Elmhirst, he framed eight point guide-lines regarding the aims, values and approach of developmental goals as well as educational goals of the institution (File 129(ii) image 22, 41). He taught sociology to the students of Shantiniketan and Sriniketan drilling in them the scientific methods of observation, enquiry and critical interpretation; he framed an outline of Sriniketan's various training programme on the basis of which the scouts, villagers and other trainees were to be trained to launch their own welfare projects. The general aim of these trainings was to introduce the boys to the wider conception of art of livelihood, that included house-crafts and handicrafts, the art of thinking and coordination of experience, and the art of expression through games, drama, design, etc. The overall objective was to multiply the centres of development of society as widely as possible.

Geddes stayed at Sriniketan for a brief period only. Due to lack of definitive documentary evidence we can only speculate but this much is sure that he left Sriniketan by the end of 1924. On April 1923 Tagore wrote to Elmhirst informing him, 'Arthur is delighted, he is doing very well in Surul' (Tagore, 'Letter' 78)[1]. From his work it seems that he was associated with the initial phase of work when communications with the villagers were just being established. During his stay he carried out extensive surveys of the villages that provided background to his Doctoral thesis. Rabindranath's explanatory model regarding reason of decay and degeneration in cultural and economic life of rural society in Bengal relied heavily on the historical priority of vibrant cultural growth during the previous century. Both Elmhirst and Geddes seem to have concurred with this view. Elmhirst tried to fashion developmental path that should be followed and expressed the need to stimulate the 'spirit of freedom' among the people that would motivate them to renew life's endless pattern and creative spirit (Elmhirst 32). Geddes, on the other hand, tried to pinpoint the factors that led to the degeneration. Elmhirst pointed out that the model of sharing in economic enterprise followed by John Cheap was an inclusive one leading to the economic prosperity of surrounding villages that was abandoned by the British administrators.[2] Geddes reasoned that the area where the villages show all the signs of decadence Tagore was so concerned about could be explained by showing how geographical factors led to the development of sociological and economic condition resulting in underdevelopment of the cultural area coterminous with the western part of Bengal (Elmhirst, 'Rabindranath Tagore and Sriniketan' 203). But first let us find out how he reacted to the situation that prevailed at Sriniketan.

An anarchic group

Giving his impression about the variegated group assembled for carrying out developmental aims of Sriniketan he wrote:

> This interesting group of men of many kinds and nations who though astonishingly anarchic in both senses of the word are yet united by the regional and international ideals of the place, and personality of the poet, one of the noblest looking men or sages, I have ever seen and one of the delightful companions (File 129(ii) image 14).

Elmhirst along with Rathindranath Tagore, Kalimohan Ghosh and others gave shape to the institutional structure of Sriniketan, pinpointed the problems affecting the rural life, framed the rules of behaviour, the role the institution should play in development process, methods of intervention and initiated contact with the villagers. His stay at Sriniketan lasted only for a brief period. Geddes' stay too did not last long but, perhaps, was not intermittent. Rabindranath wanted him to train the Sriniketan workers in village development work. He supplemented the Sriniketan workers' activities with explanations of the situation prevailing in the villages. Describing his relationship with LK Elmhirst he wrote to his father on March 23, 1923:

> In a way I am glad Elmhirst is away for it gives one more responsibility and intellectual freedom. Yet I feel him a future ally in life such as I've

seldom met or not yet at all and a friend lost through his departure, still in a way we're making a 'common' expression in the usual sense. I'm anxious that he should feel I have been to his aim in execution as well as intention, while not rigidly sticking to his by any means. There is nothing more essential than that work should be carried on with full regard for past attainment so that this shall not be lost and dull regard for past plan. Above all in India and in this ramshackle institution 'stunts' are excellent in their way *but only if related to the whole and understood as such* (emphasis added).

This holistic approach, consonant with Tagore's philosophy of *samagrata* (the whole/totality in which environment played an important role) and treating the people as fellow human beings governed his work at Sriniketan too. Elaborating the approach to developmental work he proceeded to write,

> ...we ask ourselves can we love, know and then actively help our neighbours (Arthur, Letter to Patrick Geddes, 23 March, 1923).

The idea was to attain sympathy, knowledge and power of active help. His stay at Sriniketan essentially revolved around these three elements of behaviour followed in interacting with the surrounding community. If active help was to be provided then knowledge about the situation was essential. Young Arthur had an abundance of the former and proceeded to gather the rest. His sympathy for the people also was not based from the perspective of a person of superior race or class; rather it was from empathic understanding of the situation and humanitarian zeal to deliver proper welfare measures. Therefore, the rule he emphasized was: never to advice the people without experience to back up. It is worth remembering that Geddes' stay was for a brief period only. The insight he achieved about the cultural situation speaks volume of his abilities as a sociologist. In passing we note that this too was the backbone of Sriniketan's policy of intervention, be it in social, economic or in numerous practical matters touching people's day-to-day living. This approach was inspired by the poet but both Geddes and Elmhirst made it the scientific canons of Sriniketan's work.

Giving a detail account of his work at Sriniketan Arthur wrote to his father, Patrick Geddes, on 12-3-23:

> My village investigation has not yet begun; too many problems of planning, etc., at which I seems to be of some use and am in some demand at Santiniketan and here (Sriniketan or Surul Khoti).
>
> I realise that I was little rash perhaps in saying there would be no more of the fanciful architecture of Suren Kar- Rathi Tagore's artist confidant – since Rathi's (the poet's son) house still to be build while the foundations are laid and the plan therefore are fixed...

As well as planning we are trying to clear the place up – move those broken down carts, tidy away the wrecks, the heaps, the midden, the mosquito holes and drains and actually fix camp latrines. 'Gandhi Day' – in memory of a sort of fiery visit here a few years' ago of Mahatmaji's was celebrated on Saturday by a holiday. All the servants being relieved of their duties by volunteer cooks, etc. While Pearson, by keeping tactfully in the background as a mere labourer, managed to get up corps of cleaners which I joined to see who would work and also from a policy and for fun. They worked well for an hour or two, got quite keen. This had its effect in suggesting a bigger clean up from LK and hastening its execution. Someone noticed there were hardly any Bengali among clean up corps mostly west India, etc.

My teaching here consists of two nature study (double periods of an hour and a half each, per week), two library evenings, at first discussion on plans, etc, maps ways tackling our surveys of nature and man, students of Sriniketan school are just 10 boys who came down here from Santiniketan school a year ago but they are developing into manly fellows varying very much. They are gradually taking charge of special jobs – dairy, tannery, weaving, scouting and each has a garden plot and most have chickens. The staff have a complete charge of the above, one whose specially I hope to be assistant to a wonderful village worker – pulling the people together in his gentle way with great success – Kali Babu by name.

He was asked by the poet to 'introduce to the students' of Shantiniketan, Patrick Geddes' graphic method, i.e. his sociological interpretation of history and culture, diagrammatically expressed. This he proceeded to do during July-Sept, 1923. He emphasised the use of scientific method so that the society could be studied by dispassionate observations and enquiry. This was done at a time when sociology as a discipline did not even had toe-hold in the area. The students were asked to go to villages and study them on their own and assess the situation prevailing there. One rule religiously stuck to, as pointed out above, was not to give advice without adequate experience and insiders' knowledge. The approach worked out by Arthur created the ground of Sriniketan's long series of village and other kinds of surveys that helped it to interpret the situation, formulate policies and initiate appropriate actions. Later, when Arthur needed additional information or supports for the interpretation that he was making in preparation of his thesis to be submitted to Montpellier University he sought these from Kalimohan Ghosh. But the interpretation that he provided was solely based on his critical interpretation of the data he collected. As Sriniketan's development work unfolded many aspects of people's behaviour baffled the young sociologist. He studied the socio-historical development of the area and meticulously collected data on various aspects of present rural life and wove these into a tapestry of social structure and processes and tried to unravel why the society that one time exhibited resilience and excellence now fell behind. Even his explanation of prevalence of malaria in the area tried to go beyond the reasons that appeared on the surface to be true.

Value of Research

While Elmhirst went on exploring the area, finding out the problems people suffered from, their cultural inclinations, linking the institution with the local and district administration and recruiting the required personnel, Geddes tried to find out deeper aspects that underlay people's behaviour and affected planned action. The research work he carried out was supported by the belief in the value of meticulous research and necessity to look at life from as varied angles as possible, especially, for understanding the situation of Sriniketan:

> ... the knowledge needed here can only be won by patient research – by observation in the villages and countryside synthesized in the studies ... the results, if carried to the point of publication will be of real value to co-workers and those who have to work and frame a policy. One survey was submitted to the Royal Commission of Agriculture. Economic surveys, such as, Dr Mann's 'Land Labour in a Deccan Village' though far too few – are invaluable yet, even this points to the need a further sociological and interpretative survey, as 'Land Labour and Community Life in a Bengal Village'. This demand insight, sympathy and patient work, a task which has been attempted. *To those studies in the Visva-Bharati of a more scholarly and historic nature it is the complement and fundamental for research into the value and reality of Indian civilization* (Geddes, 'Agriculture', emphasis added).

His own research and ability to arrive at empathic understanding of rural society's situation and giving emphasis that mere altruistic attitude is not going to help much followed poet's three essential preconditions of developmental work: collective action, fortification and consolidation of the groups' boundary and organization (Tagore, 'Sabhapatir Abhibhashan' 3). He emphasized that the role of community organization in developmental work of such nature was more than essential and gave examples from Europe's history. His research work, especially village surveys, likewise anticipated and prepared the groundwork of Sriniketan's future research work.

But before we dwell on this, let us find out how he tried to understand the problems faced by the villagers and Sriniketan's effort to instil co-operative spirit among villagers. When Sriniketan began its rural reconstruction work the villagers were torn apart by constant feuds resulting in mindless lawsuits against each other that only benefited the lawyers of local Bolpur town. Slowly Sriniketan was able to make the villagers realise the futility of constant feuding and instead work for collective development. Geddes, on the other hand, became interested in the basic issues affecting villagers' social life and began exploring the intricate pattern of relationship between environment, economy, poverty, and ill health affecting their culture and society.

Instilling collective spirit

One of the pillars of the poet's reconstruction of rural life was organizing the economy and the society based on co-operative principles (the other two were self-reliance and endogenous development or development from within). But despite realizing the necessity of organizing co-operative from the very outsets it took a quite a while for Sriniketan to implement this. Sriniketan did begin to organize a consumer's co-operative at Sriniketan from 1923 (Elmhirst, *Poet and Plowman* 94). It quickly became self-sufficient and led to the chalking out of a plan to open such co-operatives in the villages. But soon it had to postpone full-scale opening of co-operatives. Exploratory interactions with the villagers by Elmhirst (along with Kalimohan Ghosh) at the initial stage led to the realization of the existence of multidimensional nature of the problems faced by the villages. Co-operative endeavour and opening of co-operative organizations that would begin to address the basic issues affecting the economic life of the people was agreed upon. Over and above all these, the need to establish secure communication with the villagers and solving the issue of lack of trust that stood in the way of collective enterprise among the people drew urgent attention (Elmhirst, 'Rabindranath Tagore and Sriniketan' 206-07). The people on their own too began to respond to Sriniketan's presence and began to articulate their needs and preferences, such as establishing consumers' co-operative stores; weavers expressed their requirements of steady supply of good quality yearns and marketing of produce. This was as early as 22 February 1922. In response to this, the idea of initiating 'some form of project system' so that people 'can learn from a co-operative enterprise from the outset' was mooted (Elmhirst, *Poet and Plowman* 111). However the circumstances that began to unfold led to postponing such an idea.

Sriniketan opened its outdoor hospital at the end of 1922 with the help of American nurse, Gretchen Green. Large number of patients from far and near, especially, malaria affected patients from surrounding villages begun to come down in the hope of receiving treatment of their various ailments. It was realised that first Sriniketan must address the health condition of the people. This and other intermediary factors intervened and stood in the resolve to open co-operative organization first. It was realised that before any developmental plan was launched it was far more important to find a way to their heart first and ameliorate the living condition as far as possible. Organizing the people to tackle the raging malaria, helping them secure square meals, improving village roads, removing the menace caused by monkeys (Langur) became part of Sriniketan's 'project work'. Simultaneously effort to win the 'friendship' of the community, building a network of relationship of trust, instilling a right spirit of work among the village workers and implementing sound community organization in the villages through common actions mentioned above, helping the people solve their own problems from the perspective of common ideas and goals became the handmaiden of the 'project work'.

Geddes provided explanation of how the steps taken by Sriniketan helped to further their objectives. According to him friendship was won through 'healing old feuds', by providing medical work in the villages, helping the people to create an atmosphere of mutual interaction by establishing the village scout or *bratidals*, introduction of new crops, improving animal husbandry and so forth, the long line of such work thus made the people realise that there was 'no individual profit or pay but common good'. Explaining how this was achieved Geddes wrote:

> Fine work has been done in healing old feuds, in averting fresh ones and now strengthening the will for peace of the village elders and starting work which testify to a new solidarity. For instance, the roads in five or six villages are being re-made by their inhabitants, about a mile or more in each... Economic efficiency won by health will be seen at a glance when the mothers, housewives or the breadwinners helpless through sickness are cured of hunger and ruins are averted. Their poverty, cause and effect of disease, forbids for payment by the villagers themselves and so long treatment must be mainly charitable but should really be seen how the trust won by healing brings lasting friendship (File 129(ii) image 10-11).

It was only when the vital spirit of mutual trust showed signs of taking root once again, trust build through community organization so sorely shaken by constant buffeting by economic disasters, social divisions, diseases, disputes and dissension, Sriniketan slowly began its work of not only opening of various types of co-operatives but all round developmental work through self-help and endogenous efforts.

Another important action, deliberately taken up, was organizing scout groups called *bratidal* from among the village boys. Tagore while working in his ancestral zamindary estate Selidaha found the efficacy of organizing bratidal (boy scouts) among the village boys an important tool of endogenous village development, for instilling values of self-help and as a bridge between the villagers and outside world. He advocated that forming bratidal would also help in cementing the tie between Sriniketan as an institution and the villagers. Similarly, we find that the utility of forming boy scouts (bratidal was given a formal shape by Sriniketan) was approvingly spoken of as an enabling measure for opening new window of relationship with the villagers where there was none previously. While other workers were busy in setting up bratidal organization in the villages Geddes tried to find out the efficacy of the group as a methodological tool. He analysed and compared the prevalence of malaria in villages where bratidal worked assiduously to keep the village ponds and drains clean with villages where inhabitants were slow to form such groups and fell behind in cleanliness. The latter was evidently due to lack of community spirit and zeal. The villages where bratidal worked to keep it clean remained practically free from malaria. This helped Sriniketan to demonstrate the necessity to the villagers in creating organizations from within and the tangible gain that would accrue to them from it. Prevalence of malaria in the locality was a constant factor. But Geddes as well as the doctors pointed out that other diseases were no less frequent and caused serious health problems to the villagers. Combating these required different approach. In course of his work he concurred with the poet about the breakdown in the collective effort that underlay the degeneration and decay in the village life. The lack of effort to keep the sources of drinking water and environment clean led to various problems including health and economic problems of the villages. Therefore, he made the finer point of developmental practice, i.e. providing helps from outside do not necessarily lead to development.

Arthur's concern and his effort to arrive at better level of understanding regarding the nature and pattern of society and culture of Bengal led him to constantly seek knowledge from the poet and European intellectuals. Even when he was preparing to present his thesis to Montpellier University in France in 1927 he wrote to Tagore seeking to tap his knowledge about Bengal. Based on his investigation and knowledge gathered about rural life around Sriniketan and also about Bengal he submitted his thesis entitled, 'The Land of Tagore: Rural civilization of Western Bengal and its Geographical factors' in 1927. The thesis sought to find out the structure of civilization of Western Bengal and explain the relationship with the geographical and occupational organizations.

The thesis did not merely delve deep into the reasons of underdevelopment of western area of Bengal but also threw useful light on the functioning of Sriniketan and has contemporary relevance. He pointed out that the Elmhirst gave up the idea of 'self-sufficient' Sriniketan and decided that it needed continued financial assistance for a long time to come. His experience of working in the area convinced him that the catalytic role and 'independent strategy' envisaged for the institution would not be 'compatible with the technological process of preparation nor with development' (Geddes, *Au*

Pays de Tagore 198). Taking into account the decadence in culture and economy, misery from which the people suffered from, rigidity of caste system, inadequate education, etc., Geddes argued that for Sriniketan to attain its objective 'there must be co-ordination of knowledge, a synthesis which will guide the line of action. Without the practical feedbacks philosophy may become too abstract, too removed from life' (Geddes, *Au Pays de Tagore* 218). Interestingly, Patrick Geddes in one of his letter to Tagore (undated but most probably posted in 1927) wrote that the thesis 'illustrate the useful application of western science – in its synthetic and not merely analytical form – to Eastern problem'.

Explaining underdevelopment

In what way the thesis of Arthur Geddes was applicable in solving problems faced by western Bengal, especially, problems faced by Birbhum district within which Sriniketan was situated? Apart from depicting how the regional culture was constituted Geddes tried to find out the areas of progress made in the past and decay that set in later in the region, a point that he returned later in his essay entitled 'Regions of Bengal' (187). In this paper he tried to demonstrate the correlation of geographical divisions and cultural regions of Bengal, its decadence and progress. In his doctoral thesis he tried to explain the reasons of prevalence of malaria and low yield rate of paddy in Birbhum, Bankura and western part of *Rarh* cultural region. While the endemic nature of malaria, especially in western part of Bengal was explained by some experts as due to lack of proper drainage, marshy lands, building of artificial embankments and canals or building of bridges over rivers impeding the free flow of rivers' courses Arthur explained the prevalence of malaria and economic decay as primarily due to the dead river courses of the western Bengal. Terming the Damodar and other rivers of the region as 'dead rivers' he wrote,

The slow 'death' of the rivers brings with it not only a change in the conditions of agriculture but in those of health – primarily in increase in malaria. By 1850, the population of the Western Delta was afflicted with epidemic malaria, which is believed to have struck down something like half the many millions of its population. Ever since, poverty and malaria have remained.

The reasons seem to that the breeding of the anopheline mosquito, which is actually checked by the flow of silt-laden waters in the monsoon (the period of danger), is favoured by the formation of the small poodles and stretches of stagnant water such as are formed in the west under present conditions. That is to say, the same conditions which favour malaria are those which ruin rice growing. Malaria in part is 'poverty disease': hence the combination of underfeeding with conditions favouring infection is irresistible. The spread of these conditions eastward take place by out-breaks of violent epidemic malaria, accompanied by heavy mortality, which, as they die down, give place to endemic malaria, and henceforth this takes a steady toll lessened vitality and in life.

... Not only the people suffer, but the leaders of the community too, and hence the survival of all that makes for intellectual heritage of Bengal is encouraged... What we have lost through the fall of some of the fairest districts cannot be estimated, for those which have been struck are those which in the past contributed overwhelmingly the greatest proportion of men of religious and literary genius ('Regions' 188).

We need not enter here into the argument and counter arguments as to the factor(s) that led to prevalence of malaria in Bengal. It rages on even now. It is true, perhaps, that only one causative factor may not be behind the spread of malaria in all regions. However, Geddes' diagnosis of the problem that affected western Bengal due to the decay of the river's course is worth pondering. The 'slow death of the river' might have resulted in series of subsequent economic and other factors that began to have a cascading effect on the rural population and social structure. It may also be pointed out here that almost annual occurrence of floods in western part of Bengal these days might be connected to the slow death of river long ago pointed out by Geddes. The problem has not been addressed even now because the factors that led to siltation of river-bed of the region as suggested by Geddes long ago was never taken notice of or seriously attended to.

After submission of the thesis and award of the degree he became busy with the problems of peasant farmers and lands development of Western Mediterranean, Human Geography as well his teaching assignments. But he constantly returned to his first love that of understanding the relationship of civilization with the environment. He visited Sriniketan in 1939 and 1956. The subject of Bengal was tried to be looked at within the larger context of India as a geographical unit, the variation in the pattern of growth/decay of population, especially of western Bengal. In 1934 with this idea in his mind he wrote to Tagore:

Bengal is daily in my thought and I wish that someday I might visit India and Bengal. As I said, my study of Bengal is nearing completion. Further, I've a capable assistant helping me with preparatory maps of Indian population – as a basis of my promised work on India; of course India only be a reconnaissance but when that is made the visit of India would show me so much that I did not see (for lack of eyes!) when I was there last and that no one has described.

In 1937, he published a paper entitled 'Population of Bengal: A Contribution to geographical method'. In the paper he demonstrated relationship of density of population and its regional distributional pattern with various geographical areas of Bengal and how it changed slowly over a long stretch of time along with health and well-being of the people of the area, by using cartographical method ('geographical meaning of demography'). The paper argued that the eastern region of Bengal was on the path of development as evidenced by population growth and economic expansion while the western part of Bengal was not only in a geographically moribund state but at the same time showed depression in population growth. While the population densities of western part of Bengal rarely exceeds 500 to the square mile the eastern part 'drawn north to south from near the confluence with Brahamputra-Jamuna to the sea' have 'almost uninterrupted high density of 900 or 1000' ('Population of Bengal' 347). The latter area's population is relatively flourishing and increasing, while below that this region, the people are impoverished and sickly, and their numbers are stagnant or actually diminishing ('Population of Bengal' 347). He points out:

> In Bengal however the highest district variability is 3 per cent on the western uplands, on which I have shown the change in fifty years as +45 to +20 per cent in the jungles, down to almost 10 per cent on malarious fans and the Delta (cf. Fig. 2). In the western central Delta proper the decrease of almost 10 per cent has been accompanied by a variability of only 2 per cent, so unvarying has been the effect of endemic malaria since before the first census. In Eastern Bengal districts however, with their total increase of almost 100 per cent, the variability has been less than 1 per cent., so steady has the rate of increase been. Meantime the calamitous state of the whole of the western and central Delta calls for urgent action. There is little doubt that in this land, which less than eighty years ago was an abode of health and of high civilization, the water and silt supply for agriculture can be increased, and with this malaria can be largely controlled. Unfortunately inattention to crops and health and concentration on such modern advantages as cheap railways, roads, and canals-run across the natural drainage system and designed to serve the commerce and industry of Calcutta, London, or Dundee form part of a general disregard of the peasants' own food supply and health. It is this which has permitted, and even helped to bring about, the tragedy of general decay and death. (360)

The tragedy of 'general decay and death' that Geddes found in the rural areas surrounding Sriniketan led him to search for the causative factors that could only be unearthed by examining these on the broader canvas of Bengal as a geographical region (even on a national scale) and cultural area. His journey from a small rural area to a broader scale of Bengal and India led him to search for the peculiarities of Bengal. The conclusion that he long ago drew from his experience of working at Sriniketan perhaps have some amount of truth in it. Development began at a micro level look to be successful and long lasting for a brief period but if projected on broader regional canvas and a higher level of coordination of actions between developmental practitioners, government officials and knowledge generated by sciences could be synthesized and implemented then achieving welfare of human beings might become greater. This is hardly followed. Therefore, the tragedy created by nature multiplied by actions of human beings remains to haunt us.

[I am grateful to Prof. Neil Fraser for his comments on an earlier draft of this paper. However, I am solely responsible for any omission or commission.]

Notes:

1. Neil Fraser has come to the conclusion that Arthur Geddes stayed at Sriniketan from March 1923 to Nov. 1924. (in this volume).

2. L.K. Elmhirst op.cit. He writes, "Cheap's tradition was an intriguing one, and stirs one to dream new theories. Under what, let us hope, was his benign influence, he built up a network of huge clearing stations. He encouraged spinning and weaving in all the villages around, collated his produce and distributed the raw cotton from Surul as well as other goods for sale, and brought the whole area to a pitch of prosperity well illustrated by pukka (solid) buildings, homes and temples, in such villages, as I have already seen." (p.86)

References:

Elmhirst, L.K. *Poet and Plowman.* 2008 edition. Kolkata: Visva-Bharati, 1975. Print.

Elmhirst, L.K. "Rabindranath Tagore and Sriniketan." *Visva-Bharati Quarterly, Tagore Centenary Volume* 26. 3-4 (1951): 206-207. Print.

File 129(ii)/ image 10-11, R.B. Archive, Visva-Bharati.

File 129(ii) image, 14, Rabindra-Bhavana Archive (R.B.), Visva-Bharati.

File 129(ii) image, 14, 22, 41, Rabindra-Bhavana Archive (R.B.), Visva-Bharati.

Geddes, Arthur. "Agriculture." N. d. MS. Rabindra-Bhavana Archive, Visva-Bharati.

Geddes, Arthur. *Au Pays de Tagore: la civilisation rurale du Bengale Occidental et ses facteurs gdographiques.* Paris: Armand Collin, 1927. Print.

Geddes, Arthur. *Au Pays de Tagore: la civilisation rurale du Bengale Occidental et ses facteurs gdographiques.* Trans. Dr Meera Ghosh. Paris: Armand Collin, 1927. Print.

Geddes, Arthur. Letter to Patrick Geddes. 12 March 1923. MS. Rabindra Bhavana Archive, Visva-Bharati.

Geddes, Arthur. Letter to Patrick Geddes. 23 March 1923. MS. Rabindra Bhavana Archive, Visva-Bharati.

Geddes, Arthur. Letter to Rabindranath Tagore. 24 March 1926. MS. R.B. Archive, Visva-Bharati.

Geddes, Arthur. Letter to Rabindranath Tagore. 4 December 1934. MS. Rabindra-Bhavana Archive, Visva-Bharati.

Geddes, Arthur. "Population of Bengal: A contribution to geographical method." *Geographical Jr.* 89.4 (1937): 344-361. Web.

Geddes, Arthur. "The Regions of Bengal." *Geography* 15.3 (1929): 186-198. Web.

Geddes, Patrick. Letter to Rabindranath Tagore. 12 March 1927. TS. R.B. Archive, Visva-Bharati

Tagore, Rabindranath. "Letter to L.K. Elmhirst." 18 April 1923. Letter no.14. *Purabi: A Miscellany in Memory of Rabindranath Tagore, 1861–1941.* Eds. K. Dutta & A Robinson. U. K.: Tagore Centre, 1991. p. 78. Print.

Tagore, Rabindranath. "Sabhapatir Abhibhashan." *Palliprakriti.* Ed. Pulinbihari Sen. Kolkata: Visva-Bharati, 1986. Print.

Scientific Innovation in India

Acharya Prafulla Chandra Ray

The East's Writing Back to the West: Acharya Prafulla Chandra Ray and Postcoloniality

Biswanath Banerjee

IN A LETTEr to the wife of Chittaranjan Das, Acharya Prafulla Chandra Ray wrote,

> I can assure you, however, dear sister, that in serving my favourite science I have only one idea in my mind, namely, that through her I should serve my country... God knows, I have no other object in my life (Ray, *Life and Experiences* I: 233).

In the late 19th and early 20th century, India witnessed a steady progress and development of science, which was largely inspired by the British colonial expansion and its imperial practices. The deployment of science by the British as a facilitator for colonial rule generated a corresponding interest in science among the Western educated indigenous intelligentsia. These intellectuals and scientists sought to cultivate and utilize the knowledge of science and technology in constructing the concept of nationhood and to challenge the colonial apparatus. Among these leading scientists of India, Acharya Prafulla Chandra Ray (1861–1944) was one of the most important figures.

Despite Ray's ungrudging admiration for the progressive Western civilization and his ardent support for Western education and learning, he was harshly critical of Western belligerency, its singular passion for power and wealth, its egoism and blind contempt for the East. However, being well acquainted with modern enlightened Western culture, Ray had unhesitatingly acknowledged its remarkable scientific and technological progress, while he simultaneously critiqued the Western hegemonic claims over rationality and science and questioned its cultural superiority. Ray conceived science as a fraternity where the colonized could claim equality and therefore resist colonial stereotyping. Through his scientific researches, what Ray did try to proclaim was not to thrust off Western civilization, but rather to prove to the world the ability of the East to undertake original research, which had a rich scientific and intellectual heritage.

This article explores Prafulla Chandra Ray's complex and somewhat problematic approach towards the West, which was marked by a constant dialectic of acceptance and resistance. It focuses on Ray's first visit to Europe at the age of twenty one, when he went to do his BSc course at the University of Edinburgh, Scotland. This visit of Ray's marks a crucial juncture in his career as a scientist. It is also significant in terms of our understanding of Prafulla Chandra Ray's complex postcolonial and nationalist consciousness, evident in the corpus of his work and writings.

In reading Ray's accounts of his upbringing and his childhood experiences, we find clear references to the development of a strong nationalist spirit under his father's tutelage and through his early initiation to the Brahmo Samaj: 'Strange as it may appear, from my boyhood I was unconsciously drawn towards the Brahmo Samaj. Various were the circumstances contributing to it. My father, though outwardly conforming to the current Hindu faith, was at heart liberal to the core' (Ray, *Life and Experiences* I: 30). Ray's close acquaintance with the writings of Rammohun Roy, Akshay Kumar Dutta, Keshub Chandra Sen on the one hand, and his early initiation to the English literature on the other, made him familiar with the modern enlightened Western culture which consequently instilled in him his life-long abhorrence for irrational indigenous social practices. Ray wrote: 'The caste system, as it is in vogue in the existing Hindu Society, with its pernicious appendage of untouchability, appeared to me the very negation of the relation existing between man and man. Enforced widowhood, child-marriage and other customs were equally my abomination' (Ibid.).

The harmonious co-existence of this duality—a strong nationalist sentiment on the one hand and an inward critique of the various social evils and customs on the other—was omnipresent in Ray. Being a progressive, rationalist thinker, Ray conceived India as a modern, enlightened postcolonial nation which could be built with a synthesis of the East and the West. This syncretism of Ray is predominantly located in his account of his several tours to Europe that he made at different points of his career, which also explore a constant oscillation between his scientific self and the nationalist self.

Prafulla Chandra Ray's father, Harish Chandra Ray, had always had the ambition of sending at least one of his sons to England for higher education. However, he did not have the means to financially enable this. Prafulla Chandra, was well aware of his father's dream. When he took admission to the Metropolitan school, he decided to prepare for the Gilchrist Scholarship for Edinburgh University with the encouragement of Professor Pedler (Mahanti). Ray prepared for the scholarship while he was in Calcutta, an arduous task which involved succeeding in a highly competitive examination. Ray was successful, and became one of the first winners from India of this prestigious Scholarship.

Ray sailed for England in the middle of 1882. After 33 days of travel, Ray was received at Fenchurch Street Station by Jagadish Chandra Bose who was then a student of Cambridge University. On arriving in London, Ray was struck by the 'gorgeous visions of the metropolis of the British Empire on the Thames', as he described: 'the stupendous area it covered simply bewildered me' (Ibid. 53). He poured over maps to discover bus and underground railway routes across the city and found the cultural encounter at the metropolitan centre fascinating.

After a week's stay in London, Ray made his way to Edinburgh to begin his study for a BSc in Science. Ray was moved by the landscape of Edinburgh, as in his autobiography he wrote: 'It is surrounded by picaresque scenes and the sea (Firth of Forth) is quite near. I took my lodgings near the meadows and within a few minutes' walk of Arthur's Seat, which was my favourite resort during my holidays' (Ibid. 56). Ray was also impressed by the rich intellectual and cultural ambience of Edinburgh, which, as he described 'had then a time-honoured reputation as a seat of learning.' Ray added: 'Metaphysics and medicine, especially the latter, attracted pupils from far and near. Physical Science as represented by Chemistry and Physics found also eminent exponents' (Ibid. 54).

Ray was simultaneously impressed by the lifestyle of Scottish students, many of whom came from farming families. They were assiduously keen to do well, with great expectations set on their shoulders from hardworking families and they had very little money for revelry and alcohol. Ray admired the thrifty, hardworking, debating Scottish student.

This appreciation of Ray can be read in contrast to his bitter criticism of the contemporary educational scenario in India, against which Ray made his life-long complaints. After returning from Edinburgh, when Ray joined the Presidency College Calcutta, he got the opportunity to get acquainted with the average mentality of an Indian student, whose sole aim was to obtain a university degree, 'to secure a hallmark, which is a passport to a professional career or a clerical appointment in Government departments' (Ibid. 147). As an honest devotee of scientific study and research, Ray trenchantly criticized this 'degree-hunting mania' of an Indian youth and called the contemporary universities as the 'huge factories for mass-production of graduates' (Ibid. 259, 260). In contrast to this 'insane craze' of an Indian student to obtain a university degree, Ray praised the real thirst for knowledge of the true votaries of science in the West, as he remarked: 'In Europe there have been votaries of science during the last four centuries who have pursued it for its own sake, never expecting to reap any pecuniary benefit' (Ibid. 147, 148). Lamenting over this absence of a genuine passion in an Indian youth to acquire knowledge, Ray remarked:

The fact is there is scarcely any genuine thirst for knowledge in our land. One may have the hall-mark of two or three degrees, but that is no proof that he has acquired a love of learning. You can bring the horse to the trough, but you cannot make it drink. The passing of examinations has become the be-all and end-all of the existence of our youths. And thus we cannot expect any good result from their study of sciences. Indeed, nowhere in this world is to be found such a mad craving for securing the University degree. And our graduates bid farewell to the Goddess of learning as soon as they have passed the examination. After his graduation a young man often thinks that he has nothing more to learn. Whereas in other countries, the university career is regarded as the period for apprenticeship. He begins to specialize himself after finishing his university career (Ray, 'The Place of Science' 129, 130).

Ray made a constant comparison of the status of scientific education in India with that in Europe, and tried to foreground the drawbacks and lacunae of the contemporary education system in India, which to Ray, must be reformed by following the model shown by the West. Ray located the intellectual stagnation of India within the steady degeneration of the spirit of enquiry among the people, especially the youth. Hence, Ray's repeated references to a European's insatiable desire to know 'the *how* and *why* of phenomena' (*A History of Hindu Chemistry* I: 195) was to motivate the Indians to imbibe this very spirit within themselves. It was through this zeal and effort that India could once again regain its lost prestige which had once been earned by its ancestors.

Ray always looked at the modern West as a source of inspiration and encouragement to the Indians who should never hesitate to learn and appropriate the new discoveries and researches made by the West in the field of science and technology. He obtained his BSc from the University of Edinburgh in April 1886, being one of only 3 graduates in BSc in the Department of Physical Experimental Sciences in that year. He then stayed on a further year to get a Doctor of Science degree, for which he wrote a thesis on 'Conjugated Sulphates of the Copper-magnesium Group'. In 1888 a research paper based on the thesis was published in the Proceedings of the Royal Society of Edinburgh.

Ray is recorded in the 1888 University Calendar as the Vice-President of the Chemical Society (Fraser 44). This was the oldest Chemical Society in the world, founded by Joseph Black in 1785. As the Vice-President, Ray often had to chair meetings of the Society. It helped him pursue his vision that science could help industry in Bengal or he was able to make visits to various chemical works through the Edinburgh University Chemical Society. He mentioned in his Autobiography about his visits to Pullar's Dye Works, Perth, MacEwen's

Brewery, Edinburgh, the distillation of shale in Burntisland, and the sulphuric acid works of Tennant and Co. Glasgow (Ray, *Life and Experiences* I: 93).

In the University of Edinburgh, Ray had the experiences of working with Professor Alexander Cum Brown, who was his supervisor and a scholar of repute. Ray's experiences of working in the University laboratory at Edinburgh led him to think of forming a modern laboratory in India, which would be a model for the aspiring students and researchers of his country. After returning from Edinburgh and joining the Presidency College Calcutta, Ray, along with Sir Alexander Pedler, took initiatives to modernize the Presidency College laboratory. He had a copy of the plan of the Edinburgh University laboratory, and Pedler collected some plans of the German laboratories. It was by their joint effort that in the year 1894, that the Chemical Department of the Presidency College was finally shifted to the newly formed building with a new laboratory of its own, which was soon to become the model for other chemical laboratories in India (Ibid. 112, 113).

In 1904, Ray made his second visit to Europe as a Government Officer of India, and visited the Faraday Research Laboratory and the laboratories of the Imperial College of Science and University College London. On the continent he visited Charlottenburg (near Berlin), Berne, Geneva, Zurich, Frankfurt and finally his most-desired destination, Paris, where, apart from meeting Berthelot for the first time, he also met Sylvain Levi, an authority on Buddhist literature (*Life and Experiences* I: 131-137, Lourdusamy 159). Ray called his visit to the metropolis of France as a 'pilgrimage' to him, because, 'the Birth of Modern Chemistry is associated with it' (Ray, *Life and Experiences* I: 134).

This deep admiration of Ray (towards)for the European scientists, and his warm appreciation towards their achievements and contributions in the field of science, point to the very syncretism of Ray's postcoloniality, which was always receptive to the West, whenever it found anything (best)good in it. Ray firmly believed 'that contact of one civilization with another brings about strange and on the whole beneficial results' (Ibid. 142). Interestingly, here we locate a complex duality in Ray's approach towards the West. During his sojourn in Europe, on his visit to the laboratories of the famous European scientists, Ray marvelled at the modern scientific researches and discoveries of Levi, Berthelot, Fourcroy, Lavoisier and others. He (approached with open arms) admired the scientific vigour of the West and sought to emulate the same to restore the scientific temperament in India. At the same time, Ray was acutely conscious of contesting the West's depicting the East as scientifically barren. Thus, through his monumental work, *The History of Hindu Chemistry*, he tried to construct the history of a vibrant Hindu scientific culture, untainted by foreign influences. This knowledge of the past glory, according to Ray, would stimulate the people to regain their true self.

Thus, through a perfect synthesis between the ancient Indian scientific heritage and the intellectual and material development of the West, Ray aimed to create a progressive, hybrid Indian culture which would be unique in its character and independent in its identity.

However, despite his ungrudging admiration for Western education and learning, Ray remained forever harshly critical of the despotic British rule in India, which was marked by brute force, blind selfishness and sheer arrogance. This strong anti-colonial nationalist sentiment, which forever remained present in Ray, was first reflected in his essay, 'India Before and After the Mutiny', which Ray wrote for an essay competition in 1885, while he was studying at the University of Edinburgh. In 1886 the Rector of the University, who had been Secretary of State for India during 1867–68, set a prize essay on 'India before and after the mutiny.' Though Ray remained busy working in the laboratory and preparing for his BSc examination, it was his ardent nationalist spirit that drove him to participate in the competition and to contribute his share on the subject: 'I was a novice in the art of writing a book, especially of the description now required, but being an Indian I thought the opportunity should not be flung away and having accumulated a vast mass of materials I now made bold to put ink to paper' (Ray, *Life and Experiences* I: 62).Ray read avidly and widely on Indian history and economics, in English and in French. He read articles in the *Hindu Patriot, Fortnightly, Contemporary Reviews and Nineteenth Century* and Parliamentary debates.

As an early document of Ray's nationalist self assertion, this essay deserves a special mention. In his essay, Ray made a detailed critical assessment of the political, historical and economic conditions of India under the British Raj, and conceived the Mutiny as the First Anti-colonial Liberation Struggle of the Indians. The text eventually reveals a strong nationalist sentiment of the young author and his diatribe against the British colonial domination in India. Giving a penetrating analysis of the colonial polity and economy and its adverse implications (upon)for contemporary India, Ray intended to make his fellow Englishmen aware of the British atrocities to Indians through this essay. He appealed to the English to adopt a more generous and humane policy, which could bring a closer union between the two countries and could bridge the gulf between the two races.

In his essay on the Mutiny, Ray trenchantly criticized the ruthless economic exploitation of the British colonizers in India, which had consequently resulted in a severe financial crisis during and after the outbreak of the Mutiny. Ray here particularly criticized the absolute misgovernance (of)by the contemporary British officials and the despotic and arbitrary rule of the various governor generals employed by the British Government. This caused a total collapse of the entire branches of Indian economy and the extreme impoverishment of the people of a vast, wealthy nation.

As an ardent nationalist, Ray always sought to make his nation free from this exploitative colonial domination. After returning from Edinburgh and since his joining the Presidency College, Ray remained concerned to alleviate the economic distress of the vast multitude of his nation. Ray's concept of the postcolonial nation was fundamentally laid (in)on the economic liberation or *swaraj* from the Western colonial hegemony in which science was to play a crucial role. Ray realized that the true dissemination of science would lie in its application in industry and technology which could eventually stabilize the economic condition of the nation. Hence, Ray's repeated urge for the pursuit of original scientific researches was not devoid of the material reality of the contemporary society but was ingrained within it.

In 1892, with the help of Satish Chandra Sinha, Dr Amulya Charan Bose and Chandrabhusan Bhaduri, Ray went on to form the Bengal Chemical and Pharmaceutical Works, the company that became the pioneer of the chemical industry in India. Ray's aim behind the establishment of the company was to stop the Western economic exploitation in India, and simultaneously, to encourage the indigenous people to take up industrial and business enterprises, which would eventually bring economic self-reliance to the country.

Interestingly, in his endeavour to decolonize his nation from the foreign colonial hegemony, Prafulla Chandra Ray actually looked (at)to the West as an ideal model to follow, which had always been a model of inspiration to him in terms of its scientific and industrial development. Ray could realize the fact that scientific education and industrialization had progressed on an equal footing in Europe, where 'science comes in as a ready handmaid to industry' (Ibid. 92). For its own industrial progress, according to Ray, India must emulate the strategies and methodologies shown by the West; he suggested: 'It is evident that to revive industry in this country we are to take lessons from the West, substitute machines for the hand as far as possible, replace the efforts of individual craftsmen by co-ordination of workers, and have elaborate organization for buying our materials and distributing our products' (Ray 'The Industrial Development' 516).

But, as a *savant* of modern Chemistry, though Ray realized the need for the dissemination of Western scientific knowledge and technology in India, he also strongly advocated Mahatma Gandhi's philosophy of the *Charka* and *Khadi*, which were the potent nationalist symbols of the contemporary period. Ray conceived the *Charka* (the spinning wheel) as a secondary source of income for the ill-fed poor farmers, which could act as a potent instrument to eradicate their economic deprivation.

Ray's discourse of nationalism also embodied a complex duality between modernity and tradition. Being impressed with the modern enlightened culture of Europe, Ray unhesitatingly absorbed the scientific and intellectual spirit of the West. However, he was simultaneously influenced by the Gandhian notion of asceticism and the moral and ethical principles of the ancient Indian culture. Though Ray was associated with several industrial and business concerns, he never adhered to the materialist spirit of the West and harshly critiqued its hunger for power and wealth. This points to a harmonious co-existence of the intellectual vigour of the West and the morality or ethics of the East, which were always present in Ray.

This complex postcoloniality of Ray could be also found evident in his literary output, especially in his criticism of Shakespeare, which too embodies a duality of acceptance and resistance and the consequent creation of a 'third space.' Towards the end of his life, Ray embarked on a project of studying Shakespeare and his works, paying special attention to Shakespeare's learning, authorship and the popular culture. In this series of articles, compiled in the volume, *The Shakespearean Puzzle – Endeavours After its Solution,* Ray contested the symbolic iconic status accorded by the British to Shakespeare, and persistently compared the genius of the colonial bard with that of Rabindranath Tagore, thus dismissing the West's claim of its unparallel literary and cultural superiority.

Ray ironically termed the English idolatry of Shakespeare as 'Shakespeare fanaticism', under the guise of which the British sought to project its literary and cultural superiority and thus proclaimed its colonial supremacy over the East. Prafulla Chandra Ray's postcolonial mind remained forever alert to resist colonial stereotyping and the notions of Western literary and cultural superiority. Though Prafulla Chandra and Rabindranath had differences of opinions in terms of the concept of *swaraj,* especially on the issue of Mahatma Gandhi's nationalist programme of *Charka* and *Khadi,* both of them had a deep admiration for each other and had high respect for each other's opinions. Ray always showed his deep reverence to the Poet for his patriotism and nationalist spirit. As Shakespeare had been hailed by the British as a pride of their nation, similarly Ray had also occasion to project Rabindranath as an embodiment of Indian nationhood, whose songs and poetry had given a new identity to modern Bengal vis-à-vis India.

However, being a neutral observer and critic, Ray envisioned Elizabethan England as marked by 'free thinking' which 'emancipated their minds from the shackles of age-long prejudice and superstition' accounting for their 'strong individualistic and keen rationalistic spirit' (Ray *The Shakespearean Puzzle-Endeavours* 7). In contrast to this picture of England, Ray harshly criticized the rigid caste system of contemporary India and especially Bengal, that had been instrumental in keeping knowledge confined to a particular section of the population, apart from being a source of 'centuries of social inequalities and oppression,' raising 'walls of differences between man and man' and thus making India lie 'at the feet of nations— powerless and helpless' (Ray 'Social Reform in India' 234). Projecting Shakespearean England as a utopia of rationality, Ray perhaps tried to foreground the necessity of a similar intellectual climate in Bengal as well as in India, to be dominated by the scientific and empirical mode. This receptive attitude towards the West points to the issue of cultural negotiation and Ray's concept of 'mimicry'.

Prafulla Chandra Ray visited Europe on five different occasions. Reading his accounts of these travels in the autobiography, we come to know of Ray's altering gaze to the West and his transformation of selfhood. These narratives of travels point to Ray's altering subject positions from that of an admiring callow student to a savant, eager to belong to a scientific fraternity, and finally to a nationalist who claimed equality and demanded the establishment of national scientific industries and institutions. Being well aware of the age-long prejudices and superstitions in which the contemporary Indian society was plunged, Ray sought to imbibe the very scientific and rationalist spirit of the West. According to Ray, this would lead to India's scientific and technological advancement. But, despite this receptive attitude towards the West, in his subsequent travels also approached the West at a level of equality and as part of a global scientific fraternity. Thus, Ray's accounts of his travels to Europe present before the readers his complex postcolonial self, who was eager to absorbcolonial science, but was deeply suspicious and hostile to imperial intentions, while he remained a pioneer of developing chemical industries in Bengal.

Works Cited:

Fraser, Bashabi and Neil Fraser. "Prafulla Chandra Ray in Edinburgh and His Association with the West." *Sir P. C. Ray:The Father of Chemistry Teaching and Research in India, a Philanthropist, and an Entrepreneur*. Ed. Sunil Kumar Talapatra and Biswapati Mukherjee. Kolkata: Indian Science News Association, 2016. 37-54. Print.

Lourdusamy, J. *Science and National Consciousness in Bengal(1870–1930)*. New Delhi: Orient Longman Private Limited, 2004. Print.

Ray, Prafulla Chandra. *A History of Hindu Chemistry*. 2 vols. Calcutta: The Bengal Chemical & Pharmaceutical Works Limited, 1903 and 1909. Print.

—. "India Before and After the Mutiny." Edinburgh: Livingstone, 1886 and Calcutta: RKPK Acharya Prafulla Chandra Samilanee, 1991. Print.

—. "The Industrial Development of India." *Acharya Prafulla Chandra Ray: A Collection of Writings*. Ed. Anil Bhattacharya. Vol. I A. Kolkata: Acharya Prafulla Chandra College, 2008. 498-529. Print.

—. *Life and Experiences of a Bengali Chemist*. 2 vols. Kolkata: Chuckervertty, Chatterjee & Co., 1932 and 1935. Print.

—. "The Place of Science in the Vernacular Literature." *Essays and Discourses*. Madras: G. Nateson & Co., 1918. 122-137. Print.

—. *The Shakespearean Puzzle-Endeavours after its Solution*. Ed. Pinak Pani Dutta. Kolkata: Acharya Prafulla Chandra Sammilanee, 2003. Print.

—. "Social Reform in India." *Essays and Discourses*. Madras: G. A. Nateson & Co., 1918. 213-35. Print.

Jagadish Chanda Bose with Rabindranath Tagore

Patrick Geddes

The Scientist as Hero: The Fashioning of the Self in Patrick Geddes's *The Life and Work of Sir Jagadish. C. Bose* (1920)

Amrit Sen

CONCLUDING HIS BIOGRAPHY of Sir JC Bose, Geddes uses the metaphor of Karna whose 'life has been one of combat, and must be to the very last' (258). He further adds about this 'life work', that it is 'something of a sociological study also; and as such, one of its purposes – that of incentive to encouragement and emancipation of the student... others may be encouraged to face their difficulties, and to overcome them as far as may be, towards something greater than merely individual end' (254). Carefully constructed within this autobiography is the figure of JC Bose the scientist as hero. Why did Geddes write a voluminous biography of AJC Bose? What was the continuum of ideas that drew them together? If as a botanist he responded to the scientific discoveries of Bose, what were the motivations for the particular self-fashioning of Bose that he represents? These are some of the questions that thus paper seeks to probe.

Geddes was born in 1854 and was senior to JC Bose by almost a decade. Famed as a town planner and sociologist, he initially lectured in Zoology at Edinburgh University (1880–1888), was demonstrator in the Department of Physiology in London and held the chair of Botany at University College Dundee (1888–1919). He inspired Victor Bramford to form the Sociological Society in 1903. A scientist who did not complete any formal degree, Patrick Geddes traversed freely across disciplines. But his primary interest and major work in the last decade of the 19th century was in town planning and architecture. JC Bose on the other hand (born in 1858), was trained as a physicist and worked on semiconductors and electromagnetic waves. It was only later in 1901 that his lectures on responses to stimuli in plants were publicized. He too was therefore crossing disciplines. While Geddes might have heard of AJC Bose's reputation through the medium of print, he first came across him in the Paris Exhibition through Margaret Noble, who acted as Geddes's secretary.

Hellen Meller offers us a rather simplistic reason for Geddes writing Bose's biography. Meller argues that Bose came close to Geddes on a personal level.

He was a particularly warm hearted man, and he showed much loving concern after the deaths of Anna and Alasdair in 1917. Geddes tried to repay him by writing his biography that published in 1920 (Meller 160). Bose not only gave emotional and moral support to Geddes, he was also important in getting him work. He invited him to come and give lectures at his institute, he helped him set up Summer Schools in Darjeeling; and he got commissions for him in the early 1920s when Geddes had more or less fallen out with the British administrators and the commissions from the maharajas were drying up. It was Bose who managed to get him the contract to plan Osmania University's campus at Hyderabad. As has been said earlier, Bose had originally met Geddes at the 1900 Paris Exhibition through an introduction by Sister Nivedita and the two were drawn toward each other by an awareness of treading unconventional paths in science. Soon after the opening of his Institute, Bose wrote to Geddes, 'Your letter warmed my heart. Write to me always like this ... let me speak to you as my other self and you do the same... you have very few even in your own country who understand your aims and I am in a worse predicament' (quoted in Meller 161). Bose's view of Geddes was definitely coloured by his own experience as the lone outsider misunderstood by the world. Geddes too was aware that people often regarded him with his self-imposed mission as a crank. He himself summed up rather sadly the common reaction to his social crusade in his Indore report; 'they seem simply dreamers or else 'cranks' when they seek to accomplish something towards the future, and so obtrude upon our present' (Meller 7).

It is probably worthwhile now to recollect how Geddes fashions the self of JC Bose, the scientist as hero. Geddes provides a painstaking detail of JC Bose's father as magistrate hailing from Vikrampur, 'a peculiarly rich and active centre of Buddhist Culture' (2) with 'not all gentle folk responsive to religion and education' (12). The great rivers and the verdant landscape introduced Jagadish to the language of nature that he was to later scientifically probe. Jagadish was sent to a vernacular school 'that a child should know his own mother language before beginning English; and further that he should first know his own people, and not be kept apart by that false pride which nowadays in India tends to separate them from their less fortunate brethren' (15). Bose's recollections also identify him with Karna, 'From his low caste came rejections, came every disadvantage; but he always played and fought fair... all this too gave me a lower and lower idea of all ordinary worldly success... that the only real and spiritual advantage and victory is to fight fair, never take crooked ways. Especially significant is Bose's paying off his father's debts after joining college' (37). Geddes refers to Bose's heroic juggling of classes and research at Presidency College and his crusade against the disparity of pay in the Indian education service. Geddes writes, 'Indeed one very real reason for the writer's undertaking this biography, beyond the great contributions Bose has made to the advancement science, is found in his efforts towards raising and maintaining the professional standard and ideal above and beyond social difference altogether' (35). Geddes also mentions Bose's amazing ability to craft instruments with local artisans (57). Geddes refers to the tremendous obstacle Bose had to face from the physiologists Sir John Sanderson and others when he crossed over into plant physiology and his valiant efforts to get his scientific experiments validated. The climax of his effort is described in the establishment of the Bose Institute where Geddes was the only foreigner invited, resplendent in an Indian dress. Geddes makes two points here; firstly that Bose was placed in an especially difficult position because he found 'himself impelled over the frontiers as drawn, moving among the conceptions of different sciences and pursuing experiments in fields where inevitably they are looked upon as strangers' (253) and secondly Bose presented himself as one who has transcended racial boundaries and proved himself solely as a scientist, thereby challenging notions of the inability of Indian science. Geddes writes:

In contemplating the great cancer of his countryman, the young Indian, will be stimulated to put brain and hand to fine tasks, nothing fearing. Thus will he be inspired not only to recover the noble intellectual traditions of the Indian past, but to restate these traditions in modern terms... by impassioned inquiry and research, by resolute and unending work, by direct and personal action on positive lines and in the constructive spirit – by these things – can India or Europe or the vast enduring brotherhood of mankind be carried further along the road to their deeply needed and long awaited reconstruction (254).

Having discussed the self fashioning of Bose by Geddes, the deeper philosophical and political question that needs to be asked is – what prompted this tremendous bond and projection of the scientist as hero? The first reason seems to be Geddes's firm belief in science and planning that would lead to liberation for India. Geddes was thus quite hostile to Gandhi's ideas of the charka and rejection of science. As Lewis Mumford writes

Few observes have shown more sympathy... with the religious and social practices of the Hindus than Geddes did; yet no one could have written more scathingly of Mahatma Gandhi's attempt to conserve the past by reverting to the spinning wheel at a moment when the fundamental poverty of the masses in India called for the most resourceful application of the machine both to agricultural and industrial life (Tyrwhitt 12).

Was this realization one that drew Patrick to Bose and Tagore and prompted him to inspire Arthur Geddes to work intensively in Santiniketan?

One remembers how deeply Geddes was attracted to Rabindranath Tagore's project at Sriniketan with its application of scientific research and machinery to confront the problems facing Indian agriculture.

The self-fashioning of the young Jagadish through his father was also part of his belief in the 'family as the biological unit of society' and that from 'stable, healthy homes' come children who are able to fully participate in life.

Geddes was also fascinated by his other idea about his mistrust of money. In JC Bose's rejection of taking patents for his inventions Geddes saw a reflection of his own stance as heroic – an attribute that he locates within the Indian tradition:

> Bose has sometimes, and not unnaturally been criticized as impractical for making no profit from his inventions. But as to this he was determined from the first. His memory as a child had been impressed by the pure white flowers offered in Indian worship; and it came early to him that whatever offerings his life could make should be untainted by any considerations of personal advantage. Moreover, he was painfully impressed by what seemed to him symptoms of deterioration, even in scientific men, by the temptation of gain; and so at this time he made the resolve to seek for no personal advantage from his inventions (63).

As early as 1895, JC Bose demonstrated to a mesmerized Calcutta audience, the possibility of wireless transmission of radio waves over a distance of 75 feet. Bose presented his first results before the Asiatic Society, Calcutta, in May 1895. According to the pioneering Indian chemist, Acharya Prafulla Chandra Ray, who was a colleague and close friend of Bose at Presidency College, 'It appears that he had not then realised the importance of the new line of research he had hit upon' (quoted in Sengupta 94). Bose sent copies of his research paper to his former teacher Lord Rayleigh and to Lord Kelvin and both realized its worth. Bose went on a lecturing tour of England and Europe during 1896–1897 and then again during 1900–1902, when he visited America. After his public lecture in 1897 at the Royal Institution in London, the British press expressed 'surprise that no secret was at any time made as to its (the invention's) construction, so that it has been open to all the world to adopt it for practical and possibly money-making purposes' (quoted in Sengupta 93). An early admirer of the Bose coherer was the British navy, which used it to establish effective radio link between a torpedo boat and friendly ships. In May 1901 Bose informed Rabindranath Tagore:

> the proprietor of a reputed telegraph company... came himself with a Patent form in hand... He proposed to take half of the profit and finance the business in the bargain. This multi-millionaire came to me

a begging. My friend, I wish you could see that terrible attachment for gain in this country, that all engaging lucre, that lust for money and more money. Once caught in that trap there would have been no way out for me (J. Bose to Tagore, 17 May, 1901 quoted in Pal 576).

Exasperated by Bose's rather diffident approach towards money, Margaret Noble (better known as Sister Nivedita) and American-born Mrs. Sara Bull on their own initiative obtained in 1904 an American patent in Bose's name (for his 'galena single contact-point receiver'). Bose, however, remained unmoved and refused to encash the patent. The irony of the situation seems to have gone unnoticed. Here in Nivedita we have a spiritualist advocating the cause of patents and royalties; and a physics professor dismissing the idea! There can be no doubt, as PC Ray reminded the audience assembled in 1916 to greet Bose on his knighthood, that, 'If he had taken out patents for the apparatus and instruments which he had invented, he could have made millions by their sale' (quoted in Sengupta 94). More importantly, he would perhaps have become an Indian role-model for production of wealth through science. Was it keeping in view the possibilities of such misuse that Bose abandoned radio waves altogether?

DM Bose recollects that when JC Bose was asked as to who was the inventor of the radio, his answer used to be, 'the invention is more important than the inventor' (quoted in Pal, 12). He was so consistent about his faith of distributing the fruits of one's labour without thinking of one's personal benefits that he made it one of the rules of the constitution of the Bose Institute that, 'no invention from this Institution should be patented' (quoted in Pal, 12). Geddes explains Bose's anti-patent position by drawing attention to the Indian tradition:

> Simply stated, it is the position of the old rishis of India, of whom he is increasingly recognised by his countrymen as a renewed type, and whose best teaching was ever open to all willing to accept it (67).

Geddes's strong attraction to Bose must have also owed its genesis to the centrality of plant physiology and response in his scientific research. As early as 1888 Patrick Geddes had written:

> This is a green world, with animals comparatively few and small, and all dependent on the leaves. By leaves we life. Some people have strange ideas that they live by money. They think energy is generated by the circulation of coins. Whereas the world is mainly a vast leaf colony, growing on and forming a leafy soil, not a mere mineral mass: and we live not by the jingling of our coins, but by the fullness of our harvests. (*Cities in Evolution* 216).

In the biography Geddes quotes Bose as a powerful sympathizer for the plant world:

> I succeeded in making the dumb plant the most eloquent chronicler of its inner life and experiences by making its own history. These our mute companions, silently growing beside our door have now told us the tale of their life-tremulous as and their death spasm in script that as inarticulate as they. May it not be said that their story has a pathos of its own beyond anything that we conceive? (151)

He proceeds to add the narrative gloss: 'These revelations are as unexpected as they are startling. They show that the pretension of man and animals for undisputed superiority over their hitherto despised "vegetative brethren" does not bear the test of close inspection (180).' Interestingly an integral part of the description o the Bose Institute is the Garden around 'where sensitive and other moving plants preponderate, twiners and climbers, which cover a long and shady pergola ready to serve as a cloister with its "Philosophers Way"' (253). The final image of Bose for the Indian Villagers is of Bose in his garden, 'that is where, at might, the plants talk to him'! (255)

Geddes also saw within Bose's work a strong rootedness in his triadic concept of the 'place, work and folk'. Geddes recurrently illustrates Bose's strong sense of Indian identity, especially in his account of Bose's travels: 'this western educated modern physicist also peculiarly and widely knows his country; knows it as an Indian of Indians' (111). Geddes refers to Bose's statement 'with all these experiences, India has made me and kept me as her son. I feel her life and unity deep below all' (113). Geddes then moves to highlight this diversity and unity as a panacea for a strife from Europe: 'Must we not again look to all that is best in each country's history and civilization? Which should be found in its rural villages and cities past' (117). At the fag end of the biography Geddes asks 'what of the teeming and toiling millions of India and what can such schemes do for them?' (254)

Geddes's answer is complex here and demands critical engagement. Rather than dismiss the villager as ignorant he claims for them an intuitive knowledge:

> The Indian villager is not nearly so ignorant as by the average of literates he is judged to be... the traditional life of the people with its spiritual roots in the organic being of society and its folk-knowledge linking the generations, enables the people to get at something of the greater knowledge in their own fashion (255).

It is the fusion of the spiritual roots and scientific experimentation that both Geddes and Tagore responded to, a point that even Bose raised in his inaugural speech at Basu Bigyan Mandir:

To the theological bias was added the misgivings about the inherent bent of the Indian mind towards mysticism and unchecked imagination. But in India this burning imagination which can extort new order out of a mass of apparently contradictory facts, is also held in check by the habit of meditation. It is this restraint which confers the power to hold the mind in pursuit of truth in infinite patience, to wait, and reconsider, to experimentally test and repeatedly verify (229).

Bose's strong grounding in his language, philosophy and his country had a strong fascination for Geddes along with his ability to seamlessly move to empirical research. Bose's ability to bring together the various disciplines of science too must have fascinated Geddes. After all in his ideas of science and architecture, he had talked about 'an inseparably interwoven structure' (Tyrwhitt 57) resembling a flower and had resisted specialization:

Each of the various specialists remains too closely concentrated upon his single specialism, too little awake to those of others. Each sees clearly and seizes firmly upon one petal of the six-lobed flower of life and tears it apart from the whole (Tyrwhitt 57).

It is in this context that he had an abiding interest in Eastern philosophy, which he believed more readily conceived of life as a whole.

Bose echoed the sentiment in his presidential address at the Bengal Literary Conference in 1911:

You are aware that, in the West, the prevailing tendency at the moment is, after a period of synthesis, to return upon the excessive subdivision of learning... such a caste system in scholarship undoubtedly helps at first, in the gathering and classification of new material. But, if followed too exclusively, it ends by limiting the comprehensive of truth ... the Eastern aim has been rather the opposite, namely that, in the multiplicity of phenomena, we should never miss their underlying unity. After generations of this quest, the idea of unity comes to us almost spontaneously and we apprehend no inseparable obstacle in grasping it. (quoted in Pal 258)

Geddes's recognition of JC Bose as the international scientist with his own rigour and belonging to the pantheon of international cooperation can be seen in his inclusion as Vice President in the Indian College (Tagore was the President and Brajendranath Seal, a fellow Vice-President) within the International University at Montpellier. His agenda here was to promote 'science in definite cooperation with humanities and socialized applications, from city to village renewal... from horticulture to agriculture to... afforestation'. Within Geddes's formulation of a *studia synthesis* interacting with *agenda synergica* was the dominant notion of a 'substantial unity and harmony', a *vita sympathetica* sending an impulse of cooperative activities ... extending from individual friendships and social harmonies and to racial sympathies' (quoted in Mukhopadhyay 90).

The final chapter on the Bose Institute in the life reflects Geddes' ideas of the interaction between the local and the global: 'this new Institute may act and react with Indian thought and life as well as with the world's science, and also it may advance here industry, there agriculture, there again medicine, and above all the needed emancipation and renewal of higher education' (233). Bose too referred to his Institute as 'the House of knowledge' where 'not the quantity but quality that is of essential importance' adding 'the facilities of thus Institute should be available to water from all countries. In this I am attempting to carry out the traditions of my country, which... welcomed all scholars from different parts of the world within the precincts of its ancient seats of learning at Nalanda and Taxila' (234). Thus Bose referred to his Institute not merely as a laboratory but a 'temple' as a fit memorial for the establishment of that truth for which faith was needed. It is this principle of global cooperation that drew Geddes, Tagore and Bose together. Of special significance is Tagore's poem composed for the opening day celebrations at the Indian College Montpellier, where Tagore refers to 'the eternal dream / is borne on the wings of ageless height... until at last knowledge gleams out from the dusk / in the infinity of human sprit' (quoted in Mukhopadhyay 85).

Tagore raised the same sentiments at the Basu Vigyanyan Mandir:

> I offer my salutations to the illustrious founder of this Institute, humbly sitting by those who are deprived of the sufficiency of that knowledge which can only save them from the desolating menace of scientific devilry and the continual drainage of the resources of life, and I appeal to this Institute to bring our call to Science herself to rescue the world from the clutches of marauders who betray her noble mission into an unmitigated savagery (quoted in Sengupta 93).

Bose acknowledged his debt to Tagore:

> It was following this quest that I succeeded in making the dumb plant the most eloquent chronicler of its inner life and experiences by making its own history... The barriers which seemed to separate kindred phenomena was found to have vanished, the plant and the animal appearing as a multiform unity in a single ocean of being... The same cosmic unity has unfolded to Tagore's poetic vision and has

found expression in his philosophic outlook and in his incomparable poems... (quoted in Sengupta 95)

Noticeably the other scientist Geddes mentions here is APC Roy whose 'promise and powers have been amply justified by the high appreciation of brother chemists and success of his pupils'. Geddes's internationalism was thus based on the triad of sympathy, synergy and synthesis and in this context JC Bose could emerge as a hero.

The relationship between Rabindranath Tagore and Patrick Geddes has received considerable critical attention with congruencies in their ideas of education, internationalism and an attention to Geddes's notion of place, work and folk. However Geddes's interaction with JC Bose was equally substantial. Geddes saw in Bose the scientist as hero, the agent who could weld Indian tradition, mysticism with empirical rationality and modernity. Keenly rooted in tradition, Bose could also fulfil Geddes's vision of a community of sympathetic international scholarship that was based on a rejection of lucre. Bose's crossovers in scientific research, the movement across the mystic and the scientific, greatly fascinated Geddes. Additionally he saw both himself and Bose as outsiders and visionaries working valiantly against a system that sought to dismiss utopian thought. Geddes' fashioning of Bose as hero thus was thus a fulfillment of his own latent personality. He was not simply writing a life in order to repay Bose's kindness; it was an act of simultaneously writing himself.

Works Cited

Geddes, Patrick. *Cities in Evolution: An Introduction to the Town Planning Movement and to the Study of Civics*. London: Williams and Morgan, 1949. Print.

Geddes, Patrick. *An Indian Pioneer of Science: The Life and Work of Sir Jagadis C. Bose*. London: Longman, Greens and Co., 1920. Print.

Geddes, Patrick and Jaqueline Tyrwhitt. *Patrick Geddes in India*. London: Lund Humphries, 1947. Print.

Meller, Helen. *Patrick Geddes: Social Environmentalist and City Planner*. London: Routledge, 1990. Print.

Mukhopadhyay, Tapati. "Europe Ekti Bharatiya Visvavidyalayer Suchanaparbo: Rabindranath o Patrick Geddes", in Tapati Mulhopadhyay and Amrit Sen eds. *Rabindra Balaye Biddadjan*. Kolkata: Visva-Bharati, 2016.Print.

Pal, Palash Baran (ed). *Anustup: J. C. Bose Special Issue* 43.2 (Winter 2008). Print.

Sengupta, Debiprasad. "*Anaamaniyo Jagadish Chandra*", in *Anustup: J. C. Bose Special Issue* ed. Palash Baran Pal 43.2 (Winter 2008): 88-97. Print.

List of Contributors

BASHABI FRASER is Professor of English and Creative Writing, Director, Scottish Centre of Tagore Studies (ScoTs), Edinburgh Napier University.

TAPATI MUKHERJEE is Director, Culture and Cultural Relations and Adhyaksha, Rabindra-Bhavana, Visva-Bharati, Shantiniketan.

AMRIT SEN is Professor of English, Visva-Bharati, Shantiniketan.

NEIL FRASER is Honorary Fellow, School of Social and Political Studies, University of Edinburgh.

SAPTARSHI MALLICK is Research Scholar, University of Calcutta and Charles Wallace fellow.

KATHRYN SIMPSON is MHRA Research Associate, Queens University, Belfast.

KABERI CHATTERJEE is Associate Professor of English and Head of the Department of English, Scottish Church College, Kolkata.

THOMAS CROSBY is a Journalist based in the United Kingdom.

DIKSHIT SINHA is Former Professor of Social Work, Visva-Bharati.

BISWANATH BANERJEE is Assistant Professor of English, Adamas University, Kolkata.

(All the contributors were associated in various capacities as part of the UGC-British Council UKIERI Project on The Scotland India Continuum of Ideas: Tagore and His Circle)

Luath Press Limited

committed to publishing well written books worth reading

LUATH PRESS takes its name from Robert Burns, whose little collie Luath (*Gael.*, swift or nimble) tripped up Jean Armour at a wedding and gave him the chance to speak to the woman who was to be his wife and the abiding love of his life. Burns called one of the 'Twa Dogs' Luath after Cuchullin's hunting dog in Ossian's *Fingal*. Luath Press was established in 1981 in the heart of Burns country, and is now based a few steps up the road from Burns' first lodgings on Edinburgh's Royal Mile. Luath offers you distinctive writing with a hint of unexpected pleasures.
Most bookshops in the UK, the US, Canada, Australia, New Zealand and parts of Europe, either carry our books in stock or can order them for you. To order direct from us, please send a £sterling cheque, postal order, international money order or your credit card details (number, address of cardholder and expiry date) to us at the address below. Please add post and packing as follows: UK – £1.00 per delivery address; overseas surface mail – £2.50 per delivery address; overseas airmail – £3.50 for the first book to each delivery address, plus £1.00 for each additional book by airmail to the same address. If your order is a gift, we will happily enclose your card or message at no extra charge.

Luath Press Limited
543/2 Castlehill
The Royal Mile
Edinburgh EH1 2ND
Scotland
Telephone: +44 (0)131 225 4326 (24 hours)
email: sales@luath. co.uk
Website: www. luath.co.uk